THE BIG BLACKSTONE GRIDDLE COOKBOOK FOR BEGINNERS

THE ULTIMATE GUIDE WITH 250+ DELICIOUS & EASY GRILL RECIPES WITH PRO TIPS & ILLUSTRATED INSTRUCTIONS

Jesus Arredondo

INTRODUCTION 10

BLACKSTONE GRIDDLE RECIPES 11

1. FRIED PICKLES RECIPE 12

2. HONEY LIME FRUIT SALAD 13

3. Mushroom, Pepper, and Fontina Frittata 13

4. CLASSIC BUTTERMILK PANCAKES 15

5. Fluffiest Blueberry Pancakes 15

6. Grilled Pizza with Greens and Eggs 16

7. How To Make Tomato, Cheese, and Bacon Omelette 17

8. Grilled French Toast Stuffed with Strawberry Basil Cream Cheese 18

9. Classic French Toast 19

10. French Crepe Recipe 20

11. CLASSIC DENVER OMELETTE 21

12. The Classic Bacon, Egg, and Cheese Sandwich 22

13. Sausage, Vegetable, and Egg Scramble 23

14. Best-Ever Steak & Eggs 24

15. The Ultimate Breakfast Burrito 25

16. Mexican Scrambled Eggs 26

17. hash brown egg scramble 27

18. Crispy Hash Browns 28

19. BACON POTATO HASH 30

20. Buffalo Chicken Burgers 30

21. Teriyaki Pineapple Turkey Burgers 32

22. ex-Mex Turkey Burger Recipe 32

23. Beef burgers – learn to make 33

24. Lamb burgers with tzatziki 34

25. EASY HATCH CHILE SALSA VERDE 35

26. Chipotle Burgers with Creamy Avocado Sauce 36

27. Perfect Salmon Burgers 37

28. Chicken Caesar Burgers 38

29. Best-Ever Turkey Burger 39

30. Nut Burgers 40

31. Shrimp Burgers with Seaweed Salad 41

32. Spicy Guacamole Burger 42

33. Garlic Pork Burgers (Spanish Style) 43

34. Beetroot and lentil burgers 44

35. Giant Party Cheeseburger 45

36. Crispy Pork Tenderloin Sandwiches 46

37. Grilled Ham and Cheese with Pineapple 46

38. Croque Madame Sandwich 47

39. The Ultimate Grilled Cheese 48

40. Crispy Garlic Bread Grilled Cheese Sandwiches 49

41. Cheesy-Crust Skillet Pizza 50

42. Vegan Portobello French Dip Recipe 50

43. GRILLED VEGGIE PESTO FLATBREAD 51

44. Grilled Veggie Pizza 52

45. Baked Bacon Jalapeno Wraps 53

46. Mexican Bean Breakfast Skillet 54

47. Ultimate Breakfast Burritos 55

48. Oatmeal Pancakes with Cinnamon 56

49. Cauliflower Hash Browns 56

50. Bacon Egg and Cheese Sandwich 57

51. Crispy Garlic Broccoli with Sesame Fried Rice 58

52. Restaurant-Style Coleslaws 60

53. Griddled aubergines with yogurt & mint 61

54. Roasted Lemon Garlic Mushrooms 61

55. Roasted Red Peppers in Oil, Vinegar, and Garlic 62

56. THE BEST ROASTED ROSEMARY GARLIC POTATOES 63

57. Buttery Grilled Potatoes in Foil Packets 63

58. Grilled Ratatouille Pasta Salad 64

59. Grilled Zucchini with Miso 65

60. Tostones Recipe (Twice-Fried Plantains!) 66

61. Atomic Buffalo Turd Jalapeno Poppers 66

62. EASY AND HEALTHY DESSERT IDEAS 67

63. Glazed Ranch Carrots 68

64. Jamaican Jerk Grilled Vegetables 68

65. Roasted Garlic-Parmesan Zucchini, Squash, and Tomatoes 70

66. Green Beans with Crispy Onions 70

67. Fried Green Tomatoes 71

68. Twice-Baked Potatoes Recipe 72

69. MEXICAN STREET CORN FLATBREAD PIZZA 73

70. Garlic Pita Bread Bites 74

71. Addictive Sweet Potato Burritos 75

72. Corn Fritters 76

73. Balsamic Roasted Brussels Sprouts with Cranberries & Pecans 77

74. Crispy Brussels Sprouts with Warm Blue Cheese and Bacon. 78

75. Lemon Garlic Roasted Asparagus 79

76. Cinnamon-Spiced Candied Sweet Potatoes 79

77. Rosemary Roasted Butternut Squash 80

78. Pork, Sage, Onion & Cranberry Stuffing Log 81

79. Maple-Glazed Green Beans 82

80. JALAPENO POPPER CORN SALAD 82

81. Fried Rice Restaurant Style 83

82. Sweet Potato and Black Bean Tacos (with Honey and Lime) 84

83. Grilled Green Bean Salad With Red Peppers and Radishes Recipe 84

84. FRIED RAVIOLI 86

85. Homemade Egg Rolls 87

86. Cornbread Stuffing 88

87. Easy yogurt flatbreads 90

88. BURGERS WITH SAUTÉED MUSHROOMS, ARUGULA AND DIJON AIOLI 90

89. Pork Tenderloin with Lemon-Thyme Cream and Cabbage Apple Slaw 91

90. Grilled Vegetable Tostadas with Quick Mole Sauce 93

91. Mascarpone-Stuffed French Toast with Blackberries 93

92. Grilled Cauliflower Skewers 95

93. Roasted Figs stuffed with Goat's Cheese and Walnuts. 95

94. Skillet Peach Crisp with Ginger and Pecans 96

95. MARSALA HONEY PEARS WITH GORGONZOLA 97

96. Sweet Potato Pancakes 98

97. Cinnamon S'mores Toast 99

98. Whoopie Pies 100

99. Strawberry, Basil, and Balsamic Pizza 101

100. Chinese Five-Spice Steak with Oranges and Sesame Broccolini 102

101. Buttermilk Biscuits 103

102. Brown-Butter Apricots with Brioche and Ice Cream 104

103. Maple Fried Bananas 105

104. Chocolate-Banana Sundae 106

105. Coconut Banana Fritters 106

106. YOGURT APPLE BOWLS 107

107. Peanut Butter Sundaes 108

108. Parmesan Garlic Broccoli Fritters 108

109. Paleo Vegan Zucchini Cauliflower Fritters 109

110. Jerk Shrimp Tacos with Pineapple Salsa, Slaw, and Pina Colada Crema 110

111. Cinnamon Toast the Right Way 111

112. Doughnut Funfetti Ice Cream 112

113. Jelly Roll Pancakes 113

114. Rum Soaked Grilled Pineapple 113

115. BUTTERY HERB SAUTÉED MUSHROOMS 114

116. RANCH POTATOES 115

117. Smoky Cauliflower Bites 115

118. Baked Peaches 116

119. Fruit Skewers 117

120. Baked Apples Recipe 118

121. Strawberry Shortcake (The Best) 119

122. French Toast Pain Perdu Recipe with Almond 120

123. Honey Glazed Grilled Pineapple 121

124. Eggplant Bites 122

125. Grilled Fruit Kebabs 123

126. Zucchini-Parmesan Cheese Fritters 124

127. Zucchini Patties 125

128. Pear Crisp with Vanilla Ice Cream 126

129. HONEY PEANUT BUTTER BREAKFAST BANANA SPLITS 127

130. PINEAPPLE SHRIMP STIR FRY 127

131. Brioche French Toast 129

132. Spicy Bisquick Sausage Balls 130

133. Crock-Pot Pecan Pie Bread Pudding Recipe 130

134. Fresh Fruit With Vanilla Cream 131

135. Apple Peach Pie 132

136. Grilled Pound Cake with Berries 133

137. Coconut Chocolate Brownies 134

138. CINNAMON ROLL APPLE COBBLER 135

139. Cinnamon Toast Pumpkin Seeds 135

140. Blackberry Cobbler Recipe 136

141. Maple Walnut Ice Cream 137

142. Cinnamon-Sugar Pumpkin Seeds 138

143. Bacon-Wrapped Scallops 139

144. Chili Lime Baked Cod 140

145. Easy Honey Chipotle Salmon 140

146. Crab and cod fish cakes with tomato salsa 141

147. Cajun Blackened Tilapia 142

148. Garlic Baked Haddock 143

149. Swordfish with Gremolata 144

150. Halibut with Lemon, Spinach, and Tomatoes 145

151. Foil Pack Lime Cilantro Salmon 146

152. LEMON BUTTER SCALLOPS 147

153. Blackened Red Snapper 148

154. Coconut Pineapple Shrimp Skewers 149

155. Grilled Lobster Smothered in Basil Butter 150

156. Tuna Zucchini Cakes 151

157. Horseradish Sauce for Fish 151

158. Homemade Enchilada Sauce 152

159. Grilled Scallops with Meyer Lemon Salsa Verde 153

160. Baked halibut recipe 154

161. Spicy Grilled Shrimp 155

162. Spicy Peppered Crab Legs 156

163. Easy garlic herb butter baked salmon. 157

164. LEMON GARLIC BUTTER SHRIMP 158

165. Herb Fish 158

166. Super Grouper 159

167.Fish Mayonnaise Recipe 160

168. GARLIC BUTTERFISH RECIPE 161

169. Pineapple Shrimp 162

170. Red Snapper Ceviche 163

171. Peruvian Red Snapper Ceviche 163

172. Linguine with Clams and Fennel 165

173. chilled corn soup over lobster salad 165

174. GARLIC HONEY-LIME SHRIMP RECIPE 167

175. Spicy Red Snapper with Mango Salsa 168

176. Lime-Cilantro Tilapia 169

177. grilled swordfish skewers with Italian salsa verde 170

178. GARLIC BUTTER LOBSTER TAILS 171

179. GARLIC PARSLEY BUTTER SHRIMP 172

180. Coconut Pineapple Shrimp Skewers 173

181. Grilled BBQ Chicken 173

182. Keto Grilled California Avocado Chicken 174

183. SWEET CHILI CHICKEN 175

184. LEMON GARLIC CHICKEN THIGHS 176

185. Grilled Salsa Verde Chicken 177

186. Honey Spiced Glazed Chicken Thighs 177

187. SPICY GRILLED CHICKEN TACOS WITH AVOCADO CREMA 178

188. Hawaiian Chicken Kabobs 180

189. Cheesy Garlic Stuffed Chicken Recipe 180

190. Beer Chicken Recipe 182

191. Baked Chicken and Zucchini 183

192. EASY CHIPOTLE CHICKEN RECIPE 184

193. Spicy chicken kebabs 185

194. Grilled Thai Curry Chicken Skewers with Coconut-Peanut Sauce 186

195. Grilled Garlic Chicken Skewers 187

196. Honey Sriracha Grilled Chicken Thighs 188

197. BAKED STICKY HONEY GARLIC BUFFALO WINGS 189

198. Chicken Fajita Cobb 190

199. Greek Chicken Bites 191

200. Honey Garlic Chicken Drumsticks 192

201. Veggie-Packed Chicken Fried Rice 193

202. Buffalo chicken & blue cheese slaw 194

203. Chicken Broccoli Stir Fry Recipe 195

204. Easy Chicken Stir Fry Recipe 196

205. Cheesy Chicken Fritters 197

206. BAKED GARLIC LEMON WINGS 199

207. Chicken Fajitas with Bell Peppers 200

208. Chicken Tagine with Apricots and Almonds 200

209. Herb and Garlic Turkey Burgers 202

210. EASY GREEK LEMON CHICKEN 203

211. Sesame Ginger Chicken 203

212. Grilled Lemon-Garlic Chicken with Peach Salsa 205

213. Light Honey-Glazed Cornish Hens 206

214. Grilled Cornish Hens 207

215. Classic Barbecue Chicken 208

216. How to Smoke a Turkey on the Grill 209

217. Happy Orange Turkey 210

218. SPATCHCOCK SMOKED TURKEY 211

219. Roasted Thanksgiving Turkey 212

220. ROASTED TURKEY BREAST 213

221. Classic roast turkey 214

222. Perfect New York Strip Steak 215

223. How to Cook Strip Steak 215

224. Skillet Beef Stew 217

225. Beef Teppanyaki made Easy. 218

226. Grilled Tuscan Steak 219

227. Caprese Steak 220

228. Grilled Ribeyes with Herb Butter 220

229. Chile-Spiced Skirt Steak Tacos 221

230. Heirloom Tomato and Steak Caprese 222

229. Flank Steak with Garlic Butter Sauce 223

230. Herb-Crusted Pork Tenderloin 224

231. Grilled Flank Steak Gyros 225

232. Easy Beef and Broccoli 226

233. Herb-Crusted Beef Tenderloin 227

234. THE PERFECT STEAK WITH GARLIC BUTTER 228

235. How To Cook Pork Shoulder Steak 229

236. Glazed Country Ribs 270

237. Tangy Pork Tenderloin 271

238. Honey Mustard Pork Chops 271

239. BONELESS PORK CHOPS RECIPE 232

240. EASY HONEY GARLIC PORK CHOPS RECIPE 233

241. Slow Cooker Pork Chile Verde 234

242. Lemon-Oregano Lamb Chops 276

243. Greek-Style Lamb Burgers 277

244. Pan-Fried Pork Chops with Honey Lime Glaze 237

245. Grilled Spice-Rubbed Pork Chops with Scallion-Lime Rice Recipe 279

246. Lamb Chops with Rosemary and Garlic 280

247. PINEAPPLE BACON PORK CHOP 281

248. Tangy Pork Chops 282

249. Herb-Crusted Pork Tenderloin 241

250. Apricot Lamb Chops 285

251. GARLIC BUTTER PORK CHOPS (THE BEST!) 243

252. Basic Paprika Pork Chops 244

253. Classic Moroccan Lamb or Beef Kebabs (Brochettes) 287

254. Lamb Chops with Garlic & Herbs 288

255. Charred squash & spiced lamb 289

256. Griddled lamb with spiced new potatoes 247

257. Lamb Chops Sizzled with Garlic 247

258. GARLIC BUTTER LAMB CHOPS 248

259. Garlic and Rosemary Grilled Lamb Chops 293

260. Griddled Lamb with Fresh Pesto, Celeriac Mash & Ratatouille 250

261. Greek Butterflied Lamb Leg 251

264. Lamb kofta meatballs in curry sauce 252

265. Classic Rack of Lamb 297

266. Greek lamb chops with tzatziki 254

267. Peppercorn Garlic Pork Chops 255

268. Caprese Steak 256

269. Coffee-Crusted Beef Tenderloin Steak 301

270. Lemon Garlic Roasted Artichokes 302

271. parmesan green beans 258

272. Mushroom Stir-Fry 259

273. THE EASIEST VEGETABLE STIR FRY 260

274. EASY FRIED RICE 261

275. EASY GARLIC PARMESAN ZUCCHINI NOODLES (ZOODLES) 262

276. Sauteed Garden Fresh Green Beans 308

277.4-Ingredient Baby Bok Choy Stir Fry..309

278.Sauteed Vegetables 264

279.Super Easy Stir-Fried Cabbage...311

280.Pineapple fried rice 312

281.Easy Baked Zucchini 266

282. Green Beans and Bacon 313

283.Mesa Grill Potato Salad 268

BLACKSTONE GRIDDLE

A Blackstone Griddle: What Is It?

lackstone produces a range of griddles, but they all have a cold-rolled steel flat-top that enables precise cooking and equal heat distribution across the whole surface.

B

The options with a Blackstone griddle are infinite, ranging from breakfast spreads for a party to weeknight stir-fries and blueberry cobbler, as several TikTok videos have shown. You may prepare items that cook at various temperatures simultaneously because of the wide surface area and several burners, such as bacon and pancakes or chicken and sliced peppers (plus no extra pans to wash).

I was testing out one of Blackstone's most feature-rich models, the Pro Series 36" Outdoor Cooking Station. It offers enough storage for all of your griddle accessories, counter-height shelves, a magnetic knife strip, and a paper towel holder.

1. FRIED PICKLES RECIPE

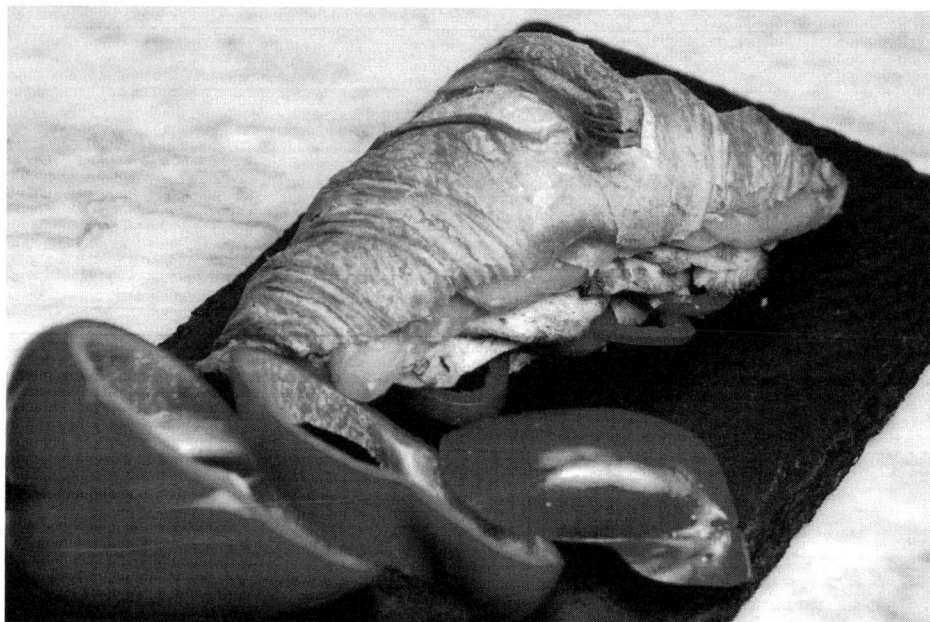

YIELD: 4-6

PREP TIME: 10 MINUTES

COOK TIME: 20 MINUTES

TOTAL TIME: 30 MINUTES

INGREDIENTS

- oil for frying (vegetable or peanut)
- 1/2 cup all-purpose flour
- 1 tsp Italian seasoning
- 1 1/2 tsps garlic powder
- 1/4 tsp salt
- 1/4 tsp black pepper
- 1 tbsp hot sauce
- 1/2 cup water
- 16 ounces dill pickle slices, drained and dried on paper towels

INSTRUCTIONS

1. In a heavy-bottomed saucepan set over medium-high heat, heat 1 1/2 to 2 inches of oil to 375 degrees Fahrenheit.
2. Combine the flour, Italian seasoning, garlic powder, salt, and pepper in a shallow bowl or rimmed plate. Mix till smooth after adding water and spicy sauce.

3. Add the dried pickles to the batter in batches and gently fold them in. Remove pickles from the batter using a slotted spoon (or Chinese Spider) and allow extra to drip off. One by one, gently stir the pickles into the oil. Fry until golden, approximately 1 1/2 to 2 minutes. Take out and allow to dry on paper towels. As batches are frying, watch the oil temperature to maintain a constant 375 degrees F.
4. Serve with ketchup and/or Comeback Sauce.

2. HONEY LIME FRUIT SALAD

PREP:10 MINS

COOK:5 MINS

TOTAL:15 MINS

INGREDIENTS

- 1 pound (500 g) of strawberries washed, hulled, and sliced
- 3 kiwi fruits peeled and sliced into half moons
- 2 mangoes peeled and diced
- 10 ounces (300 g) of blueberries washed
- 1 cup green grapes halved
- 9 ounce (250 g) can pineapple chunks or pieces (or 1/2 of fresh pineapple, peeled and diced)
- 3 tbsp honey
- 1 tbsp freshly squeezed lime juice
- 1 tbsp pineapple juice (from the canned pineapple, if using)

INSTRUCTIONS

1. In a large salad bowl, add prepared cleaned, sliced, or chopped fruits.
2. Combine the honey, lime juice, and pineapple juice in a measuring cup. Mix the fruit thoroughly after adding the syrup. If not serving right away, stir the fluids that have gathered at the bottom of the bowl one more before serving.

NUTRITION

Calories: 181kcal | Carbohydrates: 46g | Protein: 2g | Sodium: 4mg | Potassium: 459mg | Fiber: 5g | Sugar: 36g | Calcium: 45mg | Iron: 1mg

3. MUSHROOM, PEPPER, AND FONTINA FRITTATA

Prep: 15 minutes

Cook: 28 minutes

Ingredients

- 2 tbsp olive oil
- 1 thinly sliced onion
- 1 thinly sliced green bell pepper
- 1 cup sliced mushrooms
- 1 garlic clove, minced
- 8 large eggs
- 2 large egg whites
- ⅓ cup 1% low-fat milk
- ¾ tsp salt
- ¼ tsp black pepper
- 1 tbsp chopped fresh or 1 tsp dried basil
- 1 ½ tbsp butter
- 1 cup cherry tomatoes, halved
- 1 cup fontina cheese, cut into small cubes (about 5 ounces)

Directions

1. In a 10-inch oven-safe skillet or sauté pan, heat the oil. Add the onion and pepper, and cook for 5 minutes over medium heat while stirring often. Add the mushrooms, cover, and cook for three minutes while stirring often. Sauté for another minute after adding the garliCup Vegetable combinations should be removed from the heat and quickly cooled on a platter. Return pan to stove after wiping with paper towels.
2. In a large bowl, mix together the eggs, egg whites, milk, salt, pepper, and basil; put the bowl aside. For two to three minutes, heat a skillet on medium. Add the butter, rotating the pan to ensure uniform butter melting. After stirring in the veggies, gently pour the entire mixture onto the hot skillet. Sprinkle cheese and cherry tomatoes on top of the egg mixture (do not stir).
3. The frittata should be gently cooked over medium-low heat for 15–18 minutes or until it is almost done. Preheat the broiler, then set the frittata there for 2-4 minutes to finish cooking the top (carefully watch the frittata to make sure it doesn't burn).
4. After removing the frittata from the oven, let it cool on a wire rack for five minutes before shaking the pan erratically to release it. After a few more minutes of cooling, carefully place a plate on top of the frittata and flip it over. The frittata should now be right side up on a new platter. Keep chilled until you're ready to serve.

Nutrition Facts

168 calories; fat 13g;protein 10g; carbohydrates 4g; fiber 1g; cholesterol 189mg; iron 1mg; sodium 353mg; calcium 114mg.

4. CLASSIC BUTTERMILK PANCAKES

Prep Time: 10 mins

Cook Time: 4 mins

Total Time: 14 mins

Yield: 18 pancakes

INGREDIENTS

- 2 cups all-purpose flour
- 2 tsps baking powder
- 1 tsp baking soda
- 1/2 tsp kosher salt
- 1/4 cup granulated sugar
- 2 large eggs
- 2 cups buttermilk
- 4 tbsp butter, melted

INSTRUCTIONS

1. Mix the flour, baking powder, baking soda, salt, and sugar in a large basin. The eggs, buttermilk, and melted butter should all be placed in the middle well. Until almost mixed, whisk. It will be lumpy batter. While the griddle is heating, let the batter cool.
2. Over medium-low heat, preheat a large griddle or cast iron skillet. Canola oil can be softly sprayed on or greased.
3. Scoop 4 tbsp of batter onto the griddle using an ice cream or cookie scoop, allowing space between each pancake for them to bubble up and for you to turn them over. Cook the pancakes for approximately 2-3 minutes on one side, then quickly turn them over and cook them for another 2 minutes until both sides are golden brown. Just one flip.
4. Serve right away or keep warm in a 250° oven until ready to serve.

5. FLUFFIEST BLUEBERRY PANCAKES

TOTAL TIME: 20 minutes

YIELD: 2 servings

INGREDIENTS

- 3/4 cup milk
- 2 tbsp white vinegar

- 1 cup flour
- 2 tbsp sugar
- 1 tsp baking powder
- 1/2 tsp baking soda
- 1/2 tsp salt
- 1 egg
- 2 tbsp melted butter
- 1+ cup fresh blueberries
- more butter for the pan

INSTRUCTIONS

1. Making "buttermilk" here, combine the milk and vinegar, and let it settle for a few minutes.
2. The dry components should be blended. Just mix the dry ingredients with the egg, milk, and melted butter.
3. A nonstick pan should be heated to medium. Add a dab of butter to the pan to melt it (essential for giving a yummy golden brown crust).
4. Place a third of a cup of batter in the heated skillet and spread it out evenly (it will be pretty thick). On top, scatter a few blueberries. Cook until you notice little bubbles on the surface and the edges beginning to firm up. The pancakes should be cooked through and fluffy to the sky after flipping, which should take another 1-2 minutes.
5. Butter and maple syrup are recommended. But in all honesty, I sometimes prefer to consume these unadorned. MMMM, MMMM, MMMM.

6. GRILLED PIZZA WITH GREENS AND EGGS

Total:45 mins

Yield:4

Ingredients

- 1 tbsp extra-virgin olive oil, plus more for brushing and drizzling
- 6 ounces chopped
- 2 garlic cloves, minced
- 1 tsp crushed red pepper
- Salt
- Black pepper
- 1 pound store-bought pizza dough, thawed if frOuncesen
- 1 cup fresh ricotta cheese
- 4 large eggs
- Grated pecorino cheese for serving

Directions

1. Heat the 1 tbsp of olive oil in a big skillet. Stirring occasionally, sauté the Pinarello over fairly high heat for about 3 minutes, or until it has just begun to wilt. Add salt and black pepper to taste.

2. Start the grill. Stretch the pizza dough into a 15-inch-long oval on a surface that has been lightly dusted with flour. Brush the dough with olive oil. Griddle the heated grill with oil. Lay the dough, greased side down, on the grates. Grill for about 3 minutes over fairly high heat or until markings emerge on the bottom and the dough is just beginning to puff. Place the dough on a cookie sheet that has been lightly dusted with flour and brush with olive oil. Leave a 1-inch border around the dough after spooning the ricotta on top. Sprinkle the Pinarello over the top. One egg should be delicately put onto the pizza after being cracked into a little bowl. Replicate with the final three eggs. Use salt and pepper to season the pizza.

3. Reposition the pizza on the griddle. Close the grill and cook for about 5 minutes over medium heat or until the crust is browned and the egg whites are solid. Pizza should be moved to a cutting board. Olive oil should be drizzled, pecorino cheese grated on top, and the bowl divided into pieces.

7. HOW TO MAKE TOMATO, CHEESE, AND BACON OMELETTE

Prep:10 mins

Cook:5 mins

Total:15 mins

Serves:2 people

Ingredients

- 2 bacon rashers, sliced into the ½-inch thickness
- 1 small plum tomato, cut into ¼-inch cubes
- ¼ cup Gruyere cheese, grated
- 1 tbsp butter
- 3 eggs

Instructions

1. A shallow skillet should be heated to medium. Sauté the bacon in butter until crisp and barely browned.
2. Crack the eggs and beat them in a bowl.
3. Lay the eggs out. To cook evenly, swirl.
4. Keep the cheese in the center and sprinkle it on top.
5. Spread the tomatoes out without touching the pan's edge.

6. Fold the omelet in half by lifting one side.
7. The omelet should be placed on a platter. Dispense and savor!

Nutrition

Calcium: 210mgCalories: 310kcalCarbohydrates: 2gCholesterol: 278mgFat: 26gFiber: 1gIron: 1mgMonounsaturated Fat: 11gPotassium: 224mgProtein: 16gSodium: 362mgSugar: 1g

8. GRILLED FRENCH TOAST STUFFED WITH STRAWBERRY BASIL CREAM CHEESE

Prep Time: 15 mins

Cook Time: 10 mins

Total Time: 25 mins

Ingredients

- 4 ounces of spreadable cream cheese
- 1/2 cup strawberry basil preserves, divided
- 1 loaf challah bread, sliced into 1-inch thick slices
- 8 large eggs
- 2 cups whole milk
- 2 tbsp honey
- 1 tbsp pure vanilla extract
- 6 ounces blueberries
- 6 ounces raspberries
- 1 pound strawberries, sliced

Instructions

1. Your grill should be preheated to medium-low, or roughly 250–300°F, with the grates oiled.
2. Slice a pocket into the center of each piece of bread, starting at the bottom. The gap should be wide enough to insert a knife with filling into the bread without cutting all the way through.
3. Cream cheese and 1/4 cup preserves should be mixed well in a small bowl. If it appears a bit thick, that's acceptable. Spread the cream cheese mixture evenly on the baguette slices. Fill the bread and place it in a large pan (at least a 913, bigger if you have it).
4. Whisk the eggs, milk, honey, and vanilla until well blended in a large mixing basin. Pour onto the stuffed bread.
5. The french toast should be cooked through and golden brown on the prepared grill over direct heat for about 5 minutes on each side. Move it to indirect heat if it is browning too soon after being placed near direct heat.

6. In the meanwhile, combine the berries with 1/4 cup of preserves and stir until evenly covered.
7. Serve your french toast with berries on top!

Nutrition Information

Serving: 1of 6, Calories: 327kcal, Carbohydrates: 31g, Protein: 14g, Fat: 16g, Cholesterol: 279mg, Sodium: 217mg, Fiber: 5g, Sugar: 21g

9. CLASSIC FRENCH TOAST

PREP 5 MINS

COOK 10 MINS

TOTAL 15 MINS

Ingredients

- 4 large eggs
- 2/3 cup milk
- 1/4 cup all-purpose flour
- 1/4 cup granulated sugar
- 1/4 tsp salt
- 1 tsp ground cinnamon
- 1 tsp vanilla extract
- 8 thick slices of bread

Instructions

1. Heat a skillet over medium heat or the griddle to 350 degrees Fahrenheit.
2. All ingredients, save the bread, should be added to a blender or shallow dish and thoroughly mixed. It's alright if the flour doesn't blend in totally smoothly while whisking by hand.
3. Placed on a hot, oiled griddle or pan, bread pieces are dipped into the batter and thoroughly dredged on both sides.
4. Cook the loaves for a few minutes or until the bottoms begin to become golden brown. Flip the food over, then continue cooking it there.
5. Take it out onto a platter. Serve hot with syrup and some powdered sugar on top.

Nutrition

Calories: 159kcalCarbohydrates: 24gProtein: 6gFat: 3gCholesterol: 83mgSodium: 258mgPotassium: 108mgFiber: 1gSugar: 9g: 76mgIron: 1.5mg

10. FRENCH CREPE RECIPE

yield: 8

prep time: 10 MINUTES

cook time: 10 MINUTES

total time: 20 MINUTES

Ingredients

- for the crepes
- 2 eggs
- 1/4 cup butter, melted
- 2 1/2 tbsp sugar
- 1/2 cup all-purpose flour
- 1/2 cup milk
- 1/8 cup water
- 1/2 tsp vanilla
- a tiny dash of salt
- for the filling
- 1 cup heavy whipping cream
- 2-4 tbsp powdered sugar (to taste)
- 1/2 tsp vanilla extract
- fresh strawberry slices

Instructions

For the Crepes

1. All the ingredients—aside from the flour—are whisked together. A little at a time, gradually include the flour while whisking to incorporate it.
2. Give the crepe batter 10 minutes to rest. Before using, quickly mix the batter once more.
3. Heat unsalted butter in a nonstick, 6" skillet over medium heat. To get the batter to spread evenly over the pan, add two to three tsps of batter and tilt the pan from side to side.
4. The crepe should be cooked for 30 seconds on each side before using a big spatula to carefully release the edges. The crepe is ready to be flipped if it lifts. Give it another 10 to 15 seconds if it doesn't pull up very well before attempting again. The crepe should be carefully lifted out of the pan, flipped over, and cooked for an additional 10 to 15 seconds before being taken out to cool.

For the filling

1. Simply use a hand mixer or stand mixer to beat the heavy whipping cream until soft peaks form. After including the vanilla and powdered sugar, whisk the mixture until firm peaks form.
2. Each crepe should have a coating of cream on it, followed by sliced strawberries. The crepe should then be rolled up like a wrap.

11. CLASSIC DENVER OMELETTE

Prep Time: 10

Cook Time: 10

Total Time: 20 minutes

INGREDIENTS

- 1 tbsp olive oil
- 1/4 cup onion finely chopped
- 1/2 red pepper finely diced
- 1/2 green pepper finely diced
- 5 slices lean ham chopped (about 4 ounces)
- 4 whole eggs
- 4 egg whites
- 2 tbsp cool water
- 2 tbsp butter
- 1/2 cup shredded white cheddar cheese
- Salt and pepper to taste

INSTRUCTIONS

1. In a pan over medium heat, warm the olive oil. Add the peppers and onion. Cook the veggies for 4-5 minutes over medium heat or until the edges begin to brown. After another 1–2 minutes, add the ham. Keep warm, cover, and remove from heat.
2. Mix eggs, egg whites, and water in a bowl.
3. In an 8-inch nonstick pan, melt 1 tbsp of butter over low heat. Pour half of the egg mixture into the pan. Cook the eggs under cover for two to three minutes, or until they have set. Add 1/4 cup of the cheese, extinguish the flame, and let the cheese melt. Then, fold the omelet in half, crossing one side over the other to seal it.
4. Repeat the process with the remaining egg mixture, cheese, and vegetables.

12. THE CLASSIC BACON, EGG, AND CHEESE SANDWICH

Yield: 2 Sandwiches

Prep Time 5 minutes

Cook Time 15 minutes

Total Time 20 minutes

Ingredients

- 2 ciabatta rolls
- 4 tsps unsalted butter divided
- 4 slices bacon
- 4 large eggs
- Kosher salt and freshly ground pepper to taste
- ½ cup grated Havarti or other cheese
- Sriracha or other hot sauce to taste

Directions

1. The rolls should be cut in half horizontally. 2 tsps of the butter should be melted over medium-high heat in a large, heavy pan, such as cast iron. Place the sliced sides of the roll in the pan and sizzle for one to two minutes, or until the bottoms are brown. Take out and place aside.
2. Over medium-high heat, add the bacon to the pan and cook until crisp, about 4 minutes per side. Remove the bacon to a plate lined with paper towels, drain out any remaining fat in the pan, and then gently clean the interior of the pan with a wad of paper towels (the pan is hot!).
3. In a bowl, crack the eggs and whisk them just enough to include the salt and pepper. Melt the 2 tsps of butter that are left in the pan. Pour the eggs in, and as the bottom hardens up, pull the sides up with a spatula to reveal the raw egg below. Sprinkle the cheese on top when the

top is almost done cooking, but the bottom is still a little damp. Allow the eggs to cook for one more minute before folding the edges over the center to form a rectangle omelet. Cut the omelet in half after sliding it out of the pan and placing it on a cutting board so that each piece resembles a ciabatta roll.

4. On the bottom of the browned bun, place the scrambled eggs. Put the bacon on top of the eggs, drizzle on some Sriracha or other hot sauce, and then top with the roll's top slice.
5. Serve the sandwich hot, read a magazine for ten minutes during the day, and remember this time fondly for the rest of the week.

Nutrition Information

Calories: 711kcal | Carbohydrates: 28g | Protein: 36g | Fat: 50g | Cholesterol: 430mg | Sodium: 1138mg | Potassium: 248mg | Fiber: 1g | Sugar: 1g | Calcium: 408mg | Iron: 2mg

13. SAUSAGE, VEGETABLE, AND EGG SCRAMBLE

Prep:12 mins

Cook:30 mins

Total:42 mins

Yield: Serves 4

Ingredients

- 2 medium Yukon gold potatoes, peeled, cut into 1/2-inch dice
- Salt and pepper
- 2 tbsp unsalted butter
- 6 ounces smoked sausage, sliced 1/4-inch thick
- ½ medium onion, chopped
- ½ medium green bell pepper, seeded, chopped
- 1 ½ cups sliced mushrooms
- 6 large eggs
- ¼ cup whole milk

Directions

1. In a big, deep pan, add the potatoes and 2 tsps of salt. Add 1 inch of cold water on top. Bring to a boil over high heat, lower the heat to a simmer, and cook for about 8 minutes, or until the potatoes are just soft. Drain. Clean the skillet.
2. In the same skillet over medium heat, melt the butter. Include sausage. Cook for approximately 3 minutes, occasionally turning, until both sides are browned. Put in a bowl with a slotted spoon. Season the veggies in the pan with salt and pepper. Cook for

approximately 8 minutes over medium heat, stirring periodically, or until the veggies are soft.

3. In a medium bowl, whisk the eggs with the milk; season with salt and pepper. Stir together the veggies in the pan with the meat and potatoes. Pour the egg mixture in and whisk continuously for approximately a minute, or until the eggs are set but still creamy. Serve right away.

4. Stay warm. Place the (ovenproof) skillet in the oven on low heat to buy some time if the eggs are done before you're ready to eat.

Nutrition Facts

346 calories; fat 24g;protein 18g; carbohydrates 16g; fiber 3g; cholesterol 320mg; sodium 535mg.

14. BEST-EVER STEAK & EGGS

YIELDS:2 SERVINGS

PREP TIME:0 HOURS 30 MINS

TOTAL TIME:1 HOUR 0 MINS

Ingredients

- 1"-thick New York strip steak (about 13 Ounces.)
- 2 tbsp. Vegetable oil, divided
- 1 tsp. Kosher salt, plus more for seasoning to taste
- 1 tsp. Freshly ground black pepper, plus more for seasoning to taste.
- 3/4 tsp. Smoked paprika, plus more for seasoning to taste
- 2 tbsp. butter

- 4 eggs

DIRECTIONS

1. Take the steak out of the fridge and wait 30 minutes for it to reach room temperature.
2. Steak is seasoned with 1 1/2 tsps of salt, 1 tsp of pepper, and 3/4 tsp of paprika after being rubbed with 1 tbsp of vegetable oil.
3. Over medium-high heat, preheat a medium cast iron skillet. Add the steak and cook for about 5 minutes total, turning once, or until a deep golden crust forms on both sides of the meat.
4. Add butter to the pan and lower the heat to medium-low. Grab the handle of the skillet with a kitchen towel and tilt it towards you so that the melted butter collects at the bottom of the pan. To create a thicker, more golden crust, baste butter onto the steak repeatedly with a spoon. After about two to three minutes, flip the steak again. Check the internal temperature of the meat using a meat thermometer: 120-125°F for medium rare, 130°F for medium.
5. After placing the steak on a chopping board, give it about 10 minutes to rest.
6. In the meantime, shimmer the remaining oil in a nonstick pan over medium heat. Once the white is set, and the sides are just starting to brown, crack one egg into the pan and cook it for 3 to 4 minutes. Take out of the pan and add salt and pepper.
7. On the bias and against the grain, cut the meat into 1"-wide strips.
8. Serve steak with potatoes and eggs. Add extra salt, pepper, and paprika to taste before garnishing with herbs.

15. THE ULTIMATE BREAKFAST BURRITO

Prep time 15mins

Cook time 25mins

Ingredients

FOR THE PICO

- 3 Roma tomatoes, cored and finely chopped
- 1/2 cup finely chopped fresh cilantro
- 1/4 cup finely chopped red onion
- 1 lime, zested and juiced
- 1 small jalapeño, seeded and diced
- Kosher salt, to taste
- Black peppercorns, freshly ground, to taste.

FOR THE BURRITO

- 3 medium Yukon Gold potatoes
- 4 tbsp La Tourangelle Grapeseed Oil divided

- 8 ounces spicy chorizo sausage, casings removed
- 1 tbsp Simply Organic Garlic Powder
- 1 tbsp Simply Organic Onion Powder
- 1/ 2 tsp Simply Organic Cayenne
- 1 small bunch of scallions, ends trimmed and thinly sliced
- 6 large Handsome Brook Farm Pasture-Raised Organic Eggs, vigorously whisked
- 4 large tortillas
- 1 avocado, sliced
- 1 cup grated sharp cheddar cheese
- Hot sauce for serving

METHOD

1. Set the oven to 350°F.
2. Creating the pico Combine all ingredients in a medium bowl and season to taste. Keep in the fridge.
3. Potatoes should be grated, then transferred to a clean kitchen towel, and any extra liquid squeezed out. Keep covered in a kitchen towel.
4. In a cast iron pan, heat 2 tbsp of grapeseed oil over medium-high heat. Cook chorizo for about 8 minutes, breaking it up into little crumbles with a heat-resistant spatula as it cooks. Use a slotted spoon to remove and set aside.
5. Potatoes can be added to the same skillet. Add cayenne, salt, pepper, garlic powder, onion powder, and cayenne to the bowl. Place in a single layer over the pan and cook for 4 minutes, occasionally stirring, until golden brown. Another 4 minutes are needed to brown the potatoes on the other side. Take out of the pan and place aside. Clean the skillet entirely.
6. Heat the remaining 2 tbsp of grapeseed oil in the skillet over medium heat. Saute the scallions for 2 minutes or until they are soft. Scramble the eggs for 2 minutes after adding them. Take out of the skillet and place aside.
7. Divide the egg mixture, chorizo, potatoes, pico, avocado slices, and cheese among the four tortillas to make the burritos. Wrap securely after tucking in the sides. Burritos should be placed on a baking pan. Place in oven, and bake for 10 minutes, or until cheese is melted. Slice in half, then serves right away with spicy sauce.

16. MEXICAN SCRAMBLED EGGS

Prep:15 mins

Cook:10 mins

Total:25 mins

Servings:1

Ingredients

- 2 eggs
- ½ cup diced onion
- ¼ cup milk
- 2 tbsp diced green bell pepper
- 2 tbsp diced red bell pepper
- 1 jalapeno pepper, seeded and diced
- 2 tsps Mexican-style chile powder
- 1 tsp onion powder
- ½ tsp ground cumin
- 1 dash of ground cinnamon
- salt and ground black pepper to taste
- cooking spray

Directions

1. In a bowl, whisk the eggs together. Combine with onion, milk, green, red, and jalapeño peppers, cumin, cinnamon, salt, and pepper, as well as chile and onion powders.
2. Grease a sizable pan with cooking spray and heat over medium-high heat. Pour in egg mixture; cook and stir for 5 minutes per side, or until golden brown.

Nutrition Facts

233 calories; protein 16.3g; carbohydrates 16.4g; fat 11.8g; cholesterol 376.9mg; sodium 327.7mg.

17. HASH BROWN EGG SCRAMBLE

Prep Time: 5 mins

Cook Time: 15 mins

Total Time: 20 mins

INGREDIENTS

- 1–1 1/2 tbsp butter
- 1 tbsp olive oil, plus more if needed
- 1, 14-5 Ounces can of sliced or diced New Potatoes, drained
- Salt and pepper
- 1/2 tsp granulated garlic (or garlic powder)
- 1/2 tsp paprika
- 1 red pepper, diced small
- 1 medium onion, halved, thinly sliced, and cut in half again
- 6 eggs, beaten

- 1/2 cup milk
- 4 slices of American cheese
- Toast or toasted bagels with butter, optional but delicious

INSTRUCTIONS

1. In a large pan, melt the butter and olive oil over medium-high heat. Add the potatoes after the butter has melted. Add paprika, salt, pepper, granulated garlic, and other seasonings to taste. Break up the potatoes into tiny pieces before adding them to the spices (if you used sliced potatoes). Cook for three to five minutes.
2. Add the onions and peppers. Combine and gently season with the same ingredients as the potatoes. Cook for approximately 5 minutes, or until the potatoes are crispy and the peppers and onions are tender. Add a bit of additional butter or olive oil if you notice the pan is getting dry at any point while the food is cooking. The pan must be smooth for both the eggs and to prevent scorching.
3. In a mixing dish, combine the eggs, milk, salt, and pepper while the potatoes are boiling. Add the cheese into pieces and stir the eggs. Place aside.
4. Add the eggs and let them cook in the pan, untouched, for a minute, till the potatoes are crispy and the onions and peppers are soft. For the eggs, keep the heat higher. The eggs and potatoes should be combined right away after one minute and scrambled together until done. The eggs should immediately begin to melt the cheese. Remove from the pan and serve the eggs with bread, if wanted, after another 1-2 minutes, when they appear to be fully cooked.

18. CRISPY HASH BROWNS

PREP TIME5 mins

COOK TIME15 mins

TOTAL TIME20 mins

Ingredients

- 3 tbsp extra virgin olive oil
- 1 pound Russet baking potatoes
- Salt and pepper

Method

1. Peel and grate the potatoes: Use a box grater with big holes to peel and grind the potatoes.
2. Squeeze out the moisture:
3. Squeeze the shredded potatoes to remove as much liquid as you can. Use a potato ricer (or an orange or lemon press) similarly to how you would like a garlic press, with the exception that you don't push the potatoes through the ricer. Simply push the extra moisture out.
4. Work in batches, and only add half the amount of raw grated potatoes to the ricer.
5. If you don't have a ricer, wrap the uncooked, shredded potatoes in a fresh kitchen towel and squeeze until you get as much moisture out of it as you can. To make things easier to manage, work in bunches. Use a towel that you don't mind displaying some use as the potatoes can occasionally stain a fabric one.
6. Although they don't perform as well as cloth or a ricer, you may still squeeze out the moisture with strong paper towels.

Cook the hash browns:

1. In a big frying pan, heat 3 tbsp of oil to medium-high. Add the shredded potatoes and spread them out evenly around the bottom of the pan after the oil is shimmering but not smoking. The potatoes should be between 1/4 and 1/2 inches thick but not too thick in any one spot.
2. Potatoes should be salted and peppered.
3. The hash browns over:
4. Lift one edge of the potatoes and check their doneness after a few minutes. They are ready to flip if they are golden brown from frying.
5. To turn the potatoes over, either cut the huge potato cake into half or quarters and turn it with a large metal spatula (or two spatulas).
6. Cook them more until the bottoms are golden brown.

Serve:

1. Use a metal spatula to cut into quarters and serve.

19. BACON POTATO HASH

prep time:15 MINS

cook time:20 MINS

total time:35 MINS

INGREDIENTS

- 1/2 pound thick-cut bacon
- 2 tbsp reserved bacon fat
- 1 tbsp butter
- 2 small shallots, diced
- 1/2 green bell pepper, diced
- 2 medium Russet potatoes, peeled and cut in half lengthwise
- 1/4 tsp dried thyme leaves or 1/2 tbsp chopped fresh thyme
- kosher salt, to taste
- Freshly ground black pepper.

INSTRUCTIONS

2. Roughly 2 tbsp of the bacon grease that was saved after cooking about half to three-quarters of a pound of bacon were left aside.
3. The potato halves should be heated in a big saucepan of room temperature water, brought to a boil, then reduced to a simmer, and cooked for 10 to 12 minutes. The potatoes shouldn't be mushy but still slightly firm. Drain into a colander and chill down with cold tap water when the ten minutes are up. Cut into 1/2 inch cubes once it is safe to handle and has cooled.
4. Reheat the bacon grease and tbsp of butter in the same pan over medium-low heat. After the diced shallot has been softened for 5 minutes, add the green pepper and fry for an additional 2–3 minutes.
5. The potatoes, salt, and pepper are then added. Once stirred, simmer the hash for another 10-15 minutes, stirring regularly, or until potatoes are well cooked.
6. The final step is to add crumbled bacon to the potato hash, combine, and serve.

Nutrition

serving: 1g, calories: 421kcal, carbohydrates: 23g, protein: 10g, fat: 32g, cholesterol: 52mg, sodium: 418mg, potassium: 626mg, fiber: 2g, sugar: 2g, calcium: 25mg, iron: 1mg

20. BUFFALO CHICKEN BURGERS

Hands-On:35 mins

Total:35 mins

Yield: Serves 6

Ingredients

- 1 ½ pounds ground chicken
- 4 ounces diced whole-grain bread
- 5 tbsp 2% reduced fat milk, divided
- ½ cup minced onion
- ½ tsp freshly ground black pepper
- ¼ tsp kosher salt
- 5 tbsp hot sauce, divided
- 1 tbsp butter, melted
- 1 ounce (about 1/4 cup) blue cheese, crumbled
- 2 tbsp low-fat buttermilk
- 2 tbsp canola mayonnaise
- 1 cup very thinly sliced carrot
- 1 cup very thinly sliced celery
- ¼ cup very thinly sliced green onions

Directions

1. Turn on the grill or the heat in a grill pan.
2. Combine the chicken, bread, 1/4 cup of milk, onion, pepper, and salt in a medium bowl.
3. Allow the bread to absorb all of the liquid by folding it together. Avoid mashing. Make sure the mixture is loose and erratiCup
4. Six equal servings of the chicken mixture should be made. Together, bring the six (1/2-inch-thick) burgers just firmly enough to keep their shape.
5. In a small dish, mix 1/4 cup hot sauce and butter. Roll patties in the butter mixture, one at a time.
6. Mix 1 tbsp of the milk, 1 tbsp of the spicy sauce, the blue cheese, the buttermilk, and the mayonnaise in a medium bowl. Fold in the carrots and celery after adding them. While the burgers are cooking, let the lettuce wilt a little at room temperature.
7. The burgers should be grilled for five minutes on each side or until they reach 155 degrees within. They'll continue.
8. Place the burgers on a plate and top them with a third cup of celery salad. Onions should be uniformly distributed on the burgers.

Nutrition Facts

315 calories; fat 17.8g; protein 25g; carbohydrates 17g; fiber 3g; cholesterol 109mg; iron 2mg; sodium 660mg; calcium 95mg.

21. TERIYAKI PINEAPPLE TURKEY BURGERS

Total: 25 min

Prep: 25 min

Yield: 8 servings

Ingredients

- 1 can (20 Ounces.) DOLE® Pineapple Slices
- 1/2 cup teriyaki sauce
- 2 pounds ground turkey or chicken
- 1 tsp grated fresh ginger
- 1/2 cup panko bread crumbs
- 8 whole grain hamburger buns
- 8 slices of Cheddar or Monterey Jack cheese

Directions

1. Pineapple juice should be saved, about 1/2 cup. Save two slices of pineapple for a snack or other use.
2. In a small bowl, combine the teriyaki sauce and the saved pineapple juice.
3. Turkey, ginger, bread crumbs, and 1/4 cup of the teriyaki sauce are combined. 8 patties should be formed.
4. Grill patties until browned and well cooked, basting with the remaining teriyaki sauce. Grill pineapple slices until they are just beginning to become golden.
5. Burgers should be served on buns with pineapple and cheese.
6. Tip: To make 4 servings, use 1 can (8 Ounces.) DOLE® Pineapple Slices and cut the remaining ingredients in half.
7. Per Serving: 134 calories, 1g fat 17mg cholesterol, 775mg sodium, 17g carbohydrate (<1g dietary fiber, 9g sugars), 1 g protein, 13% Vit A, 10% Vit C, 21% calcium, 4% iron, <1% potassium, 3% folate

22. EX-MEX TURKEY BURGER RECIPE

Prep Time: 15 MINUTES

Cook Time: 15 MINUTES

0 MINUTES

Total Time: 30 MINUTES

Ingredients

- 1 pound lean ground turkey
- 2 avocados - mashed
- juice of ½ lime
- 4 pepper jack cheese slices
- ½ cup light mayo - or sour cream
- 1 cup shredded lettuce
- 4 hamburger buns

Tex Mex Seasoning

- 1 tsp garlic powder
- 1 tsp salt
- 1 tsp cumin
- 1 tsp coriander
- 1 tsp chili powder

Instructions

1. Mix the mashed avocado with the lime juice and season with salt to taste to make guacamole. Place aside.
2. The Tex-Mex Seasoning's ingredients are combined in a bowl. Put in halves.
3. Half of the Tex-Mex Seasoning and mayo (or sour cream) should be combined. Place aside.
4. Combine the ground turkey and the remaining Tex-Mex Seasoning in a big bowl. By hand, thoroughly combine; shape into 4 equal patties.
5. Burger patties should be cooked through and browned on the grill for about 6 minutes on each side at medium heat.
6. Add a slice of cheese to the top of each burger, close the grill, and let the cheese melt (about 1-2 minutes).
7. Put mayo sauce on the bottom bread, top with the turkey burger patty, then add a generous amount of guacamole, some shredded lettuce, and the top bun to complete the turkey burger. Dispense and savor!

Nutrition

Calories: 486 kcal, Carbohydrates: 34 g, Protein: 34 g, Fat: 25 g, Cholesterol: 68 mg, Sodium: 1087 mg, Potassium: 930 mg, Fiber: 8 g, Sugar: 5 g, Calcium: 105 mg, Iron: 3 mg

23. BEEF BURGERS – LEARN TO MAKE

Prep:17 mins

Cook:13 mins

Ingredients

- 1 small onion, diced
- 500g good-quality beef mince
- 1 egg
- 1 tbsp vegetable oil
- 4 burger buns
- All or any of the following to serve: sliced tomato, beetroot, horseradish sauce, mayonnaise, ketchup, handful iceberg lettuce, rocket, watercress

Method

1. 500 grams of beef mince should be added to a bowl along with 1 egg and 1 tiny sliced onion.
2. Cut the mixture in half. Wet your hands just enough. Make tennis ball-sized balls out of the mixture with caution.
3. Gently press down to flatten into patties that are about 3 cm thick after placing them in the palm of your hand. To ensure equal cooking, make sure the thickness of each burger is the same.
4. Place on a dish, wrap in plastic wrap and place in the refrigerator for at least 30 minutes to firm up.
5. The grill to medium heat (there will be white ash over the red hot coals – about 40 mins after lighting). Vegetable oil should be lightly brushed onto one side of each burger.
6. Place the hamburgers on the grill with the oil side up. Cook the beef for 5 minutes or until it is slightly charred. They may stick if you move them around.
7. Turn over using tongs after oiling the opposite side. Avoid pressing down on the meat since doing so will cause the juices to be lost.
8. For medium, cook a further 5 minutes. Cook your burgers for 1 minute shorter on each side if you like a pink center. Cook 1 minute longer for well done.
9. Remove the hamburgers from the grill. So that the fluids may all condense within, let the food lie on a platter.
10. Halve four hamburger buns. Place them cut-side down on the grill rack and toast for 1 minute, or until they are just beginning to sear. Place a burger into each bun, then add your preferred side salad.

24. LAMB BURGERS WITH TZATZIKI

Prep:15 mins

Cook:25 mins

Ingredients

- 25g bulghar wheat

- 500g extra-lean lamb mince
- 1 tsp ground cumin
- 1 tsp ground coriander
- 1 tsp smoked paprika
- 1 garlic clove, very finely crushed (optional)
- oil for brushing
- large burger buns, sliced tomato, and red onion to serve

For the tzatziki

- 5cm piece cucumber, deseeded and coarsely grated
- 200g pot thick Greek yogurt
- 2 tbsp chopped mint, plus a handful of leaves to serve

Method

1. Put the bulgur in a pan, add water to cover, and bring to a boil for 10 minutes. Press out any extra water by draining extremely well in a sieve.
2. Cucumber juice should be squeezed out and discarded before being combined with yogurt, chopped mint, and a little salt to produce tzatziki.
3. Work the bulghar into the lamb along with the seasoning, spices, and garlic (if used), and then form into 4 patties. Brush with a little oil, then fry or grill for approximately 5 minutes on each side, or until well done. Serve the tzatziki, tomatoes, onion, and a few mints leaves in the buns (toasted if you wish).

25. EASY HATCH CHILE SALSA VERDE

Prep Time: 10 min

Cook Time: 0 minutes

Total Time: 10

INGREDIENTS

- 4 cloves garlic
- ½ white onion
- 1 green onion
- ½ cup cilantro leaves
- 1 jalapeno
- 4-5 tomatillos
- Juice of 1 lime
- 3 roasted Hatch chiles (or 1 small can)
- 1 tsp cumin
- 2 tbsp white vinegar

- ¼ tsp salt
- ¼ tsp black pepper

INSTRUCTIONS

1. Jalapenos and Hatch chiles should be free of stems and seeds. Chop the tomatillos, pepper, and onions roughly.
2. Blend or process all of the ingredients in a food processor or blender until somewhat smooth (you still want a little bit of texture).
3. Serve with your favorite Mexican bowl or with freshly made tortilla chips.

26. CHIPOTLE BURGERS WITH CREAMY AVOCADO SAUCE

prep Time: 15 minutes

Cook Time: 10 minutes

Total Time: 25 minutes

Ingredients

- 1 Pounds. ground beef
- 2 chipotles in adobo
- 1 Tbsp adobo sauce
- 2-3 Tbsp finely chopped onion
- 1 garlic clove
- 1 tsp salt
- freshly cracked black pepper
- 4-6 cheese slices
- 4-6 hamburger buns
- 1 tomato
- lettuce

For the Creamy Avocado Sauce

- 1 avocado
- 1/4 cup plain Greek yogurt
- 1/4 jalapeno
- 2 garlic cloves
- 15-20 sprigs of cilantro
- 1 lime
- 2 Tbsp olive oil
- 1/4 tsp salt
- freshly cracked black pepper
- splash of water

- 1 Tbsp mayonnaise or cream (optional)

Instructions

1. One pound of ground beef, two minced chipotles in adobo (with stems and seeds removed), a couple of tbsp of finely chopped onion, a clove of minced garlic, a tbsp of adobo sauce, a tsp of salt, and some freshly cracked pepper should all be combined in a mixing bowl.
2. Combine together and shape into 6 smaller burgers or 4 patties of 1/4 Pounds each.
3. You are free to cook the burgers in any way you choose. Typically, I brown them in a pan over medium heat for 2–3 minutes on each side before baking them for 4-6 minutes at 425°F while adding cheese slices in the last few minutes. As the burgers are finishing up, I also put the buns in the oven.
4. Add the following ingredients to a blender or food processor to make the Creamy Avocado Sauce: 1 avocado, 1/4 cup plain greek yogurt, 1/4 jalapeño, 2 cloves of garlic, 15-20 cilantro sprigs, lime juice, 2 tsps extra virgin olive oil, 1/4 tsp salt, freshly ground pepper, and a splash of water. Together nicely. A sprinkle of cream or one tbsp of mayonnaise is further option.
5. Apply the Creamy Avocado Sauce to each hamburger bun before adding your preferred lettuce, tomato, and other toppings.

27. PERFECT SALMON BURGERS

Total: 1 hr

Active: 30 min

Ingredients

- 1 1/4 pounds center-cut salmon fillet, skin and pin bones removed
- 2 tbsp dijon mustard
- 1 tbsp mayonnaise
- 1 tbsp lemon juice
- 1/2 tsp grated lemon zest
- Pinch of cayenne pepper
- 2 scallions, chopped
- 1 cup plus 2 tbsp panko (Japanese breadcrumbs)
- Kosher salt and freshly ground black pepper
- 2 tbsp extra-virgin olive oil, plus more for brushing
- 4 brioche buns, split
- Tartar sauce and arugula for topping

Directions

1. Cut the fish into pieces that are each 1/4 inch in size. Place in a big bowl. Slice the remaining salmon into chunks, then add the chunks, mustard, mayonnaise, lemon juice, lemon zest, and cayenne to a food processor. To produce a paste, pulse. To the bowl containing the chopped salmon, add the pureed salmon mixture. Add 2 tbsp panko, 1/2 tsp salt, and black pepper to taste, along with the scallions. Mix gently until barely mixed.
2. Olive oil should be brushed on a parchment-lined baking pan. On the parchment paper, divide the salmon mixture into 4 mounds. Pat into 4-inch-wide, 3/4-inch-thick patties using wet hands. Place loosely covered in the refrigerator for at least 30 minutes.
3. Set the broiler to high. In a bowl, spread the remaining 1 cup of panko. The salmon patties should be panko-coated on both sides. In a large cast iron or nonstick pan over medium-high heat, warm the olive oil. Add the patties (if required, in batches) and cook for 3 to 4 minutes, or until the bottoms are browned, adjusting the heat as needed. Turn the patties over and cook for another 3 to 4 minutes, or until the other side is browned and they feel springy to the touch. Season with salt and transfer to a plate lined with paper towels to drain.
4. In the meantime, place the buns cut-side up on a broiler pan and broil for 1 to 2 minutes, or until toasted. Place the burgers on the buns and garnish with arugula and tartar sauce.

28. CHICKEN CAESAR BURGERS

Prep/Total Time: 30 min

Ingredients

- 1/4 cup finely chopped onion
- 2 tbsp shredded Parmesan cheese, divided
- 1 tbsp lemon juice
- 1-1/2 tsps dried parsley flakes
- 1 garlic clove, minced
- 1 tsp Worcestershire sauce
- 1/4 tsp salt
- 1/4 tsp pepper
- 1/2 pound ground chicken
- 2 hamburger buns, split
- 1/4 cup torn romaine
- 4 tsps fat-free creamy Caesar salad dressing

Directions

1. Combine the onion, 1 tbsp cheese, parsley, garlic, lemon juice, Worcestershire sauce, salt, and pepper in a small bowl. Add chicken crumbles to the mixture and stir thoroughly. Make 2 patties by shaping.

2. Burgers should be covered and cooked for 5-7 minutes on each side or until an instant-read thermometer registers 165° and the juices flow clear. Add the remaining cheese on top.
3. Serve with romaine lettuce and salad dressing on buns.

Nutrition Facts

1 each: 322 calories, 12g fat 79mg cholesterol, 801mg sodium, 29g carbohydrate (5g sugars, 2g fiber), 25g protein

29. BEST-EVER TURKEY BURGER

YIELDS:4

PREP TIME:0 HOURS 5 MINS

TOTAL TIME:0 HOURS 20 MINS

INGREDIENTS

- 1 Pounds. ground turkey
- 1 large egg, beaten
- 2 cloves garlic, minced
- 1 tbsp. Worcestershire sauce
- 2 tbsp. Freshly chopped parsley
- Kosher salt
- Freshly ground black pepper.
- 1 tbsp. Extra-virgin olive oil
- Hamburger buns
- Lettuce
- Sliced tomatoes
- Mayonnaise

DIRECTIONS

1. Combine the turkey, egg, garlic, Worcestershire sauce, and parsley in a large bowl. Add salt and pepper to taste. Make four flat patties out of the mixture.
2. Heat oil in a medium skillet over medium heat. Add the patties, and heat for 5 minutes per side, or until golden and well done. Serve with the preferred toppings on a bun.

30. NUT BURGERS

Prep Time: 10 minutes

Cook Time: 10 minutes

Resting Time: 5 minutes

Total Time: 25 minutes

INGREDIENTS

- 1 ½ cups (220 g) nuts
- 1 onion
- 2 tbsp olive oil
- 1 cup (100 g) breadcrumbs
- 2 tbsp soy sauce
- 2 tsp dried herbs
- 1 cup (240 ml) vegetable stock
- 1 tbsp chia seeds

INSTRUCTIONS

1. Olive oil should be used to sauté the chopped onion in a frying pan until it is tender, translucent, and just beginning to brown.
2. The nuts should be processed in a food processor until they are fine and hardly gritty.
3. Boiling water and stock powder or bouillon are used to make vegetable broth.

4. The ground nuts, sautéed onion, breadcrumbs, soy sauce, herbs, chia seeds, and vegetable broth should all be combined in a mixing bowl.
5. To let the chia seeds soak and the mixture somewhat cool, set it aside for five minutes.
6. Round patties from the mixture are formed. Add extra breadcrumbs if the mixture becomes a little too sticky.
7. Cook for 3–5 minutes on each side, or until crisp and browned, in a little amount of oil heated over medium-high heat in a frying pan.

NUTRITION

Calories: 329kcal | Carbohydrates: 24g | Protein: 9g | Fat: 23g | Sodium: 619mg | Potassium: 279mg | Fiber: 5g | Sugar: 2g | Calcium: 79mg | Iron: 3mg

31. SHRIMP BURGERS WITH SEAWEED SALAD

Total: 25 min

Active: 25 min

Ingredients

Patties:

- 1/2 tbsp finely chopped basil
- 1/2 tbsp finely chopped cilantro
- 1/2 tbsp fish sauce
- One 1-inch piece of lemongrass
- 3 tbsp finely chopped shallots
- One 1-inch piece of fresh ginger, peeled.
- 2 cloves garlic
- Large pinch each kosher salt and freshly ground black pepper
- 1 1/2 pounds large shrimp (16 to 20 count per pound), peeled, deveined, and roughly chopped
- 1 1/2 tsps cornstarch
- 2 tsps vegetable oil

For Serving:

- 1/4 cup mayonnaise
- 1 tsp sriracha, plus more if desired
- 4 burger buns
- Seaweed salad, for topping (see Cook's Note)
- Toasted sesame seeds for sprinkling

Directions

1. For the patties, combine all the ingredients in a food processor and pulse until everything is well combined and finely minced, leaving out the shrimp, cornstarch, and oil. You should not let the machine run while adding the shrimp and cornstarch. Pulse 5–10 times, or until a chunky paste develops. Form 4 patties out of the shrimp mixture that is approximately 3/4 inch thick. On a piece of wax paper, set aside.
2. Apply a thick layer of oil to a big pan (or grill) and heat over medium-low heat. Cook the patties for 5 to 6 minutes on each side or until well done.
3. Sriracha and mayonnaise should be mixed thoroughly in a small dish before serving. Spread on the burger buns' split sides. Each bottom bun should have a shrimp patty, seaweed salad, and sesame seeds on top. Serve the burgers with their lids on.

32. SPICY GUACAMOLE BURGER

PREP TIME 5 mins

COOK TIME 10 mins

TOTAL TIME 15 mins

INGREDIENTS

- 1 Pounds 85% lean ground chuck
- 1 tsp salt
- 1 tsp pepper
- 1 tsp paprika
- 1 tsp red pepper flakes
- 1 clove garlic minced
- Sharp Cheddar Cheese sliced.
- 2 avocados
- 1 tsp chives chopped
- 1/2 lime juiced

INSTRUCTIONS

1. Set the BBQ to a medium heat setting. Cover the BBQ to keep the heat in and let it warm up.
2. Combine the meat, salt, pepper, paprika, red pepper flakes, and garlic in a large bowl. Mix everything by hand until it is all spread equally. Form patties by dividing the ingredients into four equal halves.
3. With a fork, mash the avocado after removing it from its peel together with the chives and lime juice. Place aside.

4. Transfer the patties to the hot grill, and cook them for 5 minutes on each side for medium-rare. Add the cheese just before serving, allowing it to barely melt. Place patties on buns after taking them off the grill; top with tomatoes and guacamole, if using, and serve.

33. GARLIC PORK BURGERS (SPANISH STYLE)

Prep Time: 15 Minutes

Cook Time: 15 Minutes

Total Time: 30 Minutes

Ingredients

Saffron Aioli:

- Pinch of saffron mixed with 2 t hot water
- 1 large garlic clove, minced with a pinch of salt
- 2 t caper juice
- 1/2 c mayonnaise
- 1/4 c minced cilantro or Italian parsley

Burgers:

- 1 Pounds ground pork
- 1/4 c chopped cilantro or Italian parsley
- 2 minced garlic cloves
- 2 t smoked paprika
- 1/2 t coarse salt
- 1/4 t fresh ground black pepper
- 1 1/2 T chopped capers
- 4 thin slices of Serrano ham
- 4 slices of Bermuda onion
- 4 ounces of shredded Iberico cheese
- 3 buns of your choice

Instructions

To make the aioli:

1. In a measuring cup, soften saffron with hot water.
2. Add the rest of the ingredients and stir well. Let flavors meld together as you make burgers.

To Make Burgers:

1. Salted pepper, paprika, cilantro, and capers should all be combined with the pork. Incorporate patties. Take it easy! Patties largely depend on how big your bun is. To account for shrinking, patties should be about 3/4" larger than the bread. Because of this, I only made three burgers, but you could make four 1/4-pound patties!
2. Slices of ham and onion should be brushed with a little aioli to prevent sticking to the grill.
3. To prevent the meat from sticking to the grill, preheat the grill to medium-high heat and spray or brush cooking spray across the grates. Although every grill is different and mine isn't perfect, you should grill for roughly 5 minutes per side.
4. When placing patties on the grill, add onion slices on it. After five minutes, switch each. Put the ham and buns on the grill right now. Watch each closely to prevent burning. Once the buns are toasted, place them and the ham on the cool side of the grill.
5. Burgers should be practically done before adding cheese and letting it melt.
6. To serve: Spread each side of the bun with saffron aioli. On the bottom half of the bun, place a slice of ham. Top with onions. Add burger and top with bun.

34. BEETROOT AND LENTIL BURGERS

AND-ON TIME 20 MIN

OVEN TIME 10 MIN

Ingredients

- 325g raw beetroot
- 250g pack cooked puy lentils
- 2 garlic cloves
- 1 red chili
- 5cm piece of fresh ginger
- 6 fresh mint sprigs
- 1 medium free-range egg
- ½ tbsp curry powder
- 2-3 tbsp plain flour
- Oil for frying

To serve

- 60g crumbled feta
- 4 good quality buns
- Salad leaves
- Lemon wedges

Method

1. The oven should be heated to 200°C/fan180°C/gas 6. Peel, grate and then wrap the beets in a clean J-cloth that has been folded. As much liquid as you can, squeeze out.
2. Place the lentils and the beetroot in a bowl. Garlic, ginger, mint, and other ingredients should be finely chopped. Put the egg in. Add the curry powder, salt, pepper, and 1 to 2 tbsp of flour (just enough to hold it all together).
3. Oil is heated in a pan. Create 4 burgers out of the beetroot mixture. Dust both sides generously with flour. Fry the burgers for 2-3 minutes on each side, or until golden, after the oil is sufficiently hot.
4. The burgers should be baked for 5 to 6 minutes or until they are sizzling hot. Serve with salad leaves, a couple of lemon wedges, and feta cheese on buttered, toasted buns.

35. GIANT PARTY CHEESEBURGER

YIELDS:4 - 6 SERVINGS

PREP TIME:0 HOURS 20 MINS

TOTAL TIME:1 HOUR 15 MINS

INGREDIENTS

- 3 Pounds. ground beef
- 1 Cup bread crumbs
- 2 large eggs
- 2 tbsp. Worcestershire sauce
- 3 cloves garlic, minced
- 1/2 Pounds. sliced cheddar cheese
- 1 large boule, halved
- 2 Cup romaine lettuce
- ketchup
- mustard
- 2 large tomatoes, sliced
- 1 Cup pickle coins
- Baked French fries, for serving (optional)

DIRECTIONS

1. Set a big rimmed baking sheet in the oven at 350 degrees and cover it with foil. Apply cooking spray to foil.
2. Ground beef, bread crumbs, eggs, Worcestershire sauce, and garlic are mixed together in a big bowl with salt and pepper. Use your hands to blend everything evenly.

3. Form the meat mixture into very big patties before transferring it to the prepared baking sheet. Its diameter needs to be around 1" more than that of your bread. Bake for 50 to 55 minutes, or until the meat is well cooked and browned.
4. Blot excess oil from the patties and the area surrounding it with paper towels. Heat the broiler. Cheese should completely cover the top of the burger. Broil for approximately a minute or until cheese is melted.
5. Burger assembly: Set the boule bread's bottom half on a large serving platter. Place the enormous cooked burger on top of the lettuce. Put the top half of the boule on top of the tomato and pickle toppings after spreading ketchup and mustard all over the patty.
6. Serve heated with French fries after cutting into wedges.

36. CRISPY PORK TENDERLOIN SANDWICHES

Prep/Total Time: 25 min

Ingredients

- 2 tbsp all-purpose flour
- 1/2 tsp salt
- 1/4 tsp pepper
- 1 large egg, lightly beaten
- 1/2 cup seasoned bread crumbs
- 3 tbsp panko bread crumbs
- 1/2 pound pork tenderloin
- 2 tbsp canola oil
- 4 hamburger buns or kaiser rolls, split

Directions

1. Combine the flour, salt, and pepper in a small basin. In another small bowl, put the egg. Place the bread crumbs in a third shallow basin after mixing them.
2. 4 slices of tenderloin should be cut crosswise, and each should be pounded with a meat mallet to a thickness of 1/4 inch. Shake off the excess after coating both sides with flour mixture. To help them stick, pat after dipping in egg and then crumb mixture.
3. Oil should be heated in a big skillet at medium heat. Pork should be cooked until golden brown, about 2-3 minutes per side. Take out and let dry on paper towels. With any chosen toppings, serve in buns.

37. GRILLED HAM AND CHEESE WITH PINEAPPLE

Prep:10 mins

Total:15 mins

Ingredients

- 2 slices of sandwich bread
- 2 slices of Swiss cheese
- 2 ounces thinly sliced ham
- 2 thin rounds of pineapple
- 3 fresh basil leaves
- 1 tbsp butter

Directions

1. Sandwich bread is layered with one piece of Swiss cheese, ham, pineapple, fresh basil, and the second slice of cheese.
2. Melt butter in a pan over medium heat. Insert sandwich. Cook for 2 to 3 minutes under a cover until browned.
3. Toss; cook with a lid off until cheese melts.

38.CROQUE MADAME SANDWICH

total: 30 min

Prep: 5 min

Cook: 25 min

Ingredients

- 6 ounces unsalted butter, divided
- 2 tbsp flour
- 1 cup whole milk

- 1 bay leaf
- 1/2 tsp kosher salt, plus more for seasoning
- 1/4 cup grated Parmesan
- 8 slices of thick sourdough bread
- 8 to 12 slices of good quality ham (about 3/4 pound)
- 12 ounces Gruyere cheese, grated, divided
- Nonstick spray
- 4 eggs

Directions

1. Preheat the broiler.
2. Make the bechamel sauce: In a small saucepan, melt 1 ounce of butter over medium heat. Whisk in the flour and cook, constantly stirring, until you smell the flour and butter cooking, 2 to 3 minutes. Do not allow it to brown. Add the milk and bay leaf and cook, stirring from time to time, until the mixture thickens like a soup, 10 to 12 minutes. Remove the bay leaf and stir in the Parmesan. Transfer to a bowl to cool.
3. Arrange 4 slices of the bread on a flat surface. Top each with 2 to 3 slices of ham. Mix together half of the Gruyere cheese and the bechamel sauce. Taste for seasoning. Spread a little of the sauce on top of the ham and top each with another slice of bread.
4. Heat a large cast iron skillet and, when hot, add half of the remaining butter. Add 2 of the sandwiches and brown on one side 2 minutes. Turn on the other side and brown 2 more minutes. Transfer to a baking sheet and repeat with the remaining butter and sandwiches. Spread the remaining bechamel on top of the sandwiches and top with the other half of the Gruyere cheese.
5. Wipe any crumbs from the cast iron skillet and spray with nonstick spray. Crack 4 eggs into the skillet, leaving a little room between each. (Alternatively, fry 2 at a time). While the eggs are frying, place the sandwiches under the broiler and broil until the top becomes golden brown, 1 to 2 minutes. Season the eggs with salt and top each sandwich with a fried egg. Serve immediately.

39. THE ULTIMATE GRILLED CHEESE

Prep/Total Time: 15 min.

Ingredients

- 3 ounces cream cheese, softened
- 3/4 cup mayonnaise
- 1 cup shredded part-skim mOunceszarella cheese
- 1 cup shredded cheddar cheese
- 1/2 tsp garlic powder
- 1/8 tsp seasoned salt
- 10 slices of Italian bread (1/2 inch thick)

- 2 tbsp butter, softened

Directions

1. In a large bowl, beat cream cheese and mayonnaise until smooth. Stir in the cheeses, garlic powder, and seasoned salt. Spread 5 slices of bread with the cheese mixture, about 1/3 cup on each. Top with remaining bread.
2. Butter the outsides of sandwiches. In a skillet over medium heat, toast sandwiches for 4-5 minutes on each side or until bread are lightly browned, and cheese is melted.

40. CRISPY GARLIC BREAD GRILLED CHEESE SANDWICHES

Prep Time: 2 minutes

Cook Time: 5 minutes

Total Time: 7 minutes

Ingredients

- 2 pieces of Sliced sandwich bread
- 2 slices of Cheese cheddar are my favorite
- 2 tbsp Butter softened or melted
- Garlic powder
- Dried parsley
- Parmesan Cheese shredded

Instructions

1. 2 pieces of bread should be butter-brushed or spread, and the garlic and parsley should be sprinkled on either side.
2. Each buttered side of the bread should have a couple of tbsp of Parmesan cheese sprinkled over it. Gently press the cheese into the bread.
3. One slice of bread with the buttered side down should be placed in a nonstick pan that has been heated over medium heat. Add cheese and the final piece of bread on top. Cook until bread is golden brown, parmesan cheese is crunchy, and inside cheese is melted, flipping halfway through.

Nutrition Facts

Serving: 1 sandwich | Calories: 431 kcal | Carbohydrates: 30 g | Protein: 14 g | Fat: 41 g | Cholesterol: 119 mg | Sodium: 557 mg | Potassium: 54 mg | Calcium: 404 mg | Iron: 0.4 mg

41. CHEESY-CRUST SKILLET PIZZA

Prep:10 mins

Cook:5 mins

Additional:5 mins

Total:20 mins

Ingredients

- 1 ½ cups shredded part-skim mOunceszarella cheese
- 5 cherry tomatoes, thinly sliced
- 2 tbsp torn fresh basil leaves
- 4 small fresh mOunceszarella balls (bocconcini), thinly sliced

Directions

1. A 10-inch nonstick skillet should be heated to medium-high. In a heated pan, evenly distribute the shredded mOunceszarella cheese; cook for 2 to 3 minutes, or until the cheese is melted.
2. Place fresh mOunceszarella slices, tomato slices, and basil leaves, and room for a crust to develop over the melted cheese; bake for 2 to 3 minutes, or until the top is bubbling, and the sides are browned.
3. Pizza may now be removed from the griddle by using a spatula. Pizza should be thinly sliced and placed on a cutting board after cooling for a minute.

Cook's Notes:

❖ The crust is delicate and thin, so don't overload with toppings. But do try with other toppings (pepperoni, ham, pineapple, or BBQ chicken).

Nutrition Facts

385 calories; protein 31g; carbohydrates 6.4g; fat 25.6g; cholesterol 98.2mg; sodium 608.5mg.

42. VEGAN PORTOBELLO FRENCH DIP RECIPE

Prep Time: 15 min

Cook Time: 15 min

Ingredients

- 1 large sweet onion
- 2 med bell peppers
- 1/4 tsp salt
- 2 tsp minced garlic
- 16 Ounces portobello mushroom caps (4 large)
- 2 Tbs water or veg broth (if needed to prevent sticking)
- 1 tsp Italian seasoning
- 1 3/4 cup low sodium veggie broth
- 2 Tbs low sodium soy sauce
- 1 Tbs vegan Worcestershire sauce
- 2 tsp molasses
- 1/4 tsp liquid smoke (or smoked paprika)
- 1 Tbs corn starch or arrowroot

Instructions

1. 1Thinly slice the onion and peppers, then put them in a large pan with salt.
2. 2 Use 1-2 tbsp of vegetable broth or water to prevent sticking while you toss the onions and peppers constantly over medium heat until they start to soften.
3. 3Add 2 tsps of minced garlic and mix.
4. 4Slice mushrooms into pieces that are 1/4" thick.
5. 5Add mushrooms to skillet and cook until they start to lose liquid and become smaller in size. Mix in the Italian seasoning.
6. 6Combine the ingredients for the au jus—vegetable broth, soy sauce, Worcestershire, molasses, liquid smoke, and cornstarch—in a small basin.
7. 7 When the mushroom liquid has nearly completely evaporated, slowly pour in the Au Jus.
8. 8Simmer mushrooms in au jus until sauce starts to thicken a little. To taste, add salt and pepper to the food.
9. Sandwiches can be put together on the bread of your choosing.

43. GRILLED VEGGIE PESTO FLATBREAD

yield: 4

prep time: 15 MINUTES

cook time: 25 MINUTES

total time: 40 MINUTES

INGREDIENTS

- 4 Naan bread
- ½ cup cherry tomatoes halved

- 1 red pepper sliced into rings
- 1 small yellow squash sliced thin
- 1 small green zucchini sliced thin
- 4 slices of red onion cut ¼" thick
- 2 slices of eggplant cut ½" thick
- 3 tbsp olive oil
- ½ tsp salt
- ½ tsp black pepper
- ¾ cup mOunceszarella cheese
- ¾ cup pesto (homemade recipe below)

INSTRUCTIONS

1. Heat the grill.
2. Toss all of the vegetables together with olive oil, salt, and pepper.
3. Use a grilling basket and include vegetables in it.
4. Grill vegetables until they are slightly browned, often tossing (remove and keep warm)
5. Grill the naan bread until grill marks appear.
6. Flip over and repeat on the opposite side.
7. One side of the naan bread should be covered evenly with pesto.
8. On the naan bread, divide the vegetables.
9. additional cheese
10. Place once more on the grill, cover, and cook until cheese melts (about 5 minutes)
11. Slice and present

NUTRITION INFORMATION:

Amount Per Serving: CALORIES: 259TOTAL FAT: 20gCHOLESTEROL: 14mgSODIUM: 390mgCARBOHYDRATES: 14gFIBER: 2gSUGAR: 4gPROTEIN: 7g

44. GRILLED VEGGIE PIZZA

Prep: 30 min

Bake: 10 min

Ingredients

- 8 small fresh mushrooms, halved
- 1 small zucchini, cut into 1/4-inch slices
- 1 small sweet yellow pepper, sliced
- 1 small sweet red pepper, sliced
- 1 small onion, sliced
- 1 tbsp white wine vinegar

- 1 tbsp water
- 4 tsps olive oil, divided
- 2 tsps minced fresh basil or 1/2 tsp dried basil
- 1/4 tsp salt
- 1/4 tsp pepper
- 1 prebaked 12-inch thin whole wheat pizza crust
- 1 can (8 ounces) of pizza sauce
- 2 small tomatoes, chopped
- 2 cups shredded part-skim mOunceszarella cheese

Directions

1. Mushrooms, zucchini, peppers, onions, vinegar, water, three tbsp of oil, and spices should all be combined in a big bowl. Move to a grill basket or wok. Grill under cover for 8 to 10 minutes, turning once until the meat is tender.
2. Grill in preparation for indirect heat. Spread pizza sauce on the crust and brush with the remaining oil. Add cheese, tomatoes, and grilled veggies as garnish. For 10 to 12 minutes, or until the sides are gently browned, and the cheese is melted, grill the food covered over indirect medium heat. Pizza should be rotated halfway through cooking for an evenly browned crust.

Nutrition Facts

1 slice: 274 calories, 11g fat 22mg cholesterol, 634mg sodium, 30g carbohydrate (6g sugars, 5g fiber), 17g protein.

45. BAKED BACON JALAPENO WRAPS

Prep:10 mins

Cook:25 mins

Total:35 mins

Servings:12

Ingredients

- 1 (8 ounces) package of cream cheese
- 12 fresh jalapeno peppers, halved lengthwise and seeded
- 6 slices of bacon, cut into halves

Directions

1. Set oven to 425 degrees Fahrenheit (220 degrees C).

2. Jalapeno pepper halves with cream cheese inside have each been wrapped in a slice of bacon. To stop the bacon from unraveling while baking, fasten it with toothpicks. Place the cream cheese side down on a baking sheet with the covered jalapeño peppers.
3. Set an outside grill on high heat and give the grates quick oiling.
4. Bake in the preheated oven for 10 minutes, then flip the pan over and bake for an additional 10 minutes, or until the bacon is well browned.
5. Transfer the jalapeno wraps to the hot grill and cook for two to three minutes on each side, or until the bacon is crisp.

Nutrition Facts

94 calories; protein 3.3g; carbohydrates 1.4g; fat 8.5g; cholesterol 25.6mg; sodium 161.3mg.

46. MEXICAN BEAN BREAKFAST SKILLET

Prep Time 1 minute

Cook Time 15 minutes

Ingredients

- 1 tsp. ground cumin
- one 19 ounces can of black beans rinsed and drained well
- one 19 ounces can of stewed tomatoes use flavored if you can see Italian spiced or peppers,
- 5 eggs
- 1/4 cup of grated low-fat cheese
- chopped cilantro for garnish
- salt & pepper to taste

Instruction

1) Set the oven to 450 degrees Fahrenheit. In a cast iron pan, mix the beans, tomatoes, and cumin.

2) Cook the tomato liquid until it almost entirely evaporates, stirring periodically. Up to 10 minutes may be required, but it will be well worth it! If you don't have much time, drain the tomato liquid and simmer for a few minutes.

3) Create five little pockets in the bean mixture, one for each egg.

4) Bake the eggs for 5 minutes at 450 degrees Fahrenheit or until they are still jiggly and undercooked.

5) After taking the pan out of the oven, cover it with cheese.

6) Put the dish back in the oven and continue baking until the cheese has melted.

7) Take the dish out of the oven, then top with cilantro before serving.

Nutrition

1275 calories, 172 grams of carbohydrates, 91 grams of protein, 27 grams of fat, 825 milligrams of cholesterol, 1776 milligrams of sodium, 3525 milligrams of potassium, 55 grams of fiber, and 20 grams of sugar 625 mg calcium, 24.6 mg iron

---

47. ULTIMATE BREAKFAST BURRITOS

Total Time

Prep/Total Time: 20 min.

2 servings

Ingredients

- 1 tsp olive oil
- 1/2 cup of chopped fresh mushrooms
- 1/4 cup of chopped green pepper
- 1/4 cup of chopped sweet red pepper
- 1 cup of egg substitute
- 1/4 tsp pepper
- 2 whole-wheat tortillas (8 inches), warmed
- 1/4 cup of shredded reduced-fat cheddar cheese
- 2 tbsp salsa
- 2 tbsp fat-free sour cream

Directions

1) Heat the oil in a small nonstick pan over medium-high heat. Cook the veggies until tender, stirring periodically. The pan should be taken off the heat and kept heated.

2) In the same pan, combine the egg substitute and pepper; cook and stir over medium heat until the eggs have thickened and there is no longer any liquid egg. Turn off the heat under the pan.

3) After putting the vegetable mixture and scrambled eggs into each tortilla, top with cheese, salsa, and sour cream. The tortilla should be rolled up by folding the bottom and sides over the contents.

Nutrition

1 burrito has 294 calories, 8 grams of fat, 13 milligrams of cholesterol, 585 milligrams of sodium, 31 grams of carbohydrate (6 grams of sugar, 3 grams of fiber), and 21 grams of protein.

48. OATMEAL PANCAKES WITH CINNAMON

Prep:35 mins

Total:35 mins

Yield: Makes 20

Ingredients

- 2 cups of all-purpose flour (spooned and leveled)
- 1/4 cup of packed brown sugar
- 1 tbsp baking powder
- 1 tsp salt
- 1/2 tsp ground cinnamon
- 2 cups of old-fashioned rolled oats
- 2 cups of milk
- 2 large eggs
- 1/4 cup of vegetable oil, plus more for skillet

Directions

1) To finely crush 1 cup of oats, pulse flour, sugar, baking powder, salt, cinnamon, and food processor several times. Whisk the milk, eggs, and oil in a large mixing basin. In a mixing basin, stir together the dry ingredients and 1 cup of oats until slightly moistened.

2) Set a large pan (cast iron or nonstick) or griddle to medium heat. Lightly grease a skillet. Utilizing 2 to 3 tbsp of batter per pancake, cook for 1 to 2 minutes, or until a few bubbles have burst. Cook the pancakes for another 1 to 2 minutes, or until the undersides are browned. Add additional butter and oil and repeat.

49. CAULIFLOWER HASH BROWNS

PREP:10 mins

COOK:20 mins

TOTAL:30 mins

Ingredients

- 3 cups of riced cauliflower from about 1 ¼ pound or ½ medium head cauliflower or thawed frOuncesen riced cauliflower
- 1 large egg
- 3/4 cup of shredded sharp cheddar cheese

- ¼ cup of grated Parmesan
- ½ tsp kosher salt
- ¼ tsp ground black pepper
- ¼ tsp garlic powder
- ¼ tsp onion powder
- ¼ tsp smoked paprika or 1/8 tsp cayenne pepper
- Nonstick cooking spray

Instructions

1. Place racks in the center and top thirds of the oven. Preheat the oven to 400 degrees F. Cover a rimmed baking sheet generously with nonstick spray or parchment paper.
2. Place the cauliflower rice in a microwave-safe bowl. Microwave on high for 2 minutes, uncovered.

Nutrition

80 kcal 3 g CARBOHYDRATES

6 g PROTEIN 5 g FAT 34 mg CHOLESTEROL 197 mg POTASSIUM 1 g FIBER 1 g SUGAR CALCIUM: 127 milligrams

50. BACON EGG AND CHEESE SANDWICH

Prep Time:5 mins

Cook Time:15 mins

Oven bacon time:25 mins

Total Time:40 mins

Ingredients

- 8 slices of thick-cut bacon see notes below
- 4 large deli-style hard rolls see notes below
- 4 tsp butter divided
- 8 large eggs
- 8 slices of yellow American cheese
- 4 tsp water for melting cheese
- salt and pepper to taste
- Ketchup is optional; to taste

Instructions

1. Preheat the oven to 400 degrees F and position the racks in the center. Wire racks should be placed on top of two foil-covered baking sheets. Cook for 20-25 minutes, or until crispy and cooked to your liking, by spreading thick-cut bacon equally on wire racks.
2. To keep the bacon warm, place it on a platter and cover it with foil. Divide the 4 rolls in half and place each half on a large piece of parchment paper to make wrapping simpler. s
3. In a large nonstick pan or flat griddle, melt a tbsp of butter over medium heat. Cook 2 eggs on one side for 2 minutes before flipping. If you want the egg yolks broken, break them with the edge of a spatula, or leave them alone for an over-easy egg sandwich.
4. Two slices of cheese should be on only one of the eggs.
5. After adding a tsp of water to the pan, cover with a tight-fitting lid. Remove the cover after 30 seconds and place the egg on the bottom of the roll without the cheese. On top of the cheese, crack an egg. Top with bacon, salt, pepper, and ketchup and wrap in parchment paper. Remove any extra water from the pan and cook the next three sandwiches the same way.
6. Split the paper in half and cover with foil to keep warm or serve immediately after making all four sandwiches. Enjoy!

Nutrition

Calories: 490kcal | Carbohydrates: 5.2g | Protein: 44.9g | Fat: 31.7g | Cholesterol: 443mg | Sodium: 1600mg | Potassium: 210mg | Sugar: 5g | Calcium: 226mg | Iron: 3mg

51. CRISPY GARLIC BROCCOLI WITH SESAME FRIED RICE

40 mins

2 people

Ingredients

- 150g brown basmati rice
- Ahead of broccoli

- 2 garlic cloves
- 200g chestnut mushrooms
- 200g rainbow chard
- 1 chili
- A handful of coriander
- 1 egg
- 1 tbsp tamari
- 1 tbsp sesame oil
- Sea salt
- 300ml boiling water
- 2 tbsp olive oil
- Freshly ground pepper
- 1 tbsp cold water

Method

1. Half-fill a bowl with cold water and whisk for 1-2 minutes, or until the water becomes murky. Drain and rinse before putting it in a small saucepan. A pinch of salt and 300 mL of boiling water. Cover it with a blanket, bring it to a boil, and then turn the heat down to very low. Simmer for 25 minutes, or before all of the water has been absorbed, then remove from the heat and cover to steam in the pan. The rice will stay heated in the pan.
2. Preheat the oven to 200 degrees Celsius/Fan 180 degrees Celsius/Gas 6 (200 degrees Celsius/Fan 180 degrees Celsius/Gas 6). Cut the broccoli into chunky florets and place it on a roasting tray. 1 tbsp oil, 1 tsp salt, and pepper. Bake for 20 minutes or until soft and caramelized with a nutty flavor.
3. Peeled garlic cloves should be roughly cut. 1 tbsp oil, heated in a large pan over medium heat. When the pan is hot, add the garlic and cook for 1-2 minutes, or until golden and crispy, turning regularly. Pour into a mixing bowl.
4. Slice the chestnut mushrooms thinly. The stems and leaves of the chard should be shredded. For less heat, finely chop the chile after half it and remove the seeds and pith. Set aside the coriander leaves and thinly chop the coriander stems for later.
5. Reduce the heat to medium in the garlic-cooking pan. Cook for 4-5 minutes, or until the mushrooms, chard, chiles, and coriander stems are glossy. Add 1 tbsp cold water if the pan becomes too dry.
6. With a wooden spoon, move the vegetables to one side of the pan. Crack the egg in the vacant place. Raise the heat to medium-high and gently break and scramble the eggs with a spoon for 1-2 minutes.
7. Toss the cooked rice in the veg pan with 1 tamari and 1 tbsp sesame oil. Stir carefully to ensure uniform distribution, then heat for 2 minutes.
8. Place the roast broccoli florets on top of the mushroom fried rice. Finish with the crispy garlic and coriander leaves.

52. RESTAURANT-STYLE COLESLAWS

Prep:15 mins

Additional:1 hr

Total:1 hr 15 mins

Servings:8

Ingredients

- 1 (16 ounces) package of coleslaw mix
- 2 tbsp minced onion
- ⅓ cup of white sugar
- ½ tsp salt
- ⅛ tsp ground black pepper
- ¼ cup of milk
- ½ cup of mayonnaise
- ¼ cup of buttermilk
- 1 ½ tbsps white wine vinegar
- 2 ½ tbsps lemon juice

Directions

1. Combine the coleslaw and onion in a large mixing bowl.

2. In a separate bowl, mix together the sugar, salt, pepper, milk, mayonnaise, buttermilk, vinegar, and lemon juice until smooth. Chill for 1 hour after pouring the dressing over the coleslaw and onion.

Nutrition

184 calories; 1.4 g protein; 17.1 g carbs; 12.6 g fat; 10.6 mg cholesterol; 247.9 mg sodium

53. GRIDDLED AUBERGINES WITH YOGURT & MINT

Prep:10 mins

Cook:50 mins

Serves 4

Ingredients

- 4 small aubergines, sliced into 1cm/½in thick rounds
- 2 tbsp olive oil
- 150g pot natural yogurt
- juice of ½ lemon
- 2 garlic cloves, crushed
- small bunch of mint leaves, coarsely chopped

Method

1. Toss the aubergine slices with olive oil and a tsp of salt and pepper in a mixing bowl. On a griddle pan set to high heat, cook the slices on both sides until tender and lightly browned; you'll need to do this in batches. Allow it to cool slightly before serving on a serving plate.
2. Combine the yogurt, lemon juice, garlic, and mint in a separate bowl. Season with salt and pepper to taste. Serve at room temperature with the yogurt mixture drizzled over the griddled aubergine pieces.

54. ROASTED LEMON GARLIC MUSHROOMS

yield: 4

prep time: 10 MINUTES

cook time: 25 MINUTES

total time: 35 MINUTES

Ingredients

- 1 pound cremini mushrooms (aka baby Bellas), cleaned and sliced
- 3 garlic cloves, minced
- 2 tbsp extra virgin olive oil
- 1 tbsp fresh rosemary, minced
- ½ lemon, juice
- ½ lemon, zest
- Salt and pepper to taste

Instructions

1) Set the oven to 400 degrees Fahrenheit. Using parchment paper, line a large baking sheet.

2) Combine the mushrooms, garlic, olive oil, rosemary, lemon juice, lemon zest, salt, and pepper in a large mixing bowl.

3) Place the mushrooms in a single layer on the baking sheet (a little overlap is okay).

4) Cook the mushrooms for 20 to 25 minutes, or until they are soft. Use salt and pepper to taste to season. Eating as soon as you can is preferred.

55. ROASTED RED PEPPERS IN OIL, VINEGAR, AND GARLIC

Prep:10 mins

Cook:0 mins

Total:10 mins

Servings:4 servings

Ingredients

- 3 whole roasted red peppers or a dOuncesen roasted piquillo peppers
- 2 cloves garlic
- 1/4 cup of Spanish sherry vinegar or balsamic vinegar
- 1/4 cup of extra-virgin olive oil

Make

1. Use a dinner-sized basin or plate with a lip to keep the oil and vinegar from pouring over the side.
2. If using bell peppers, remove any seeds before roasting. Cut each pepper into four pieces and place it in a dinner bowl or bowl.
3. Because piquillo peppers are small, they're already the right size for individual servings (approximately 3 inches long). Drain the piquillo peppers and scatter them about the bowl or platter.

4. Peeled and minced garlic cloves are required. Mix minced garlic with a few tbsp each of vinegar and oil in a small bowl. After whisking, carefully pour over the peppers.
5. Serve with rustic bread pieces as a tapa or as a side dish with dinner. As the main course, these peppers go nicely with grilled meat or shellfish.

56. THE BEST ROASTED ROSEMARY GARLIC POTATOES

PREP TIME5 minutes

COOK TIME40 minutes

TOTAL TIME45 minutes

INGREDIENTS

- 3 Pounds. red potatoes, cut into 1-inch pieces
- 3 cloves of garlic, minced
- 2 tbsp. fresh rosemary (thyme works great here too)
- 2 tbsp. extra virgin olive oil
- 1-2 tsp kosher salt

INSTRUCTIONS

1. Preheat the oven to 425 degrees Fahrenheit and set the baking sheet inside to heat.
2. Coat all of the ingredients in a large mixing bowl.
3. Roast potatoes on a preheated oven sheet for 35-45 minutes, turning halfway through.

NUTRITION

191 CALORIES TOTAL 5 g FAT 0g FAT CHOLESTEROL: 280 mg SODIUM 34 g CARBOHYDRATES 30g NET CARBOHYDRATES 4 g FIBER 4 g SUGAR 4 g PROTEIN

57. BUTTERY GRILLED POTATOES IN FOIL PACKETS

Prep Time20 mins

Cook Time35 mins

Total Time55 mins

Ingredients

- 3 pounds Yukon gold potatoes
- ½ cup of butter

- 1 tbsp kosher salt
- Freshly cracked black pepper
- 2 tbsp minced garlic
- ½ cup of diced white onion
- ¼ cup of olive oil

Instructions

1. Scrub the potatoes thoroughly to remove any debris from the skin. (If using a Russet potato, remove the peel first.)
2. Set aside potato pieces that are no thicker than 14 inches.
3. With a cold stick of butter, spread a thin layer of butter in the center of two 18x12 inch sheets of foil. Butter tracings should be around 12x9 inches.
4. Place half of the sliced potatoes in a thin, even layer on top of one of the butter rectangles. Season to taste with half of the salt and a generous amount of freshly cracked black pepper. On top, 1 tbsp garlic and 14 cup onion are scattered. On top of the original layer of butter, put 4–6 pats of butter.
5. Repeat the stacking and seasoning process with the remaining potatoes right on top of the first layer. Pour olive oil over the entire dish.
6. Top with the second sheet of foil and fold all of the sides toward the center to seal the package.
7. Over medium-high heat, grill for 15–20 minutes on the first side before rotating and grilling for another 10–15 minutes. (Cook for longer for crispier potatoes.) The package will puff up throughout the cooking process, which is typical.
8. Remove the potatoes from the grill and set them to cool slightly before removing the foil wrapper. Before serving, sprinkle with fresh parsley or chives, if desired.

Nutrition

Serving: 0.3pounds | Calories: 266kcal | Carbohydrates: 28g | Protein: 3g | Fat: 16g | Cholesterol: 27mg | Sodium: 875mg | Potassium: 657mg | Fiber: 4g | Sugar: 2g | Calcium: 26mg | Iron: 1mg

58. GRILLED RATATOUILLE PASTA SALAD

Active Time 25 minutes

Total Time 40 minutes

Ingredients

- 2 medium zucchini (about 1½ Pounds.), halved lengthwise
- 1 medium or 2 small eggplants (about 1 Pound.), cut into 1" wedges
- ¾ cup of extra-virgin olive oil, divided
- 2½ tsp. Kosher salt, divided
- 1 tsp. Freshly ground black pepper, divided
- 10 Ounces. penne or casarecce pasta

- 1 large or 2 medium heirlooms or beefsteak tomato (about 1 Pound.), cut into 1" pieces
- 8 Ounces. Clinging (mini fresh mOunceszarella balls), drained, halved
- 2 Tbsp. White balsamic or white wine vinegar
- 1 Tbsp. thyme leaves
- 1 cup of basil leaves

Method

1. Preheat your grill to medium-high. Toss zucchini, eggplant, and 14 cups of oil on a rimmed baking sheet with 1 tsp salt and 12 tsp pepper. 8–12 minutes, occasionally turning, until steaming, tender, and completely burnt. Return the baking sheet to the oven to cool.
2. Cook the pasta according to the package directions.
3. Slice the grilled vegetables into bite-size pieces and place them in a large mixing bowl. 12 cup oil, tomato, cheese, vinegar, thyme, 112 tsp salt, 12 tsp pepper. Drain the pasta and pour it into the bowl with the vegetables as soon as possible. Toss everything together well, then sprinkle over the basil.
4. Vegetables can be grilled up to three days in advance. Refrigerate everything in an airtight container.

59. GRILLED ZUCCHINI WITH MISO

Prep:20 mins

Total:30 mins

Yield: Serves 4 to 6

Ingredients

- 2 tbsp white or yellow miso
- 4 tsp reduced-sodium soy sauce
- 4 tsp unseasoned rice vinegar
- 2 tbsps vegetable oil
- Kosher salt and freshly ground pepper
- 8 small zucchini (about 2 pounds total), halved lengthwise
- Toasted sesame seeds for serving

Directions

1) Combine miso, soy sauce, vinegar, oil, and 1/4 tsp. Pepper in a mixing bowl. Prepare the grill to medium-high heat for direct heat grilling. Salt the zucchini, then grill it for 10 to 12 minutes, turning it once or twice, until it's crisp-tender and browned in spots. After brushing on half of the glaze and rotating to coat evenly, grill after another 1 to 2 minutes. Before serving, apply the remaining glaze and top with sesame seeds.

60. TOSTONES RECIPE (TWICE-FRIED PLANTAINS!)

PREP TIME10 mins

COOK TIME10 mins

TOTAL TIME20 mins

INGREDIENTS

- 2 large green plantains were peeled and sliced into 2" slices
- 1/2-1 cup of vegetable oil, avocado oil, or your oil of choice with a high smoke point (enough to cover the slices)
- Salt to taste

INSTRUCTIONS

- In a deep nonstick skillet, heat the oil over medium-high heat.
- Place the thick plantain slices in a skillet with enough oil to coat them completely. Watch the video for more details, but in general, you want enough oil so that the plantains' tops are visible, but the remainder of the slice is frying in it.
- All sides of the slices should be cooked for around 5 minutes. Remove the pan from the heat and absorb any remaining oil with paper towels.
- Using a plantain press or a folded paper towel, smash the plantains to about 1/2 inch thick.
- Fry the now-smashed plantains in the same skillet for about 4-5 minutes, or until golden brown on both sides.
- Before seasoning with salt, remove from the pan and drain on paper towels. (You may put the oil in an airtight jar and use it later if you like.)

NUTRITION

Serving: 1 servingCalories: 229 kcalCarbohydrates: 19 gProtein: 1 gFat: 18 Sodium: 2 mgPotassium: 298 mgFiber: 1 gSugar: 9 gVitamin C: 11 mgCalcium: 2 mgIron: 1 mg

61. ATOMIC BUFFALO TURD JALAPENO POPPERS

Prep Time: 20 minutes

Cook Time: 3 hours

Total Time: 3 hours 20 minutes

Ingredients

- 10 jalapeno peppers

- 10 slices of bacon, cut in half
- 10 mini sausages or smokies, or 20 if they are very small
- 1 cup of cream cheese
- 1 cup of grated Monterey jack
- 1 tsp chipotle or chili powder
- 2 shallots, minced

Instructions

1) Halve each jalapeno lengthwise. Remove the seeds and membrane using a spoon. After seeding the bell peppers, cut them in half.

2) Combine the cream cheese, Monterey Jack, chipotle powder, and shallots in a mixing bowl. Fill the hollowed-out peppers with the cheese mixture.

3) Spread the cream cheese with the smoke. The jalapeño should be encircled by 1/2 a slice of bacon. In the event that the bacon does not stay snugly wrapped, a toothpick may be required to hold it in place.

4) Set the smoker to 225°F and smoke the ABTs for two to three hours, or until the bacon is crisp.

Nutrition

Calories: 123kcalCarbohydrates: 2gProtein: 4gFat: Cholesterol: 28mgSodium: 188mgFiber: 1gSugar: 1g

62. EASY AND HEALTHY DESSERT IDEAS

yield: 18

prep time: 10 MINUTES

total time: 10 MINUTES

INGREDIENTS

- 1/2 cup of peanut butter
- 1/2 cup of chopped chocolate
- 6 rice cakes
- 1 tsp almond flour
- 1 tsp coconut oil
- pinch of salt

INSTRUCTIONS

1. Microwave for 20-30 seconds at a time until the chocolate and coconut oil is completely melted. Stir in between each stage to speed up the process. The chocolate melted in one minute in the microwave.
2. Add the peanut butter and stir until totally smooth.
3. Break or crumble the rice cakes and combine them with the other ingredients.
4. Add a tsp of almond flour at a time until the rice cakes are thoroughly coated with chocolate.
5. On a baking sheet lined with parchment paper, spread the ingredients evenly.
6. Refrigerate until hard, at least 2 hours.
7. Cut it up and eat it! Because these bars melt readily at room temperature, keep them refrigerated.

63. GLAZED RANCH CARROTS

Total Time

Prep/Total Time: 25 min.

12 servings

Ingredients

- 2 pounds of fresh baby carrots
- 1/2 cup of butter, cubed
- 1/2 cup of packed brown sugar
- 2 envelopes of ranch salad dressing mix
- Minced fresh parsley

Directions

1. Combine the carrots and 1 inch of water in a saucepan. Heat the water to a rolling boil. Reduce the heat to low, cover, and cook for 8-10 minutes, or until the potatoes are crisp-tender. Drain and set aside the water.
2. In the same pan, combine the butter, brown sugar, and salad dressing mix and swirl to incorporate. Add the carrots last. Over medium heat, cook and stir for 5 minutes, or until glazed. Garnish with parsley if desired.

Nutrition

3/4 cup of 156 calories, 8g fat 20mg cholesterol, 1067mg sodium, 22g carbohydrate (13g sugars, 1g fiber), 1g protein.

64. JAMAICAN JERK GRILLED VEGETABLES

Prep Time: 30 minutes

Cook Time: 20 minutes

Servings: 12 servings

Ingredients

- 1 tbsp ground allspice
- 1 tbsp onion powder
- 1 tsp ground nutmeg
- 1 tsp ground ginger
- 1/2 tsp garlic powder
- 1/2 tsp cayenne pepper
- 1 1/2 tbsp dried thyme
- 1/2 tbsp kosher salt
- 1/2 tbsp fresh ground pepper

Vegetables

- 1 medium eggplant sliced lengthwise
- 2 medium zucchini sliced lengthwise
- 2 portabello mushroom stems removed
- 2 red bell peppers cored and sliced in half
- 1 pound of thin asparagus tough ends snapped off
- 2-3 tbsps olive oil

Yogurt Sauce

- 2 cups of plain nonfat Greek yogurt
- 1/4 cup of fresh lime juice + zest of 1 lime
- 1/2 cup of minced scallions

Instructions

1. To make the spice mix, combine all of the spices, salt, and pepper in a small bowl.
2. Vegetables should be cleaned and cooked according to the instructions. In a large mixing bowl, drizzle olive oil over the vegetables. Toss gently to coat with oil.
3. Toss the vegetables with the spice combination and carefully toss to incorporate it. After coating the vegetables, set aside for 10-15 minutes to rest.
4. Preheat the grill to medium-high temperature.
5. Grill the vegetables in batches until they are soft and lightly browned on both sides, about 8-10 minutes for each batch.
6. Allow it cool for a few minutes before cutting it into serving pieces.
7. In a mixing bowl, combine Greek yogurt, lime juice, zest, and scallions to make the yogurt sauce. Season with a touch of salt if desired.
8. Serve over brown basmati rice and a yogurt sauce if desired.

65. ROASTED GARLIC-PARMESAN ZUCCHINI, SQUASH, AND TOMATOES

Servings: 6 servings

Prep10 minutes

Cook30 minutes

Ready in: 40 minutes

Ingredients

- 2 small zucchini (1 Pound), cut into 1/2-inch thick slices
- 2 small yellow squash (1 Pound), cut into 1/2-inch thick slices
- 14 Ounces Flavorino or small Campari tomatoes, sliced into halves
- 3 Tbsp olive oil
- 4 cloves garlic, minced (1 1/2 Tbsp)
- 1 1/4 tsp Italian seasoning
- Salt and freshly ground black pepper
- 1 cup of shredded (2.4 Ounces) finely Parmesan cheese
- Fresh or dried parsley for garnish.

Instructions

1. Preheat the oven to 400 degrees Fahrenheit (200 degrees Celsius). Line an 18 by 13-inch rimmed baking sheet with parchment paper or aluminum foil.
2. In a small bowl, combine the olive oil, garlic, and Italian spice. Combine the zucchini, squash, and tomatoes in a large mixing bowl. Toss lightly with your hands to evenly coat the top with the olive oil mixture.
3. Fill the prepared baking dish halfway with the mixture and spread it out evenly. Season with salt and pepper to taste. Sprinkle with Parmesan cheese before serving. In a preheated oven, roast for 25-30 minutes until veggies are tender and Parmesan is golden brown. Serve hot, with parsley on top if desired.

66. GREEN BEANS WITH CRISPY ONIONS

PREP TIME15 mins

COOK TIME10 mins

INGREDIENTS

- 1 pound fresh stringless green beans
- 1 cup of water

- 1/4 cup of dry white wine
- salt and black pepper to taste
- 2 tsp minced garlic
- 2 tbsps butter
- 1/2 cup of canned French fried onions

INSTRUCTIONS

1) Green beans should be trimmed off their ends and finely sliced using a green bean cutting tool, a kitchen shredding knife, a knife, or a food processor equipped with a shredding blade.

2) In a large pan, combine the beans, water, wine, garlic, salt, and black pepper.

3) Bring to a boil, then lower the heat to a simmer, cover the pot, and cook for 10 minutes. Drain.

4) Add fried onions that are crispy and seasoned with salt and pepper (Durkee/French style).

67. FRIED GREEN TOMATOES

PREP TIME10 mins

COOK TIME20 mins

TOTAL TIME30 mins

SERVINGS4 servings

Ingredients

- 3 medium-sized, firm green tomatoes

- Salt
- 1 cup of all-purpose flour
- 1 tbsp Cajun seasoning
- 1/2 cup of milk or buttermilk
- 1 large egg
- 1/3 cup of fine white cornmeal
- 1/2 cup of fine dry bread crumbs
- 1/4 cup of peanut, canola, or olive oil for frying

Method

1. Season unpeeled tomatoes with salt and cut them into 1/2 inch pieces. Before serving, season the slices with salt. After slicing the tomatoes, set them aside for about 5 minutes to rest.
2. I'm slicing green tomatoes to show how to make fried green tomatoes.
3. In small dishes, combine the following ingredients:
4. While the salted green tomato slices are resting, divide them into three small bowls: 1) flour and Cajun seasoning (if using), 2) breadcrumbs and cornmeal, and 3) buttermilk and egg.
5. In a mixing bowl, whisk together the egg and buttermilk.
6. Three bowls are required to create fried green tomatoes.
7. Place the ingredients in three bowls to make fried green tomatoes.
8. To bread the tomato slices, follow these steps:
9. Heat the oil in a skillet over medium heat. Green tomato slices are dipped in flour-seasoning, buttermilk-egg mixture, cornmeal-breadcrumb mixture, and cornmeal-breadcrumb mixture before finishing with the cornmeal-breadcrumb mixture.
10. A flour mixture is used to coat green tomatoes.
11. The egg mixture is dipped into the floured green tomato.
12. Green tomatoes are breaded and dipped in batter.
13. Cook the breaded tomatoes in the following order:
14. Cook half of the tomato slices at a time in the pan for 3-5 minutes on each side or until brown.
15. Place the cooked tomatoes on paper towels to drain.
16. These fried green tomatoes are wonderful with a spicy sauce or remoulade.

68. TWICE-BAKED POTATOES RECIPE

PREP TIME5 mins

COOK TIME1 hr 15 mins

TOTAL TIME1 hr 20 mins

INGREDIENTS

- 2 Russet potatoes
- ½ Cup of cooked bacon
- ½ Cup of sour cream
- 2 tbsp Worchestershire sauce
- ½ Cup of grated cheddar cheese

INSTRUCTIONS

1. Preheat the Ninja Foodi Grill or air fryer to 400°F.
2. Scrub your potatoes with warm water to remove any debris.
3. Using a paper towel, dry the potatoes.
4. russet potato
5. 15 times with a fork, poke the potatoes
6. In the Ninja Foodi Grill or air fryer, cook the potatoes at 400F until they achieve an internal temperature of 208-210F.
7. After the potato has cooled enough to handle, cut the top lengthwise.
8. Scoop the hot potato flesh into a large mixing bowl without piercing the peel.
9. Combine the potato, sour cream, Worcestershire sauce, cheddar cheese, and bacon bits in a mixing bowl.
10. 10)With a soft rubber spatula, fold the ingredients into the potato until smooth but with some potato lumps.
11. Season with salt and pepper to taste.
12. Using the spatula, return the potato filling to the potato skins.
13. twice baked potato
14. Finish cooking the loaded potatoes in your Ninja Foodi Grill or air fryer.
15. fried potato in an air fryer
16. Cook the potatoes a second time until the internal temperature reaches 145°F.
17. after the potato has been fried a second time
18. Serve immediately.

NUTRITION

Serving: 1potatoCalories: 526kcalCarbohydrates: 41gProtein: 22gFat: 31gCholesterol: 87mgSodium: 717mgPotassium: 1139mgFiber: 3gSugar: Calcium: 298mgIron: 2mg

69. MEXICAN STREET CORN FLATBREAD PIZZA

Prep Time: 5 minutes

Cook Time: 15 minutes

Total Time: 20 minutes

Yield: 8 servings

INGREDIENTS

- 2 flatbreads (store-bought naan or homemade flatbread)
- ⅓ Cup of sour cream
- ¼ Cup of mayonnaise
- 1 clove of garlic, minced
- zest of 1 lime
- juice of 1 lime (about 1 tbsp)
- Pinch cayenne pepper
- 1 (15 Ounces.) can of corn, drained
- 4 Ounces. shredded pepper jack cheese
- ⅓ Cup of crumbled cotija or queso fresco
- ¼ tsp chili powder optional
- Kosher salt

For serving:

- fresh chopped cilantro
- lime wedges
- crumbled cotija

INSTRUCTIONS

1. Preheat the oven to 500°F.
2. In a mixing bowl, combine sour cream, mayonnaise, garlic, 1 lime's zest and juice, cayenne pepper, and a couple of heavy pinches of Kosher salt.
3. Place the flatbreads on a baking sheet and equally distribute the sauce between the two flatbreads, reserving 2-3 tbsp for topping the flatbreads after they've baked.
4. Make a uniform layer of shredded cheese by distributing it evenly among the flatbreads.
5. Evenly distribute the corn among the flatbreads.
6. Crumbled Cotija cheese can be sprinkled on top.
7. To taste, add more chili powder and a few pinches of salt.
8. Preheat the oven to 400 degrees Fahrenheit and bake for 14-16 minutes. After that, broil for 1-2 minutes.
9. Serve with any remaining sauce and fresh chopped cilantro on top!

70.GARLIC PITA BREAD BITES

Prep:15 mins

Cook:10 mins

Total:25 mins

Servings:20

Ingredients

- 1 (10 ounces) package of pita bread, cut in half
- 3 tbsps butter
- 1 tsp crushed garlic
- 1 tsp dried Italian-style seasoning
- 2 tbsps grated Parmesan cheese

Directions

1) Set the oven to 180 degrees Celsius or 350 degrees Fahrenheit (175 degrees C).

2) Split the pita bread in half, then cut each half into about 2-inch pieces. On a medium baking sheet, let cool.

3) Melt the butter in a small skillet over medium heat before adding the garlic and dry Italian spice. Over the pita bread pieces, pour the mixture.

4) Modify the amount of Parmesan cheese on the bread as required. Bake for 10 minutes, or until just barely browned, in a preheated oven.

Nutrition

56 calories; protein 1.5g; carbohydrates 7.9g; fat 2g; cholesterol 5mg; sodium 95mg.

71. ADDICTIVE SWEET POTATO BURRITOS

Prep:15 mins

Cook:25 mins

Total:40 mins

Servings:12

Ingredients

- 1 tbsp vegetable oil
- 1 onion, chopped
- 4 cloves garlic, minced
- 6 cups of canned kidney beans, drained
- 2 cups of water
- 3 tbsp chili powder
- 4 tsp prepared mustard
- 2 tsp ground cumin

- 1 pinch of cayenne pepper, or to taste
- 3 tbsps soy sauce
- 4 cups of mashed cooked sweet potatoes
- 12 (10 inches) flour tortillas, warmed
- 8 ounces shredded Cheddar cheese

Directions

1. Preheat the oven to 350 degrees Fahrenheit (180 degrees Celsius) (175 degrees C).
2. Heat the oil in a medium skillet and sauté the onion and garlic until soft. Mash the beans with the onion combination in a mixing dish. 2 to 3 minutes, and gently stir in the water until it is hot. After removing the pan from the heat, stir in the soy sauce, chili powder, mustard, cumin, and cayenne pepper.
3. Spread the bean mixture and mashed sweet potatoes evenly across the tortillas, then top with cheese. Place the tortillas on a baking sheet and fold them over the contents like a burrito.
4. In a preheated oven, bake for 12 minutes or until well warmed.

Nutrition

505 calories; protein 20g; carbohydrates 76.6g; fat 8.5g; cholesterol 19.8mg; sodium 1028.5mg.

72. CORN FRITTERS

Prep:10 mins

Cook:20 mins

Total:30 mins

Servings:12

Ingredients

- 3 cups of oil for frying
- 1 cup of sifted all-purpose flour
- 1 tsp baking powder
- ½ tsp salt
- ¼ tsp white sugar
- 1 egg, lightly beaten
- ½ Cup of milk
- 1 tbsp melted shortening
- 1 (12 ounces) can of whole kernel corn, drained

Directions

1) Heat the oil to 365 degrees F in a big pot or deep fryer (185 degrees C).

2) Combine the flour, baking powder, salt, and sugar in a medium mixing basin. Whisk the egg, milk, and melted shortening in a mixing bowl, then stir it into the flour mixture. Well, combine the corn kernels.

3) Cook the fritter batter until golden spoonfuls are placed into the hot oil. Use paper towels to absorb any additional liquid.

Nutrition

133 calories; protein 2.7g; carbohydrates 14g; fat 7.8g; cholesterol 17.5mg; sodium 224.5mg.

73. BALSAMIC ROASTED BRUSSELS SPROUTS WITH CRANBERRIES & PECANS

Prep Time: 10 minutes

Cook Time: 25 minutes

Total Time: 35 minutes

Yield: 4 side servings

INGREDIENTS

- 1 ½ pound Brussels sprouts
- 2 tbsps extra-virgin olive oil
- ¼ tsp fine sea salt
- ⅓ Cup of dried cranberries
- ⅓ Cup of pecans, roughly chopped
- 1 tbsp thick balsamic vinegar

- ⅓ Cup of finely grated Parmesan cheese and/or a few thin pats of butter
- Salt and pepper to taste (use flaky sea salt if you have it)

INSTRUCTIONS

1. Preheat the oven to 425° Fahrenheit (200 degrees Celsius). To make cleaning easier, line a large, rimmed baking sheet with parchment paper.
2. Before serving, trim the nubby ends of your Brussels sprouts and discard any discolored or broken leaves. Cut each sprout in half lengthwise from the flat base to the top.
3. On your prepared baking sheet, combine the halved sprouts, olive oil, and salt. Toss the sprouts in the dressing until they are thoroughly coated. Place the sprouts in a single layer with the flat sides down.
4. Roast the sprouts for 20 to 25 minutes, tossing halfway through, until soft and thoroughly browned on the edges. When the nuts are almost done (about 3 to 5 minutes), add them to the pan and return them to the oven (this is an easy way to toast the pecans).
5. Meanwhile, place the cranberries in a shallow dish halfway filled with warm water. This will puff them up even more. Set aside the sprouts while they are baking.
6. Combine the roasted Brussels sprouts and toasted nuts in a mixing bowl or bowl. Drain the cranberries and sprinkle them on top. Drizzle the balsamic vinegar over the top, then top with Parmesan and/or butter pats for added richness. Season with salt and pepper to taste. Serve warm or at room temperature (it's excellent either way).
7. This dish is best served right away, but leftovers will keep for two to three days in the refrigerator if covered. Reheat the bowl slightly before serving.

74. CRISPY BRUSSELS SPROUTS WITH WARM BLUE CHEESE AND BACON.

TOTAL TIME35 mins

INGREDIENTS

- 1 1/2 pounds Brussels sprouts washed, trimmed, and halved
- 1 tbsp extra virgin olive oil
- 1/2 tsp garlic salt
- 1/4 tsp freshly ground pepper
- 4 ounces of blue cheese crumbled
- 3 strips of natural thick-cut bacon cooked and crumbled

INSTRUCTIONS

1. Preheat the oven to 425°F (200°C). Line a baking pan with tinfoil.
2. In a mixing bowl, combine Brussels sprouts, olive oil, garlic salt, and pepper.
3. Roast for 15 minutes, stir and then roast for another 10-15 minutes, or until desired brownness and crispiness are attained. Remove the dish from the oven and place it on an oven-safe serving dish.
4. Crumbled blue cheese can be sprinkled on top. Preheat the broiler in the oven.
5. Broil for a couple of minutes or until the blue cheese is melted.

6. Remove the bowl from the oven and top with crispy bacon. If desired, drizzle with balsamic glaze.

NUTRITION

Calories: 273kcalCarbohydrates: 16gProtein: 14gFat: 19gCholesterol: 32mgSodium: 838mgPotassium: 769mgFiber: 6gSugar: 4g

Calcium: 223mgIron: 3mg

---

75. LEMON GARLIC ROASTED ASPARAGUS

Prep Time 7 minutes

Cook Time 13 minutes

Total Time 20 minutes

Ingredients

- 1 Pound. Asparagus spear tough ends removed
- 1 ½ Tbsp. Olive oil or avocado oil
- ½ tsp. Salt
- ¼ tsp. black pepper
- 1 garlic clove crushed
- ½ lemon juice and zest

Instructions

1. Preheat the oven to 400 degrees Fahrenheit (200 degrees Celsius).
2. To remove the rough ends, snap the asparagus spears at the place where the hard and delicate parts meet. Replace the asparagus spears with the remaining ones.
3. In a small bowl, combine the oil, salt, pepper, and crushed garliCup
4. Arrange asparagus spears on a parchment paper-lined baking sheet. (If you want to take it to the next level, arrange the asparagus stems on an oven-safe wire rack.) This allows the hot air in the oven to touch the asparagus from all sides!)
5. Coat all sides of the spears with garlic oil using a pastry brush.
6. In a preheated oven, bake asparagus for 11-13 minutes, or until tender and bright green.
7. Pour the juice of half a lemon over the asparagus just before serving. Enjoy!

---

76. CINNAMON-SPICED CANDIED SWEET POTATOES

Active:35 mins

Total:1 hr 55 mins

Yield:8 to 10

Ingredients

- 4 pound orange-fleshed sweet potatoes, peeled and cut crosswise into 2-inch pieces, then cut lengthwise into 1-inch wedges
- 1 cup of packed light brown sugar
- 1 tbsp kosher salt
- ¼ tsp ground cloves
- ¼ Cup of unsalted butter, cubed
- 4 (2-inch) cinnamon sticks

Directions

1) Set the oven's temperature to 350 degrees Fahrenheit (180 degrees Celsius). A 3- to 4-quart baking dish should be filled with sweet potato wedges. Sweet potatoes are seasoned with sugar, salt, and cloves. The sweet potatoes should be covered in butter and surrounded with cinnamon sticks. Bake sweet potatoes in a preheated oven for about 1 hour and 15 minutes, turning them over after 15 minutes. The baking sheet should be taken out of the oven and set aside for ten minutes. Before serving, take the cinnamon sticks out.

77. ROSEMARY ROASTED BUTTERNUT SQUASH

Prep:20 mins

Cook:45 mins

Total:1 hr 5 mins

Servings:6

Ingredients

- 1 butternut squash, peeled and cubed
- 2 cloves garlic, minced
- 2 sprigs of fresh rosemary, finely chopped
- 2 tbsps olive oil, or more to taste
- sea salt to taste
- ground black pepper to taste

Directions

1. Preheat the oven to 400 degrees Fahrenheit (200 degrees Celsius) (200 degrees C).
2. In a large mixing basin, whisk together the butternut squash cubes, garlic, rosemary, olive oil, salt, and black pepper. Half-fill a big baking dish with the batter.

3. 45 to 50 minutes in a hot oven, until golden brown and caramelized squash.

Nutrition

136 calories; protein 2.2g; carbohydrates 24.8g; fat 4.7g; sodium 62.1mg.

78. PORK, SAGE, ONION & CRANBERRY STUFFING LOG

prep time: 30 MINUTES

cook time: 1 HOUR

total time: 1 HOUR 30 MINUTES

Ingredients

- 1.5 bags of Mrs. Crimble's Sage & Onion stuffing mix (or 225g equivalent)
- 800g gluten-free sausages or sausage meat
- 75g dried cranberries
- 400g unsmoked streaky bacon
- 8 fresh sage leaves

Instructions

1. Soak the dried cranberries in 100ml boiling water for 15 minutes, then pour off any excess liquid and set aside.
2. Follow the package directions for making the stuffing mix.
3. In a mixing bowl, squeeze the sausage flesh from the sausage skins and combine it with the filling ingredients. Break up any clumps as you go until you have a smooth, cohesive mixture.
4. Greaseproof paper that has been lightly spritzed with oil should be used to line a big oven pan. Place the bacon rashers on greaseproof paper, gently overlapping them, and alternate pieces on the top two-thirds and bottom two-thirds of the paper. The completed bacon "sheet" should be 30cm in width and 20cm in height. No gaps should exist between the rashers.
5. Place two-thirds of the stuffing on top of the bacon, then form it into a long log shape with your hands (image below). Make a trench in the log's center and place the cranberries in the middle of the trench. If there is any leftover stuffing, roll it into balls and place it on top of the cranberries.
6. Wrap the bacon around the stuffing log until it is completely covered in bacon. Wrap the baking paper around the log and tuck the ends of the bacon rashers underneath the filled log. Wrap the stuffing log with greaseproof paper, then cling film, and store it in the refrigerator if you're making it ahead of time.
7. Alternatively, remove the baking paper and preheat the oven to a 180°C fan. After 55 minutes, remove the pan from the oven, sprinkle the sage leaves on top, and bake for another 5 minutes.

79. MAPLE-GLAZED GREEN BEANS

PREP: 10 mins

COOK: 12 mins

Ingredients

- 1 1/2 pounds fresh green beans, ends trimmed
- 4 bacon strips, chopped
- 1 medium yellow or sweet onion, diced
- 1 tsp soy sauce
- 1/3 cup of dried cranberries
- 1/4 cup of maple syrup
- 1/4 tsp salt
- 1/4 tsp pepper

Instructions

1. Bring a large pot of salted water to a rolling boil. Depending on how tender you want your green beans, cook for 6 to 10 minutes.
2. To halt the cooking process, drain and place in a big dish of cold water. (You may skip this step if you like, but it will help keep the vibrant green color.)
3. Cook bacon until crispy in a large nonstick pan. After removing with a slotted spoon, place on a paper towel-lined platter.
4. Cook the onion for 3 to 5 minutes in the bacon grease, or until soft.
5. Mix the soy sauce, cranberries, maple syrup, salt, and pepper in a pan. Toss the green beans in the sauce to coat them.
6. Serve in a bowl or on a serving tray with bacon on top.

80. JALAPENO POPPER CORN SALAD

Yield: 8 people

Prep Time 10 mins

Total Time 10 mins

Ingredients:

- 2 jalapeno peppers
- 4 cups of corn kernels, cooked and cooled
- 1 cup of sour cream
- 1 cup of mayonnaise
- 2- Ounces cream cheese, softened
- 2 tsp cumin

- 1 tsp garlic powder
- 1 tsp onion powder
- 1 tsp chili powder
- 1 tsp paprika
- 1 cup of shredded cheddar cheese
- 1 cup of shredded pepper jack cheese
- ½ Cup of cooked chopped bacon
- salt and pepper, to taste

Instructions:

1) Take off the membranes and seeds from the jalapenos before slicing them.

2) Combine the jalapenos and the rest ingredients in a mixing basin.

3) Allow chilling for two hours before using.

81. FRIED RICE RESTAURANT STYLE

Prep:15 mins

Cook:30 mins

Total:45 mins

Servings:8

Ingredients

- 2 cups of enriched white rice
- 4 cups of water
- ⅔ Cup of chopped baby carrots
- ½ Cup of frOuncesen green peas
- 2 tbsps vegetable oil
- 2 eggs
- soy sauce to taste
- 2 tbsp sesame oil, to taste

Directions

1. In a saucepan, combine rice and water. Heat the water to a rolling boil. Reduce the heat to low and cook for 20 minutes, covered.
2. In a small saucepan, boil carrots for 3 to 5 minutes in water. Peas should be blanched in boiling water before draining.
3. Preheat your wok to high. After putting in the oil and tossing in the carrots and peas, cook for 30 seconds. Crack the eggs into the vegetables and quickly mix them in to scramble them.

Mix in the cooked rice well. After mixing in the soy sauce, toss the rice with it. Toss with sesame oil, then toss again.

82. SWEET POTATO AND BLACK BEAN TACOS (WITH HONEY AND LIME)

Ready in: 38 minutes

Prep10 minutes

Cook28 minutes

Ingredients

- 1 1/2 Pounds of sweet potatoes, peeled and diced into 1/2-inch cubes
- 4 Tbsp divided olive oil
- 1 tsp cumin
- 1 tsp paprika
- 1/2 tsp ground coriander
- 1/4 tsp cayenne pepper
- Salt and freshly ground black pepper
- 1 cup of chopped yellow onion, diced
- 1 1/2 tsp minced garlic
- 1 (14.5 Ounces) can of black beans, drained and rinsed
- 1 cup of frOuncesen yellow corn, thawed and drained
- 3 Tbsp honey
- 3 Tbsp fresh lime juice
- 2 Tbsp chopped fresh cilantro
- 10 Corn or flour tortillas
- Sliced avocado, romaine lettuce, cotija, or feta cheese for serving

Instructions

1. Preheat the oven to 425 degrees Fahrenheit. Place sweet potatoes on a baking sheet lined with foil. Toss with 1 tbsp olive oil to coat evenly.
2. Toss to mix evenly with cumin, paprika, coriander, and cayenne pepper, seasoning moderately with salt and pepper to taste. Bake for 15 to 20 minutes, until tender, in a preheated oven, stirring halfway through.
3. Meanwhile, heat the remaining 1 tbsp oil in a large pan over medium-high heat. When the pan is heated, add the onion and cook until it is caramelized (golden brown on the edges and soft), about 5 to 6 minutes, adding the garlic in the final 30 seconds of cooking.
4. Reduce the heat to low and stir in the drained black beans, corn, honey, and lime juice. Heat until well warmed. Add the roasted sweet potatoes and cilantro to the mix. Serve with chosen toppings on warm tortillas.

83. GRILLED GREEN BEAN SALAD WITH RED PEPPERS AND RADISHES RECIPE

Active:15 mins

Total:30 mins

Serves:4 to 6 servings

Ingredients

- 1 tbsp fresh juice from 1 lemon (15ml)
- 1 tsp Dijon mustard
- 4 tbsps divided extra-virgin olive oil (60ml)
- Kosher salt and freshly ground black pepper
- 2 scallions, white and light green parts only, thinly sliced
- 1 red bell pepper, thinly sliced (about 4 ounces; 110g)
- 6 to 8 small radishes, thinly sliced (about 3 ounces; 85g)
- 1 pound trimmed green beans (450g)
- A small handful of minced fresh parsley leaves

Directions

1. Combine the lemon juice and mustard in a large mixing basin. Drizzle in three tbsps of olive oil in a steady stream, stirring continually. Salt & pepper to taste. Set aside the scallions, bell peppers, and radishes. Toss the green beans with the remaining tbsp of olive oil and season with salt and pepper in a separate bowl.
2. Grilling Instructions: (See note.) One complete chimney of charcoal should be lit. Pour out and arrange the coals over half of the charcoal grate once all of the charcoal has been ignited and covered with gray ash. Place the cooking grate on the grill, cover it, and let it heat up for 5 minutes. Set half of a gas grill's burners to the maximum heat setting, cover, and preheat for 10 minutes. The grilling grate should be cleaned and oiled.
3. To keep the green beans from dropping into the grill grates, place them directly over the embers, perpendicular to the grill grates, or use a thin-grated vegetable basket if you have one. Cook for 3 minutes, occasionally turning, until blistered, charred, and tender-crisp. Step 5 is the next step.
4. To Prepare Food Indoors: (See note.) Preheat broiler to high and position rack as near to broiler as feasible. Arrange the beans in a single layer on a rimmed baking sheet or broiler pan coated with foil. Broil for 2 to 5 minutes, depending on broiler power, until beans are blistered and gently browned. Step 5 is the next step.
5. Add the beans to the bowl with the dressing, scallion, radish, and pepper. Toss in the parsley to mix. Add salt and pepper to taste the salad. Serve hot or cold, depending on your preference.

84. FRIED RAVIOLI

PREP TIME15 mins

COOK TIME30 mins

TOTAL TIME45 mins

INGREDIENTS

- 4 cups of canola oil
- 6 eggs
- 1/2 cup of half-and-half
- 2 cups of all-purpose flour
- 1 tsp salt
- 1/2 tsp pepper
- 1 cup of seasoned breadcrumbs
- 1 cup of panko breadcrumbs
- 24 kinds of ravioli - cheese or meat, fresh or frOuncesen (Thaw if frOuncesen.)
- 1/4 cup of shredded parmesan cheese
- 1 tbsp minced fresh parsley
- 1 cup of marinara sauce - warmed
- 1 cup of pesto sauce
- 1 cup of ranch dressing

INSTRUCTIONS

1) To a depth of 2.5 inches, fill a skillet with canola oil (approximately 4 cups). Over medium heat, warm the oil until it reaches 400 degrees F. (To test whether the oil is ready, add a few breadcrumbs.) When the oil begins to bubble around them, it is ready to fry.)

2) In another bowl, combine the eggs and half-and-half. In another bowl, mix the flour, salt, and pepper. In a third bowl, mix the breadcrumbs together.

3) The egg wash should be applied to each ravioli first, followed by the flour mixture, the egg wash again, and lastly, the breadcrumbs. The breaded ravioli should be arranged on a serving dish. Continue by using the remaining ravioli.

4) Drop three or four breaded ravioli into the oil, fry for approximately two minutes. Whenever required, turn once while the food is being fried.

5) Remove from the oil and let dry on a platter covered with paper towels. Use the remaining breaded ravioli to repeat. Serve on a serving platter with a sprinkle of parmesan cheese and chopped fresh parsley. Before serving, toss with ranch dressing, pesto, and marinara sauce (or sauces of your choice.)

85. HOMEMADE EGG ROLLS

Prep Time25 minutes

Cook Time5 minutes

INGREDIENTS

- 2 tsp vegetable oil
- 3/4 pound ground pork
- salt and pepper to taste
- 1 tsp minced garlic
- 1 tsp minced ginger
- 3 cups of coleslaw mix
- 1/4 cup of sliced green onions
- 1 tbsp soy sauce
- 1 tsp toasted sesame oil
- 12 egg roll wrappers
- 1 egg beaten
- oil for frying

INSTRUCTIONS

1. 2 tbsp vegetable oil, heated in a big pan over medium-high heat Season the ground pork with salt and pepper before adding it.
2. Cook, breaking up the pork with a spatula as required, until it is browned and cooked through. After adding the garlic and ginger, cook for 30 seconds.
3. In a mixing dish, combine the coleslaw mix and green onions. 3-4 minutes, or until cabbage is wilted
4. After adding the soy sauce and sesame oil, turn off the heat.
5. Fill each egg roll wrapper with about 2-3 tbsp of filling and fold according to package directions, sealing the edges of the wrappers with the beaten egg as you go.
6. Pour 2-3 inches of oil into a large pot.
7. Preheat the oil to 350°F (180°C). Fry 3-4 egg rolls at a time until golden brown on all sides, about 3-5 minutes, turning once or twice.
8. Drain on paper towels before serving with a dipping sauce of your choice.

NUTRITION

Calories: 146kcal | Carbohydrates: 8g | Protein: 6g | Fat: 7g | Cholesterol: 21mg | Sodium: 177mg | Potassium: 124mg | Vitamin A: 15IU Calcium: 17mg | Iron: 0.8mg

86. CORNBREAD STUFFING

YIELDS:8 SERVINGS

PREP TIME:0 HOURS 20 MINS

TOTAL TIME:1 HOUR 50 MINS

INGREDIENTS

FOR THE CORNBREAD

- Cooking spray for pan
- 1 1/2 Cup yellow cornmeal
- 3/4 Cup all-purpose flour
- 1/4 Cup packed brown sugar
- 2 tsp. baking powder
- 1/2 tsp. baking soda
- 1 tsp. kosher salt
- 1 Cup whole milk
- 1/2 Cup buttermilk
- 2 large eggs
- 3 tbsp. Melted butter cooled slightly.

FOR THE STUFFING

- 3 tbsp. Butter, plus more for pan
- 1 large onion, chopped
- 2 stalks of celery, chopped
- Kosher salt
- Freshly ground black pepper.
- 3 cloves garlic, minced
- 2 tbsp. Freshly chopped sage
- 2 tsp. Fresh thyme leaves
- 2 eggs
- 1 cup low-sodium chicken broth
- Freshly chopped parsley for garnish.

DIRECTIONS

1) Set the oven to 400 degrees Fahrenheit and generously grease or spray a 9" x 13" baking pan. Combine cornmeal, flour, brown sugar, salt, baking soda, and baking powder in a large mixing bowl.

2) Combine the milk, buttermilk, eggs, and melted butter in a separate, large mixing basin. Use a fork to quickly combine the dry ingredients with the wet ones.

3) Bake for 20 to 25 minutes, or until a toothpick inserted in the center of the cake comes out clean. Before disintegrating and transferring it to a large mixing bowl, let it cool fully. Baste a large baking dish with butter and preheat the oven to 375 degrees Fahrenheit.

4) Melt the butter in a large pot over medium heat. Season with salt and pepper after incorporating the onion and celery. Add the garlic, sage, and thyme and simmer for 1 minute or until aromatiCup

Simmer for 8 minutes or until the vegetables are soft. After taking it off the heat, whisk in the crushed cornbread. To taste, add salt and pepper to the food.

5) Combine eggs and chicken broth in a small bowl. Toss the cornmeal mixture with the sauce before adding it to the lined baking dish. Bake for 30 minutes, or until warm throughout and the top is toasted.

87. EASY YOGURT FLATBREADS

Prep:20 mins

Cook:5 mins

Ingredients

- 500g plain flour
- 1 tsp salt
- 1 tsp golden caster sugar
- 1 tsp fresh yeast or 1/3 tsp fast-action dried yeast
- 150ml full-fat milk
- 150g pot natural yogurt
- 60g clarified butter or ghee

Method

1. Combine the flour, salt, sugar, and yeast in a large mixing bowl. Warm the milk in a pot until it is lukewarm. With the exception of 1 tbsp of yogurt, add the rest of the yogurt to the milk and thoroughly combine it. Melt the butter in a separate bowl and stir it into the milk and yogurt until smooth.
2. Gradually include the flour, then knead for 10 minutes until you have a springy dough. Allow it to rise in a warm place for 1 hour or until it has doubled in size.
3. Form the dough into 10 even-sized balls. Preheat the grill to medium-high and heat a large baking tray below it for about 10 minutes. Using the leftover yogurt, flatten the dough balls and roll them into rough teardrop shapes. Grill for 2-3 minutes on each side, or until golden, on a warm baking pan. Keep an eye on them since they might burn quickly.

88. BURGERS WITH SAUTÉED MUSHROOMS, ARUGULA AND DIJON AIOLI

yield: 4 BURGERS

total time: 45 MINS

INGREDIENTS

- 1 pound of lean ground beef; feel free to use fattier beef if you prefer

- 1 1/2 tbsp olive oil
- 1 tsp salt
- 1 tsp pepper
- 2 tbsps of unsalted butter
- 12 ounces of sliced baby Bella mushrooms
- 4 ounces fontina cheese, sliced
- 4 ounces sharp cheddar cheese, sliced
- 2 cups of fresh arugula
- 1/2 lemon, juiced
- 4 whole wheat buns, toasted
- mustard aioli
- 1 1/2 tbsp dijon mustard
- 1 large egg yolk
- 2 tsp fresh lemon juice
- 1/2 cup of olive oil
- 2 tbsp wholegrain mustard
- 1 tbsp horseradish
- a pinch of salt + pepper

INSTRUCTIONS

1. In a large mixing bowl, season the ground beef with salt and pepper. 1 tbsp olive oil, mixed with the meat, and set aside for 30 minutes at room temperature.
2. While the meat is resting, place mushrooms in a big pan over low heat. 1 tbsp olive oil, 1 tbsp butter, then throw in the mushrooms to coat. Cook for 10-15 minutes, covered, or until the veggies have softened and become moist. Season with salt and pepper once soft, then remove from the fire and cover.
3. While the mushrooms are cooking, whisk together dijon mustard, egg yolk, and lemon juice in a large mixing dish. Drizzle in the olive oil slowly while continually whisking until the mixture emulsifies and comes together. Season with a touch of salt and pepper after whisking in the whole grain mustard and horseradish. Take it out of the equation.
4. Toss the fresh arugula with half a tbsp of olive oil and a squeeze of lemon juice. Add a bit of salt and pepper to taste.
5. 1 tbsp butter, melted in a large skillet over high heat Form the meat into four equal patties, then cook until done to your satisfaction in a pan. For medium-well, I cook mine for around 5 minutes per side, but it depends on how thick you like your burgers. In the last 1-2 minutes of cooking, top each burger with a couple of slices of both kinds of cheese.
6. Before constructing the burgers, spread a little quantity of mustard aioli on the bottom of each bun. On top of the burger, place mushrooms, aioli, and a handful of arugula.

89. PORK TENDERLOIN WITH LEMON-THYME CREAM AND CABBAGE APPLE SLAW

Prep:20 mins

Cook:12 mins

Roast:25 mins

Stand:3 mins

Total:1 hr

Servings:4

Ingredients

- 1 ¼ pound natural pork tenderloin, trimmed of fat
- ¼ tsp salt
- ¼ tsp ground black pepper
- 1 tbsp olive oil
- 2 tsp butter
- 3 cups of Napa cabbage, cut into 1/4-inch thick slices
- 1 medium apple, cored and chopped
- 1 tsp cider vinegar
- ⅛ tsp salt
- ⅛ tsp ground black pepper
- ¼ Cup of reduced-sodium chicken broth
- 2 tbsps lemon juice
- ½ tsp snipped fresh thyme
- 2 ounces reduced-fat cream cheese (Neufchatel), softened
- Fresh thyme sprigs

Directions

1. Preheat the oven to 425°F (200°C). Using a quarter tsp of salt and a quarter tsp of pepper, season the pork. In a large nonstick skillet, heat the oil over medium-high heat. For about 5 minutes, brown the pork on both sides. Place the pork on a rack in a roasting pan and roast for 25 to 35 minutes, or until an internal temperature of 145°F is achieved when a thermometer is used. Cover the bowl with foil and remove it from the oven. Standing time should be at least 3 minutes.
2. Meanwhile, melt butter in the remaining drippings in the same pan over medium heat. Cook until the cabbage begins to wilt slightly. Cook for 3 minutes more, or until the apple is soft and the cabbage is cooked through. Transfer to a medium bowl, mix in the vinegar, and season with 1/8 tsp salt and 1/8 tsp black pepper to keep warm.
3. In a small bowl, combine the chicken broth, lemon juice, and thyme. Pour the broth mixture into the drippings in the hot skillet. In a separate bowl, whisk together the cream cheese and heat until smooth.
4. Pork should be sliced and served with a warm apple cabbage salad. To serve, top with a dollop of lemon thyme cream. Garnish with fresh thyme sprigs if desired.

90. GRILLED VEGETABLE TOSTADAS WITH QUICK MOLE SAUCE

Prep:60 mins

Cook:10 mins

Grill:5 mins

Ingredients

- 1 recipe Quick Mole Sauce (recipe below)
- 4 medium zucchini and/or yellow summer squash, quartered lengthwise
- 1 medium eggplant, cut into 1/2-inch slices
- 1 large red onion, cut into 1/2-inch slices
- 2 tbsps olive oil
- 16 4 inches toasted corn tortillas
- 1 8 ounces carton of sour cream
- 1 cup of crumbled queso fresco or feta cheese
- Avocado slices and/or Fresh Cilantro

Directions

1) Quickly prepare the mole sauce.

2) Sprinkle salt and black pepper over the zucchini, squash, eggplant, and onion after coating them with olive oil.

3) Place veggies on an uncovered grill rack and cook for 5 to 8 minutes, flipping once halfway through. (If using a gas grill, warm it to begin.) Turn down the heat to medium. Place the veggies on a rack above a source of intense heat. Cook as previously advised, covered.) Cut the veggies into very small pieces.

4) Place toasted tortillas, Quick Mole Sauce, sour cream, cheese, avocado, and cilantro on top of the grilled veggies. 8 people can be fed by this bowl.

Nutrition

464 calories; total fat 28g; saturated fat 8g; cholesterol 25mg; sodium 514mg; potassium 935mg; carbohydrates 48g; fiber 9g; sugar 16g; protein 11g; thiamin 0mg; riboflavin 0mg; niacin equivalents 2mg; folate 93mcg; calcium 172mg; iron 2mg.

91. MASCARPONE-STUFFED FRENCH TOAST WITH BLACKBERRIES

Prep Time: 25 minutes

Cook Time: 5 minutes

Servings: 4

Ingredients:

- 1 cup of maple syrup
- 1 1/2 tsp. Orange flower water
- 1/2 tsp. vanilla extract
- 1/4 Pounds. mascarpone cheese
- 1 Tbs. sugar
- 1 tsp. Fresh lemon juice
- 1/2 tsp. vanilla extract
- 8 slices of firm-textured bread, such as brioche or challah, each 1/2 inch thick, with crusts

For the batter:

- 2 eggs
- 1/2 cup of milk
- 1/2 tsp. vanilla extract
- 1/8 tsp. salt
- 1 Tbs. unsalted Butter
- 2 cups of blackberries

Directions:

1. To make the orange blossom maple syrup, warm the maple syrup in a small pot over low heat. In a small basin or pitcher, whisk together the orange blossom water and vanilla essence until well blended. Before serving, warm the bowl. Alternatively, store it refrigerated in an airtight container for up to 3 days. Warm over low heat before serving.
2. In a mixing bowl, combine the mascarpone, sugar, lemon juice, and vanilla. 2 tbsp mascarpone mixture, spread over 4 slices of bread, leaving a 1/4-inch plain border on all sides. Top with the remaining bread slices.
3. In a mixing bowl, whisk together the eggs, milk, vanilla, and salt to form the batter. Pour the batter into a baking dish.
4. 1 1/2 tbsp butter, heated in a large frypan over medium heat and kept warm until foaming but not browning
5. Place one sandwich at a time in the batter and wait 5 seconds. Set the sandwiches aside for another 5 seconds after turning them over. With a broad spatula, carefully lift the sandwiches from the batter, allowing any excess to fall back into the baking dish, and transfer to the hot pan. Cook for 3 minutes, until golden brown. Cook for another 2 minutes, or until browned on the opposite side, using the remaining 1 1/2 tbsp butter in the pan. Using a clean, broad spatula, transfer the sandwiches to a cutting board.
6. Cut each sandwich in half on the diagonal. Serve immediately with the syrup, which should be split among individual servings and garnished with blackberries. 4 people serving.

7. Adapted from Williams-Sonoma Essentials of Breakfast and Brunch by Georgeanne Brennan, Elinor Klivans, Jordan Mackay, and Charles Pierce (Oxmoor House, 2007).
8. Delicious Cauliflower Skewers

92. GRILLED CAULIFLOWER SKEWERS

prep time:10 MINS

cook time:10 MINS

total time:20 MINS

INGREDIENTS

- 1 head cauliflower
- 1 tsp salt
- 1/2 tsp black pepper
- 2 tbsp divided lemon juice
- 1/4 cup of olive oil
- 3 tbsp grated Parmesan
- 1 tbsp chopped parsley

INSTRUCTIONS

1. Soak wooden skewers in cold water for 15 minutes.
2. Sliced cauliflower into florets or purchased cauliflower that has already been cut. Rinse well and air dry.
3. Season with salt and pepper to taste. 1 tbsp lemon juice and a dab of olive oil
4. Thread 4 thick florets per skewer onto the skewers.
5. Preheat the grill to 450 degrees F. Clean the grates by removing them.
6. Carefully place the cauliflower on the grill and cook for 5-7 minutes per side, turning once.
7. Place the ingredients in a mixing bowl. Drizzle lemon juice over the top.
8. Serve with parmesan cheese and parsley as garnish.

NUTRITION

Calories: 114, Fat: 9g, Cholesterol: 1mg, Sodium: 456mg, Potassium: 286mg, Carbohydrates: 5g, Fiber: 1g, Sugar: 1g, Protein: 2g, Calcium: 51%, Iron: 0.5%

93. ROASTED FIGS STUFFED WITH GOAT'S CHEESE AND WALNUTS.

Prep Time5 mins

Cook Time8 mins

Ingredients

- 6 Fresh Figs
- 3 Tbsp Goat's cheese
- 15 g Walnuts
- Honey

Instructions

1. Preheat the oven to 200 degrees Celsius.
2. Cut a cross through the tops of the figs, but leave the base attached.
3. Chop the nuts finely and combine with the goat's cheese.
4. Fill the figs with the cheese mixture. A tsp per person should be enough.
5. 6-8 minutes of roasting
6. Serve with a generous sprinkle of honey.

94. SKILLET PEACH CRISP WITH GINGER AND PECANS

PREP TIME10 mins

COOK TIME35 mins

TOTAL TIME45 mins

Ingredients

For the crisp topping:

- 1/2 cup of (66 grams) oat flour (see recipe note)
- 1/2 cup of (78 grams) all-purpose flour
- 1/3 cup of old-fashioned rolled oats
- 1/4 cup of light brown sugar
- 1/2 tsp fine sea salt or table salt
- 3/4 cup of pecans, roughly chopped
- 1/2 cup of unsalted butter cut into small pieces, well chilled

For the peaches:

- 2 pounds peaches, sliced 1/2-inch thick (about 6 medium, or 6 cups of sliced)
- 1/2 tsp ground ginger
- 1/3 cup of crystallized candied ginger, diced small
- 1/4 cup of granulated sugar
- 2 tbsp lemon juice (about 1/2 lemon)
- 2 tbsps unsalted butter for the pan

Method

1. Preheat the oven to 350 degrees Fahrenheit (180 degrees Celsius).
2. In a small bowl, whisk together the two flours with a fork—oat flour clumps together more than all-purpose flour. In a mixing basin, combine the rolled oats, brown sugar, and salt. Before everything is fully mixed, add the pecans.
3. Finally, work the butter into the crumbly topping until it is buttery and crumbly. In your fingertips, it should easily cluster together.
4. In a medium mixing bowl, combine the sliced peaches, ground ginger, crystallized ginger, sugar, and lemon juice. Stir everything together well with a spatula.
5. Recipe for Peach Crumble In a mixing bowl, combine the peaches and ginger.
6. Bake for 5 minutes, or until the remaining 2 tbsp of butter has melted in the cast iron pan.
7. Remove the skillet from the oven and distribute the peach-ginger mixture evenly throughout the pan. Apply small dabs of the crisp topping equally across the tops of the peaches.
8. Toss the peaches in a pan with the crisp peach mixture.
9. Toss the crumbs into the peach crumble recipe.

10. Follow these steps to make the crisp:
11. Bake for 30 to 35 minutes, or until the filling has bubbled and turned golden brown on top.
12. You must wait at least an hour before scooping into this, which will be challenging. The liquids would otherwise spill all over the place, possibly scorching your mouth.
13. If covered, this will last 3 to 4 days in the refrigerator. Simply reheat in a low oven for around 10 minutes.

95.MARSALA HONEY PEARS WITH GORGONZOLA

PREP TIME: 5 MINS

COOK TIME: 5 MINS

TOTAL TIME: 10 MINS

INGREDIENTS:

- 2 Tbsps Olive Oil (not Extra Virgin) see my note above
- 2 pears, unpeeled and uncored, says Nigella, but I say core those pears!
- 3 Tbsps Marsala
- 2 Tbsps Honey
- 50g Walnut Halves
- 500g Gorgonzola

INSTRUCTIONS

4. Heat the oil in a large frying pan over medium heat. In the meantime, peel and core the pears and cut them into eighths. (Because I cored my pears, my bowl has no stems)!
5. Cook the pears for 3-4 minutes on each side or until soft.

6. Combine the Marsala and honey in a cup or small basin. Allow the Marsala to boil and thicken before pouring it over the pears.
7. Transfer the pears to a wide serving plate, leaving the syrupy sauce in the pan.
8. Stir-fried the walnuts for about a minute in the same pan, or until they've browned slightly and gotten sticky all over.
9. Transfer the walnuts to a serving tray, along with any remaining pan juices, and top with Gorgonzola.

96. SWEET POTATO PANCAKES

YIELDS:8 SERVINGS

PREP TIME:0 HOURS 25 MINS

TOTAL TIME:0 HOURS 45 MINS

INGREDIENTS

- 1 3/4 Cup all-purpose flour
- 2 tsp. baking powder
- 1/2 tsp. baking soda
- 2 tbsp. packed brown sugar
- 1 tsp. kosher salt
- 1 tsp. cinnamon
- 1/4 tsp. ground nutmeg
- 1/4 tsp. ground ginger
- 1 3/4 Cup buttermilk
- 2 small sweet potatoes, roasted and pureed until smooth (about ¾ Cup of puree)
- 2 large eggs
- 1 tsp. pure vanilla extract
- Butter, for cooking and serving
- Toasted pecans for serving
- Maple syrup, for serving

DIRECTIONS

1) Combine the flour, baking powder, baking soda, salt, brown sugar, cinnamon, nutmeg, and ginger in a large mixing bowl.

2) Combine buttermilk, sweet potato puree, eggs, and vanilla in a separate basin.

3) Gently stir the wet and dry components together with a wooden spoon.

4) Melt butter on a large griddle or nonstick skillet over medium heat. Reduce the heat to medium-low when the butter has foamed, and then pour only 12 cups of pancake batter into the skillet. Cook

for a further 3 minutes after flipping the pancake, or until bubbles appear in the batter and the bottom is golden brown.

5) Continue with the remaining batter. More butter, roasted almonds, and maple syrup are added on top.

97. CINNAMON S'MORES TOAST

Total: 10 min

Active: 10 min

Yield: 4 servings

Ingredients

- 1 tbsp sugar
- 1/4 tsp ground cinnamon
- 4 slices of cinnamon swirl bread
- 4 tsp butter, at room temperature
- 4 tbsp semisweet chocolate chips
- 1 cup of mini marshmallows

Directions

1. Preheat the oven to broil and place a rack near it.
2. Combine the sugar and cinnamon in a small bowl.
3. Place the bread on a sheet pan and brown both sides under the broiler. 1 tsp butter on each piece of bread once it has been cooked. Evenly distribute the cinnamon sugar among the bread slices. Chocolate chips should be put on top in equal proportions. Finally, sprinkle 1/4 cup mini marshmallows on top of each slice.
4. Place the marshmallows on the broiler for about 1 minute, or until golden brown, keeping an eye on them so they don't burn. Serve immediately.

Ready in: 48 minutes

Prep30 minutes

Cook18 minutes

Ingredients

Cookies

- 2 cups of (283g) unbleached all-purpose flour (scoop and level to measure)
- 1/2 cup of (45g) unsweetened cocoa powder (scoop and level to measure)
- 1 tsp baking soda
- 1/2 tsp salt
- 1 cup of packed (200g) light brown sugar, break up any clumps
- 1/2 cup of (120ml) buttermilk
- 1/2 cup of (120ml) vegetable oil
- 1 large egg
- 1 1/2 tsp vanilla extract
- 1/2 cup of (120ml) hot water

Filling

- 8 Tbsp (113g) salted butter, at room temperature
- 6 Tbsp (85g) unsalted butter, at room temperature
- 2 1/4 cup of (270g) powdered sugar
- 1 tsp vanilla extract
- 10 Ounces. Marshmallow fluff (aka marshmallow creme, about one and a half 7 Ounces jars)

Instructions

1. Preheat the oven to 375°F and arrange the oven racks in the top and bottom thirds. Using parchment paper, line 18 by 13-inch baking pans.
2. In a medium mixing bowl, combine flour, cocoa powder, baking soda, and salt. Take it out of the equation.
3. Using an electric hand mixer or the paddle attachment on a stand mixer, combine brown sugar, buttermilk, vegetable oil, egg, and vanilla extract in a large mixing bowl.
4. Pour in hot water and stir until smooth, then add the flour mixture and stir until just combined.
5. Using a medium cookie scoop or 1 1/2 Tbsp at a time, scoop the batter onto prepared baking sheets, spacing 2-inches apart.
6. Bake the first two sheets at the same time, turning halfway through, until the cookies bounce back when touched or a toothpick inserted in the center comes out clean, 8 to 10 minutes total.
7. Allow 5 minutes to cool before transferring to a wire rack to cool completely. In the center of the oven, bake the last sheet of cookies for 8 to 10 minutes.

For the filling

1. In the bowl of an electric stand mixer fitted with the paddle attachment, cream together salted Butter, Unsalted Butter, and powdered sugar on low speed (or using a hand mixer).
2. Increase to high and whip for 4 minutes, or until light and fluffy. Add the vanilla essence and mix well.
3. Remove the bowl from the stand mixer and, using a rubber spatula, stir in the marshmallow fluff until barely combined.
4. Chill the mixture for about 20 minutes before folding it again to thicken it. With a piping bag fitted with a large round tip, pipe half of the cookies, then sandwich a second biscuit on top.
5. Refrigerate cookies in an airtight container lined with parchment paper for up to 3 days in a single layer. Allow 30 minutes at room temperature to rest before serving.

99. STRAWBERRY, BASIL, AND BALSAMIC PIZZA

Prep Time: 15 mins

Cook Time: 35 mins

Total Time: 50 minutes

INGREDIENTS

- 16 ounces prepared whole-wheat pizza dough
- 1 ½ cup of (6 ounces) shredded mOunceszarella
- 5 ounces of goat cheese
- 1 ½ cup of (about ½ pound) chopped strawberries, leafy ends removed and sliced into ¼-inch thick rounds
- 1 tbsp fresh basil, chiffonade into short little strips

- freshly ground black pepper
- Balsamic reduction
- ½ Cup of balsamic vinegar
- 2 tbsps honey

INSTRUCTIONS

1. Preheat the oven to 350 degrees Fahrenheit (180 degrees Celsius) (180 degrees Celsius). Roll out the pizza dough into a 12 to 14-inch circle on a floured board. The pizza crust was topped with shredded mOunceszarella, large chunks of goat cheese, and strawberries. Bake for 35 to 40 minutes, or until the cheese is bubbling and golden and the dough is crisp below, on a lightly oiled baking sheet (or a pizza stone if you have one).
2. In the meanwhile, make the balsamic reduction. In a small saucepan, combine the vinegar and honey after slowly simmering the liquid over medium-low heat until it has reduced in volume by half, set aside (approximately 10 to 15 minutes).
3. Sprinkle basil and freshly ground black pepper over the pizza when it has done baking. As seen in the images, slice it and drizzle balsamic vinegar over the top with a spoon. Serve!

100. CHINESE FIVE-SPICE STEAK WITH ORANGES AND SESAME BROCCOLINI

Active Time40 minutes

Total Time45 minutes

Ingredients

- 3 small oranges (about 1 Pound)
- 1 1/2 tsp. Chinese five-spice powder
- 1 tsp. light brown sugar
- 2 1/4 tsp divided kosher salt
- 1 hanger steak (about 1 1/4 Pounds.), cut in half lengthwise, center gristle removed
- 2 Tbsp. vegetable oil
- 3 bunches broccolini (about 1 1/2 Pounds.), trimmed, halved lengthwise if large
- 2 Tbsp. toasted sesame oil
- 1/2 tsp. crushed red pepper flakes
- 1 tsp. toasted sesame seeds, plus more for serving
- 3 scallions, thinly sliced
- Flaky sea salt
- Steamed rice and hot sauce

Method

1. 2 tbsp orange zest from 1 orange, coarsely grated in a small bowl. All oranges that have been sliced in half should be set aside.
2. In the same bowl as the zest, combine the five-spice powder, brown sugar, and 2 tsp. Kosher salt. All over the meat, rub the spice mixture.

3. Heat the vegetable oil in a large, heavy skillet (preferably cast iron) over high heat. Cook the steak for 15–20 minutes total, often flipping, until both sides are browned, and an instant-read thermometer placed in the center registers 130°F for medium-rare. After 5 minutes of cooking, arrange the orange halves cut side down around the steak and cook for another 5 minutes, or until well browned. Arrange the oranges on a serving plate. Allow the steak to rest on a chopping board for 10 minutes before slicing.
4. Cook broccolini in an even layer in the same skillet over high heat. Cook, stirring periodically, for 3 minutes, or until completely blackened. Cook for another 3 minutes, stirring regularly, until the veggies are tender and slightly browned all over. Put everything in a big mixing bowl. Over the top, squeeze the juice of two orange halves. Combine the sesame oil, red pepper flakes, 1 tbsp sesame seeds, and the remaining 1/4 tsp kosher salt in a mixing bowl.
5. Place the meat on a dish to serve. Place the broccolini mixture alongside it. On top, scallions, sea salt, and the remaining sesame seeds are scattered. Serve with charred orange halves to squeeze over top, rice, and spicy sauce on the side if desired.

101.BUTTERMILK BISCUITS

Prep Time20 minutes

Cook Time10 minutes

Total Time30 minutes

Ingredients

- 4 cups of self-rising flour 1 pound by weight
- 1/2 cup of very cold Butter 1 stick or 4 ounces by weight
- 1 1/3 cup of buttermilk plus extra if needed and for brushing
- all-purpose flour for dusting the work surface

Instructions

1. Preheat the oven to 425°F (200°C). Combine the self-rising flour and baking powder in a large mixing bowl.
2. Half-cut the butter stick. One half should be sliced lengthwise into four batons, then cut across the batons to produce little cubes. The remaining half of the butter should be cut into as thin pats as feasible. Toss the butter cubes and pat in the flour with your hands until well coated. Then, one by one, scrape dried glue off your fingertips by massaging each pat and cube of butter between your fingers. Continue rubbing the butter into pea-sized irregular chunks until all of it is gone.
3. All of the buttermilk should be poured over the bowl's internal borders, save around 2 tbsp. Keep some buttermilk on hand just in case. With a hard spoon, silicone or rubber spatula, or flexible dough/bench scraper, toss the buttermilk into the butter and flour mixture until a scrappy dough forms. If the mixture is still too dry, add the remaining buttermilk. Squeeze a small amount of dough between your fingers. If it holds together, you're ready to travel. If the dough is still dry when pushed, add a tbsp of buttermilk at a time until it comes together.

4. Using all-purpose flour, scrape the dough out onto a clean work surface (NOT self-rising flour). Apply just enough pressure to swiftly and gently shape the dough into a 2-inch thick rectangle. As you press out the dough, gently incorporate any crumbling edges back into the dough mass.

5. Slide both hands under one side of the dough (around 9 o'clock if you think of the dough as a clock face), bring it up, and fold the dough over the other side like a book at 3 o'clock. Once more, pat the dough ball into a 2-inch thick rectangle. Place your palms beneath the dough's bottom at 6 o'clock and fold it up toward 12 o'clock. To make a 2-inch rectangle, fold from 9 o'clock to 3 o'clock, patting, then fold from 6 o'clock to 12 o'clock, patting. Each time you do this, the dough should stay together a little better.

6. With a floured rolling pin, roll out the dough into any shape you choose, aiming for a 3/4-inch to 1-inch thickness. Flour a sharp round or square biscuit or cookie cutter with an open top. Without spinning or whirling the blade, cut straight down into the biscuit dough. Cut the biscuits as close together as possible, leaving as little space as possible between them. If you don't have a sharp biscuit cutter, form squares by cutting straight down into the dough with a sharp knife.

Nutrition

Calories: 117kcal | Carbohydrates: 15g | Protein: 2g | Fat: 4g | Cholesterol: 11mg | Sodium: 48mg | Potassium: 38mg Calcium: 20mg | Iron: 0.2mg

102.BROWN-BUTTER APRICOTS WITH BRIOCHE AND ICE CREAM

Prep:30 mins

Total:30 mins

Servings:4

Ingredients

- 1 pound ripe or overripe apricots (about 5), halved, pitted, and sliced into roughly 1-inch-thick wedges
- 1/2 cup of sugar, divided
- 4 slices brioche (each 3/4 inch thick)
- 10 tbsps divided unsalted butter
- Pinch of coarse salt
- 1 tbsp water
- 1 pint of vanilla ice cream

Directions

1. Gently toss the apricots with 3 tbsp sugar. In a rimmed bowl, thoroughly coat both sides of each brioche slice with the remaining 5 tbsp sugar. Meanwhile, melt 2 tbsp butter in a large saute pan over medium heat until foaming. Heat 2 to 3 minutes after adding 2 brioche slices

to the pan until the bottoms are golden brown. Flip the slices and cook until golden brown on the other side with 1 tbsp of butter. Transfer the remaining 2 slices to a bowl and repeat.

2. Clean the pan and set it to medium-high heat. Cook for 3 minutes, stirring regularly until the remaining 4 tbsp butter is golden brown and fragrant. Stir in the apricots and salt, and heat for another minute or so until the apricots are cooked through.

3. Remove the pan from the heat and slowly drizzle in the distilled water to make a smooth sauce. Divide the brioche among four plates. Apricots, sauce, and ice cream on top of each serving. Serve immediately.

103.MAPLE FRIED BANANAS

PREP TIME1 min

COOK TIME4 mins

TOTAL TIME5 mins

INGREDIENTS

- 2 ripe bananas
- 1 tsp butter
- 1 tsp maple syrup
- ¼ tsp ground cinnamon

INSTRUCTIONS

1. Peel and cut the bananas into 12-inch thick slices.
2. Cook the butter, syrup, and cinnamon in a frying skillet over medium heat until hot and bubbling.

3. Cook for a few minutes until the banana slices are golden and cooked through, then turn and finish cooking.
4. Before serving, reheat the dish.

NUTRITION

Calories: 133kcalCarbohydrates: 30gProtein: 1gFat: 2gCholesterol: 5mgSodium: 19mgPotassium: 432mgFiber: 3gSugar: 17gCalcium: 13mgIron: 1mg

104.CHOCOLATE-BANANA SUNDAE

Hands-On:10 mins

Total:10 mins

Yield: Serves 4

Ingredients

- 4 small bananas
- 1-pint vanilla ice cream
- 1/4 cup of chocolate sauce
- 1/4 cup of sweetened shredded coconut

Directions

1. Peeled and sliced bananas are required. Using four bowls, divide the ice cream. Toss in the bananas, chocolate sauce, and coconut.

Nutrition

374 calories; protein 6g; carbohydrates 42g; sugars 16g; fiber 1g; fat 20g; calcium 2mg; sodium 98mg; cholesterol 120mg.

105.COCONUT BANANA FRITTERS

Total:1 hr

Yield: Serves 6 to 8

Ingredients

- 1 ⅓ cup of divided all-purpose flour
- ⅔ Cup of coconut flour
- 2 tbsp sugar

- ½ tsp salt
- 1 ½ tsp baking powder
- Vegetable oil for frying
- 12 very ripe baby (aka burro) bananas, 8 red bananas, or 6 regular bananas
- Coconut ice cream
- 1 tbsp toasted white sesame seeds

Directions

1. Combine 2/3 cup all-purpose flour, coconut flour, sugar, salt, and baking powder in a mixing bowl. 2 cups water, slowly whisked in until smooth If the mixture is too thick, add 1 to 2 tbsp at a time until it achieves a thick pancake batter consistency. Rest for at least 20 minutes and up to an hour.
2. Meanwhile, fill a large saucepan with enough oil to cover the sides by 3 inches; with a deep-fry thermometer inserted, heat to 350°F over medium-high heat (15 to 20 minutes).
3. Baby or red bananas should be split lengthwise in half. If you're using regular bananas, cut them in half crosswise on the diagonal. Toss the bananas with the remaining 2/3 cup of all-purpose flour in a mixing dish and coat them thoroughly. Place a cooling rack on a baking sheet.
4. Dredge a few banana slices in batter and carefully drop them into the oil. Increase the heat to keep the temperature at 350°. Using a slotted spoon, move the bananas to a wire rack after 7 to 10 minutes of frying. Remove cooked batter bits from the oil and discard. Repeat with the remaining bananas and batter, returning the oil to 350° between batches.
5. Place 2 to 3 banana slices in each bowl. Serve with an ice cream scoop and toasted sesame seeds on top.

Nutrition

459 calories; calories from fat 39%; protein 7.9g; fat 20g; carbohydrates 62g; fiber 4.8g; sodium 309mg; cholesterol 50mg.

106. YOGURT APPLE BOWLS

Prep Time: 15 mins

Total Time: 15 mins

Yield: 4

INGREDIENTS

- 2 Opal Apples, sliced in half
- 1 cup strawberry yogurt

INSTRUCTIONS

1. Using a melon baller, remove the flesh from each apple half. Allow enough space for the yogurt to fit within the bowls by not cutting through the corners or bottoms.
2. 1/4 cup yogurt should be added to each apple dish.
3. As desired, toppings can be added. Grab a spoon and get started!

107. PEANUT BUTTER SUNDAES

Prep/Total Time: 15 min

Ingredients

- 1 cup of sugar
- 1/2 cup of water
- 1 cup of creamy peanut butter
- Vanilla ice cream
- Salted peanuts

Directions

1) Combine the sugar and water in a saucepan. Simmer for one minute, or until the sugar dissolves, after bringing to a boil. Add the peanut butter after turning the heat off. Blend on high until smooth in a blender. Before pouring over ice cream, give it some time to chill. If desired, add peanuts on top. Any leftovers should be kept in the fridge.

Nutrition

2 tbsps: 191 calories, 11g fat 0 cholesterol, 100mg sodium, 21g carbohydrate (18g sugars, 1g fiber), 5g protein.

108. PARMESAN GARLIC BROCCOLI FRITTERS

Prep: 10 mins

Cook: 10 mins

Total: 20 mins

Ingredients

- 3 cups of broccoli florets and stem, roughly chopped into 2cm/1 inch pieces (see notes) (about 1 medium head of broccoli)
- 2 tbsp oil (vegetable, olive oil, canola)

BATTER

- 1 minced garlic clove

- 1/2 cup of plain flour
- 1/4 cup of grated Parmesan
- 1 egg
- 2 tbsp milk (low fat or full fat)
- 1/2 tsp salt
- Black pepper

YOGHURT SAUCE

- 1/4 cup of plain yogurt
- 2 tsp lemon juice
- Salt and pepper

Instructions

1. Steamed or cooked broccoli should be very soft (but not mushy). Using a steamer, cook 3 minutes on high in the microwave.
2. Use a potato masher to roughly "squish" the broccoli. Not to make it seem like mashed potatoes, but to crush it slightly so that it may be flattened with a spatula after frying to produce fritters with a smooth surface instead of large lumps sticking out.
3. To make the Yogurt Sauce, properly combine all of the ingredients.
4. In a small bowl, lightly beat the egg with a fork. Combine the remaining Batter ingredients and stir until thoroughly combined. The batter may look thick at first, but after you add the broccoli, it will soften up as it releases moisture as you crush it.
5. Incorporate the broccoli into the mixture, ensuring sure it is well distributed.
6. 1 tbsp oil, heated in a medium-sized fry pan
7. Scoop 1/4 cup batter onto the pan and gently flatten with a spoon to a thickness of 1cm/1/3". Make 3 fritters at a time.
8. Cook each side for 2 to 3 minutes, or until golden brown. Carry on with the rest of the batter.
9. Serve with extra lemon wedges and the Yogurt Sauce if desired.

NUTRITION

Serving: 85gCalories: 126cal Carbohydrates: 11.9g Protein: 5.4g Fat: 1.6g Cholesterol: 31mg Sodium: 266mg Potassium: 172mg Fiber: 1.5g Sugar: 1.4g Calcium: 80mg Iron: 0.9mg

109. PALEO VEGAN ZUCCHINI CAULIFLOWER FRITTERS

Prep Time: 5 minutes

Cook Time: 5 minutes

Total Time: 10 minutes

Servings: 8 burgers

Ingredients

Original version

- 1/2 head cauliflower, approximately 3 cups of chopped
- 2 medium zucchini
- 1/4 cup of coconut flour
- 2 large eggs
- 1/2 tsp sea salt
- 1/4 tsp black pepper

Egg-Free version

- 1/2 head cauliflower, approximately 3 cups of chopped
- 2 medium zucchini
- 1/4 cup of all-purpose flour can be gluten-free if needed
- 1/2 tsp sea salt
- 1/4 tsp black pepper

Instructions

1. Grate the zucchini in a food processor or a high-powered blender.
2. Cook for 5 minutes or until the cauliflower is fork soft. In a food processor or blender, pulse the cauliflower until it is broken down into tiny bits. It will turn to mush if you overprocess it.
3. Using a dishtowel or nut milk bag, squeeze as much moisture out of the shredded veggies as possible.
4. In a mixing bowl, combine the flour of choice, egg (if using), salt, pepper, and any other ingredients. Mix everything up thoroughly. Form the ingredients into small patties or burgers (I got about 8).
5. 1 tbsp coconut oil, melted in a big pan. Cook 4 fritters/burgers in a pan over medium heat for 2-3 minutes per side. Carry on with the rest of the fritters/burgers.
6. Serve with a low-carb burger bun or your favorite dipping sauce.

Nutrition

Serving: 1burger | Calories: 54kcal | Carbohydrates: 6g | Protein: 4g | Fat: 2g | Sodium: 188mg | Potassium: 255mg | Fiber: 3g Calcium: 24mg | Iron: 1mg | NET CARBS: 3g

110. JERK SHRIMP TACOS WITH PINEAPPLE SALSA, SLAW, AND PINA COLADA CREMA

Ready 45 minutes

4 Servings

INGREDIENTS

- 1 pound (16-20) shrimp; peeled and deveined
- 1/2 cup of jerk marinade

- 2 cups of cabbage sliced
- 1/2 cup of pina colada crema (see below)
- 12 small corn tortillas; warmed
- 2 cups of grilled pineapple salsa (I added 1/2 red pepper; diced this time.)
- 1/2 cup of sour cream (or Greek yogurt)
- 3 tbsps pineapple
- 2 tbsps coconut cream
- 1 tbsp rum (or 1 tsp rum extract)

INSTRUCTIONS

1. In the jerk marinade, marinate the shrimp for at least 20 minutes and up to overnight.
2. Skewer the shrimp and cook over medium-high heat until done, about 1-3 minutes on each side.
3. Toss the cabbage with half of the crema.
4. Start with the slaw, then add the pineapple salsa and shrimp, and end with a dollop of crema.
5. Colada Pina Colada Crema

111. CINNAMON TOAST THE RIGHT WAY

YIELDS:8 servings

PREP TIME:0 hours 10 mins

COOK TIME:0 hours 15 mins

TOTAL TIME:0 hours 25 mins

Ingredients

- 16 slices of bread (whole wheat is great!)
- 2 sticks salted butter, softened
- 1 Cup sugar (more to taste)
- 3 tsp. ground cinnamon
- 2 tsp. Vanilla extract (more to taste)
- 1/8 tsp. ground nutmeg

Directions

1. Preheat the oven to 350 degrees Fahrenheit (180 degrees Celsius).
2. Mash softened butter with a fork. Add the sugar, cinnamon, vanilla, and nutmeg, if using. Everything should be completely combined.
3. Cover the whole surface of the bread pieces, including the edges.
4. On a cookie sheet, toast the bread. With the cookie sheet in the oven, bake for 10 minutes. 5 minutes in the broiler, until golden brown and bubbling. Keep an eye on it to avoid it burning!
5. Cut the slices in half diagonally after removing them from the oven.

112. DOUGHNUT FUNFETTI ICE CREAM

PREP TIME 1 hr

COOK TIME 0 mins

TOTAL TIME 1 hr

INGREDIENTS

- 12 Ounces milk (1½ cup of)
- 12 Ounces heavy cream (1½ cup of)
- 1 cup of granulated sugar
- ⅛ tsp salt
- 6 egg yolks
- 1 1/2 tsp Princess Cake; Cookie Bakery Emulsion (see note below)
- 1 large frosted doughnut, cut into small pieces
- 2 TBSP sprinkles of your choice

INSTRUCTIONS

1) In a medium saucepan, combine the milk, cream, sugar, and salt. Heat the mixture over medium heat. While the milk warms up, whisk it occasionally. Whisk the yolks in a medium dish to break them up while you wait for the milk to come to a boil.

2) When the milk reaches a simmer, turn off the heat and whisk the egg yolks while gently pouring in about a third of the hot milk mixture. This prevents the eggs from cooking by keeping them from boiling.

3) Reheat the pan, then gently pour the heated egg mixture in a while mixing the milk. Cook, whisking regularly until the custard slightly thickens and coats the back of a spoon. Using a candy or deep-fry thermometer, aim for 175 degrees Fahrenheit (80C).

4) Using a fine-mesh strainer, remove the ice cream custard from the pan and pour it into a large basin or container. Include the Princess Cake & Cookie emulsion. When the custard reaches room temperature, cover it with cling film and refrigerate it until fully cold. As the custard cools, whisk it occasionally. (To speed up the process, submerge the bowl in an ice bath while whisking it.) Prior to serving, the custard can be cooked and stored in the refrigerator.

5) Use your ice cream maker to churn the custard in accordance with the manufacturer's instructions. Add the doughnut pieces and sprinkles when the ice cream is almost done churning and has reached a soft-serve consistency. Stir the mixture just long enough to combine the ingredients. Though it will be very soft, the ice cream may now be served. To make it more rigid and easier to scoop, freeze it for an hour in an ice cream container, or plastic container. Enjoy!

NUTRITION

CALORIES: 220 kcal | CARBOHYDRATES: 21 g | PROTEIN: 3 g | FAT: 13 g | CHOLESTEROL: 139 mg | SODIUM: 68 mg | POTASSIUM: 78 mg | FIBER: 0 g | SUGAR: 18 g CALCIUM: 75 mg | IRON: 0.4 mg

113. JELLY ROLL PANCAKES

prep time: 5 MINS

cook time: 5 MINS

total Time: 10 MINS

INGREDIENTS

- 4 eggs
- 3 cups of milk
- 1 tsp vanilla
- 3 cups of flour
- 1/2 cup of sugar
- 1/2 tsp salt

INSTRUCTIONS

1) In a blender or mixer, combine all the ingredients and process until completely smooth.

2) Cook the batter as ordinary pancakes by melting a little butter in a pan. Cooking over low heat until the edges are just beginning to get golden is the key.

3) Delectable toppings include butter, powdered sugar, syrup, jam, and Nutella.

114. RUM SOAKED GRILLED PINEAPPLE

Prep Time 10 minutes

Cook Time 12 minutes

Total Time 22 minutes

Ingredients

- 1/2 cup of dark rum
- 1/3 cup of brown sugar
- 1 pineapple peeled, cored & cut into 1/2" slices
- 1 1/2 tbsp cold Butter or vegan butter
- pinch of sea salt

- ice cream or 'nice cream to serve

Instructions

1. Whisk together the rum and brown sugar in a mixing basin until smooth.
2. In a 9x13" baking dish, arrange the pineapple slices and pour the rum and brown sugar mixture over them. Allow 2-6 hours for the pineapple to soak, flipping halfway through to allow the rum to soak into both sides.
3. Remove the pineapple from the rum and place it in a small saucepan. Bring the salted caramel sauce to a boil over medium-high heat, then reduce to approximately 2/3 of its original volume. Stir in the cooled butter and spices after removing the skillet from the heat. After gently turning the saucepan to incorporate the butter, set it aside.
4. Preheat a grill pan over medium-high heat. Cook the pineapple slices in batches on the hot grill for 3-5 minutes on each side, or until caramelized and grill marks emerge. Prepare for some smoke from the sugars if you're cooking inside.
5. To serve, place the pineapple ring in a shallow bowl or plate and top with a little scoop of ice cream or 'nice cream in the center, followed with salted caramel.

115. BUTTERY HERB SAUTÉED MUSHROOMS

PREP TIME10 MINUTES

COOK TIME5 MINUTES

TOTAL TIME15 MINUTES

Ingredients

- 2 Tbsps butter
- 8-ounce button mushrooms sliced
- 1 tbsp fresh thyme finely chopped
- 1 tbsp parsley finely chopped
- 1 tbsp rosemary finely chopped
- 3 cloves garlic finely chopped
- salt and pepper

Instructions

1) Melt the butter in a medium saucepan over medium-high heat. Salt and pepper to taste, along with the mushrooms, thyme, Parsley, rosemary, and garlic, should be added.

2) Sauté the vegetables until they are soft, about 3 to 4 minutes. If desired, add extra finely chopped Parsley on top.

Nutrition

Calories47kcal (2%)Carbohydrates2g (1%)Protein1g (2%)Fat4g Fat2g (10%)Cholesterol10mg (3%)Sodium36mg (2%)Potassium133mg (4%)Fiber1g (4%)Sugar1g (5%)Calcium12mg (1%)Iron1mg (6%)

116. RANCH POTATOES

READY IN: 55mins

SERVES: 8

INGREDIENTS

- 8 -10 medium potatoes, peeled and cut into 1/2 inch cubes
- 1can cream of mushroom soup, undiluted
- 1 1/4cup of milk
- 1envelope ranch dressing mix
- 1 1/2cup of shredded cheddar cheese, divided
- salt and pepper
- 6 slices of bacon, cooked and crumbled

DIRECTIONS

1. In a saucepan, place the potatoes.
2. Immerse yourself with water.
3. Bring to a boil, then reduce to low heat and simmer for another 10-12 minutes, or until the potatoes are nearly done. Drain.
4. Drain the potatoes and place them in a buttered 13x9-inch baking dish.
5. Pour the soup, milk, salad dressing mix, 1 cup of cheese, salt, and pepper to taste over the potatoes in a mixing bowl.
6. On top, sprinkle the crumbled bacon and the remaining cheese.
7. Bake for 25-30 minutes at 350°F, or until potatoes is soft.

117. SMOKY CAULIFLOWER BITES

Prep/Total Time: 20 min.

4 servings

Ingredients

- 3 tbsps olive oil
- 3/4 tsp sea salt
- 1 tsp paprika
- 1/2 tsp ground cumin
- 1/4 tsp ground turmeric
- 1/8 tsp chili powder

- 1 medium head cauliflower, broken into florets

Directions

1. Preheat the oven to 450°F (230°C). In a mixing bowl, combine the first six ingredients. Coat the cauliflower florets with the sauce. Half-fill a 15x10x1-inch baking pan with butter. Roast, stirring halfway through, for 15-20 minutes.

Nutrition

1 cup of 129 calories, 11g fat 0 cholesterol, 408mg sodium, 8g carbohydrate (3g sugars, 3g fiber), 3g protein. Diabetic Exchanges: 2 fat, 1 vegetable.

118. BAKED PEACHES

PREP:5 mins

COOK:30 mins

TOTAL:35 mins

Ingredients

- 3 fresh, very ripe peaches halved and pitted
- 2 tbsps extra virgin olive oil
- 2 tbsp pure maple syrup or honey
- 1 tbsp brandy bourbon or rum
- 1 tbsp coconut sugar or light brown sugar

- 1 tsp pure vanilla extract
- 1 tsp ground cinnamon
- ¼ tsp kosher salt
- Vanilla ice cream, Greek yogurt, or heavy cream for serving

Instructions

1) Set the oven's temperature to 350 degrees Fahrenheit (180 degrees Celsius). Use nonstick spray to lightly coat a 9x9-inch baking dish (or one of comparable size) big enough to contain the peach halves in a single layer. Pick a bowl that will accommodate your peaches neatly and without taking up too much space. Put the peaches on the plate with the sliced side up.

2) Combine the oil, maple syrup, brandy, coconut sugar, vanilla, cinnamon, and salt in a medium mixing bowl. Allow the mixture to spill over the edges of the peaches after filling them halfway.

3) Bake the peaches uncovered for 30 minutes or until they are soft and cooked through. While still warm, garnish with a dollop of heavy cream, Greek yogurt, or a scoop of vanilla ice cream, as desired.

Nutrition

half calories: 104kcalCARBOHYDRATES: 14gPROTEIN: 1gFAT: 5g 1gPOTASSIUM: 158mgFIBER: 1gSUGAR: CALCIUM: 15mgIRON: 1mg

---

119. FRUIT SKEWERS

prep time: 10 MINS

cook time: 20 MINS

total time:30 MINS

INGREDIENTS

- 12 chunks of pineapple
- 12 chunks of honeydew melon
- 12 slices of kiwi
- 24 grapes — I used a globe
- 12 strawberries
- 24 blueberries
- 12 bamboo skewers

For the dipping sauce:

- 1 cup of Greek yogurt

- 2 tbsp honey
- 1 tsp lemon juice
- 1/2 tsp vanilla extract

INSTRUCTIONS

1. Thread 1 strawberry, 1 pineapple chunk, 1 honeydew chunk, 1 kiwi slice, 2 grapes, and 2 blueberries onto a bamboo skewer. Repeat with the remaining ingredients.
2. Serve right away on a platter.

120. BAKED APPLES RECIPE

PREP TIME15 mins

COOK TIME20 mins

TOTAL TIME35 mins

INGREDIENTS

- 4 apples
- 2 Tbsp butter softened
- 1 Tbsp sugar
- 1/4 Cup caramel plus more for drizzling
- 1/4 cup chopped pecans
- 1/2 tsp ground cinnamon
- 1/4 Cup quick oatmeal

INSTRUCTIONS

1. After cleaning the grill, preheat it to 350 degrees F.
2. Apples should be cleaned before eating. Slice off 1/4 of the apples and scoop out the cores with a sharp paring knife or apple corer. Cut the holes to a diameter of about an inch. 1/2" of the bottom should be left alone.
3. In a small mixing bowl, combine the remaining ingredients. The filling should be stuffed into the apples.
4. Each apple should be placed on a heavy-duty foil sheet (about 12 in. square). Fold the foil over the apples and fasten it with a tuck.
5. Cook, covered, over medium heat for approximately 20 minutes, or until apples are tender.
6. Take them off the grill when they're done cooking, and carefully open the foil to allow the steam to escape. Place apples in a bowl and top with caramel and ice cream.

NUTRITION

Calories: 327kcalCarbohydrates: 44gProtein: 3gFat: 18g holesterol: 16mgSodium: 89mgPotassium: 297mgFiber: 6gSugar: 32g Calcium: 45mgIron: 1mg

121. STRAWBERRY SHORTCAKE (THE BEST)

PREPARATION45 MIN

COOKING55 MIN

COOLING3 H

MAKES8 TO 10 SERVINGS

INGREDIENTS

Cake

- 1 cup of (250 ml) unbleached all-purpose flour
- 1 tsp (5 ml) baking powder
- 1/4 tsp (1 ml) salt
- 3 eggs, separated
- 1 pinch of cream of tartar
- 1 1/4 cup of (310 ml) sugar
- 1/2 cup of (125 ml) unsalted butter, softened
- 1 tsp (5 ml) vanilla extract
- 1/2 cup of (125 ml) milk
- Vanilla Strawberries
- 1 vanilla bean
- 1 1/2 cup of (375 ml) sliced fresh strawberries
- 1 tbsp (15 ml) sugar

Whipped Cream

- 1 1/2 cup ofs (375 ml) 35% cream
- 3 tbsps (45 ml) sugar
- 1 tsp (5 ml) vanilla extract
- Fresh strawberries, whole or cut into wedges for garnish
- Bottom of Form

PREPARATION

Cake

1. Preheat the oven to 180 degrees Celsius (350 degrees Fahrenheit) with the center rack in position. Using parchment paper, line the bottom of a 20-cm (8-inch) springform pan. Take it out of the equation.
2. In a mixing bowl, combine the flour, baking powder, and salt. Take it out of the equation.

3. In a separate bowl, whisk the egg whites and cream of tartar with an electric mixer until soft peaks form. Continue to beat until stiff peaks form, adding 125 mL (1/2 cup) sugar at a time. Take it out of the equation.
4. In a third bowl, beat together the remaining sugar, butter, egg yolks, and vanilla extract using an electric mixer. At low speed, alternate adding the dry ingredients and the milk.
5. Fold in a quarter of the meringue to lighten the batter. With a spatula, carefully fold in the remaining meringue. Pour into the previously prepared pan.
6. Preheat the oven to 350°F and bake for 55 minutes, or until a toothpick inserted in the middle comes out clean. Remove as soon as possible from the mold and cool completely on a wire rack.

Vanilla Strawberries

1. Split the vanilla bean in half lengthwise. Using the tip of a knife, scrape the seeds from the vanilla pod.
2. In a mixing basin, combine the strawberries, sugar, vanilla seeds, and pod. Allow for 15 minutes of maceration. Drain. Remove the pod. Take it out of the equation.

Whipped Cream

1. In a mixing basin, whip the cream, sugar, and vanilla extract with an electric mixer until stiff peaks form. Remove yourself from the equation.

Assembly

1. Cut the cake in half horizontally to form two portions. Spread 250 ml (1 cup) of whipped cream on the cut side of each slice. Place a slice of cake with whipped cream on top of the drained vanilla strawberries. Cover with the remaining whipped cream-side-up cake slice. Finish by dusting the cake with the remaining whipped cream. Serve with a garnish of fresh strawberries.

122. FRENCH TOAST PAIN PERDU RECIPE WITH ALMOND

yield: 4

prep time: 5 MINUTES

cook time: 8 MINUTES

total Time: 13 MINUTES

Ingredients

- 4 thick slices of day-old brioche
- 2 eggs
- 1/3 cup of whole milk (80 ml)
- 1 tsp orange zest (2 grams)

- 1 tsp orange liqueur or vanilla extract (5 ml)
- 1 tsp granulated sugar (4 grams)
- 1 cup of fresh strawberries (144 grams) stems removed, sliced
- 2 tbsp unsalted butter (28 grams) divided for the pan
- powdered sugar to garnish
- maple syrup, to drizzle on top
- sliced almonds to garnish

Instructions

1) Combine the eggs, milk, orange zest, orange liqueur, and granulated sugar in a medium bowl with a shallow lip. To mix the ingredients and fully break up the eggs, whisk them together.

2) Melt 1/2 tbsp of butter in a medium skillet over medium heat, tilting the pan to spread the melted butter evenly.

3) Use a fork to dip a slice of brioche into the liquid batter, being sure to coat both sides. In the heated pan, cook the brioche for one minute on each side or until golden and crisp. After each fry, melt 1/2 tbsp of butter in the pan and repeat with the remaining brioche slices.

4) Slice each piece of brioche in half diagonally, then garnish with strawberry and almond pieces. Add powdered sugar to the top and drizzle with maple syrup.

123. HONEY GLAZED GRILLED PINEAPPLE

Total: 2 hr 14 min

Prep: 10 min

Inactive: 2 hr

Cook: 4 min

Yield: 4 servings

Ingredients

- 1/4 cup of honey
- Juice of 2 limes (depending on how juicy the limes are)
- 1/2 tsp ground cinnamon
- 1/2 pineapple, cut into 3/4-inch thick rings, core removed
- 3/4 cup of vanilla ice cream

Directions

1. In a baking dish, combine the honey, lime juice, and cinnamon. Allow the pineapple slices to marinate in the glaze for 2 hours, turning halfway through.
2. Preheat your grill pan to medium-high.
3. Place the pineapple slices on the already-heated grill. On both sides, grill for 2 minutes, or until the glaze caramelizes and grill marks emerge.
4. Serve the pineapple slices with a scoop of ice cream on top on separate plates. Pour the remaining honey syrup over the top.

124. EGGPLANT BITES

Prep Time15 minutes

Cook Time15 minutes

Total Time30 minutes

Ingredients

- 1 eggplant
- 1 tsp salt
- 1 ½ cup of seasoned bread crumbs
- 2 tsp onion powder
- 2 tsp garlic powder
- 1 tsp parsley
- ½ tsp tarragon
- 1 ½ tsp salt
- 1 tsp black pepper
- 2 eggs
- olive or avocado oil spray
- parmesan cheese
- marinara sauce

Instructions

1) Peel the eggplant and chop it into small pieces. 1 tsp salt plus 1 tsp water plus 1 tsp salt plus 1 tsp salt plus 1 tsp salt plus 1 tsp

2) Combine the breadcrumbs with salt, pepper, tarragon, Parsley, onion powder, and garlic powder in a mixing bowl. To fully incorporate all of the dry ingredients, whisk them together.

3) In a small mixing bowl, stir the eggs until they are scrambled.

4) Place a paper towel over the eggplant to absorb any extra moisture.

5) After immersing each eggplant, bite in the egg wash and breadcrumbs, and place it on an oiled rack in the air fryer or oven.

6) Set the oven to 400 degrees Fahrenheit and bake the food for 15 to 20 minutes, or until golden brown.

7) If you're using an air fryer, preheat your oven to 400 degrees Fahrenheit and air fried your food for 5-7 minutes, or until golden brown.

8) When finished, place the cooked eggplant pieces in a bowl or basin and sprinkle with freshly grated parmesan cheese. The cheese will melt onto the pieces because they are already nice and heated. Serve with the marinara sauce of your choice.

125. GRILLED FRUIT KEBABS

PREP TIME10 mins

COOK TIME2 mins

TOTAL TIME12 mins

INGREDIENTS

- 1 cup of pineapple chunks
- 1 banana (cut into 1-inch pieces)
- 1 cup of kiwi (cut into half-medallions)
- 1 cup of strawberries
- coconut oil spray
- 2 tbsp maple syrup
- 1 1/2 cup of vanilla yogurt (for dipping)

INSTRUCTIONS

1. On the grill, fruit kebabs
2. Before threading 1-inch fruit slices onto the skewers, soak them in water for 20 minutes. Repeat the process to make as many skewers as you like.
3. Drizzle with olive oil and maple syrup.
4. The grill should be sprayed with coconut oil.
5. Place fruit skewers over a hot grill for approximately 10 minutes, or until softened and charred, turning once or twice.
6. Right now, have fun! Serve with a dollop of yogurt if preferred.

NUTRITION

Calories: 137kcalCarbohydrates: 30gProtein: 4gFat: 1gCholesterol: 3mgSodium: 43mgPotassium: 397mgFiber: 2gSugar: 24gCalcium: 133mgIron: 1mg

126. ZUCCHINI-PARMESAN CHEESE FRITTERS

Prep:15 mins

Cook:10 mins

Additional:10 mins

Total:35 mins

Servings:10

Ingredients

- 3 large finely grated zucchini
- ½ tsp salt
- Batter:
- 1 egg
- 5 tbsps all-purpose flour
- 4 tbsp Parmesan cheese
- ¼ tsp salt
- ground black pepper to taste
- oil for frying
- Toppings:
- 1 tbsp grated Parmesan cheese, or to taste
- 1 pinch salt
- ¼ cup of sour cream for topping

Directions

1) Add salt and zucchini to a mixing bowl and stir to incorporate. Give this ten minutes to occur. The mixture should thoroughly drain after being poured into a clean dish towel or cheesecloth and squeezed.

2) In a mixing bowl, combine the egg, flour, Parmesan cheese, salt, and pepper. Include the drained zucchini, then.

3) In a medium-sized pan over medium-high heat, warm the oil. By spoonfuls, add the batter to the pan. Each batch of fritters should be cooked for 5 minutes or until golden brown on both sides. Serve on a serving platter after seasoning with salt and Parmesan cheese. Serve with sour cream right away.

Nutrition

138 calories; protein 3.4g; carbohydrates 6.7g; fat 11.4g; cholesterol 23.3mg; sodium 248mg.

127. ZUCCHINI PATTIES

Prep Time15 minutes

Cook Time10 minutes

Total Time25 minutes

Ingredients

- 2 cups of grated zucchini well-drained (approximately 3 medium zucchini)
- 1 tbsp finely chopped onion
- 1/4 cup of Parmesan cheese (25 grams)
- 1/4 cup of flour (32 grams)
- 2 large eggs
- 2 tbsps mayonnaise
- 1/4 tsp oregano
- 1/4 tsp salt
- 1-2 dashes of black pepper
- 1-2 tbsps olive oil

Instructions

1. In a medium mixing bowl, combine all ingredients except the olive oil.
2. In a medium to a large frying pan, heat the olive oil over medium heat. Place a heaping large spoonful of the mixture in the pan and brown on both sides.
3. Drain briefly on a paper towel-lined bowl, then serve immediately. Enjoy!

Nutrition

Calories: 126kcal | Carbohydrates: 4g | Protein: 3g | Fat: 10g | Cholesterol: 84mg | Sodium: 150mg | Potassium: 137mg | Sugar: 1g Calcium: 80mg | Iron: 0.6mg

128. PEAR CRISP WITH VANILLA ICE CREAM

YIELDS:4 servings

PREP TIME:0 hours 15 mins

COOK TIME:0 hours 40 mins

TOTAL TIME:0 hours 55 mins

Ingredients

- 4 whole (to 5) Large Pears (Bosc Work Well)
- 2/3 Cup Sugar
- 1/4 tsp. Salt
- Topping Ingredients
- 1 1/2 cup All-purpose Flour
- 1/3 cup Sugar
- 1/3 Cup Firmly Packed Brown Sugar
- 1/2 tsp. Cinnamon
- 1/2 Cup Pecans, Very Finely Chopped
- 1 stick of Melted Butter

Directions

1) Set the oven's temperature to 350 degrees Fahrenheit (180 degrees Celsius).

2) Before using, pears must be peeled, cored, and diced. Mix 2/3 cup sugar and 1/4 tsp salt in a mixing basin. Remove it from the equation.

3) Combine the flour, sugar, brown sugar, cinnamon, and nuts in another basin. All the ingredients should be combined in a mixing bowl. Melted butter should be added gradually while being continuously mixed with a fork.

4) Cover the pears in a baking dish with the crumb topping.

5) Set the oven to 350°F and bake the food for 30 minutes.

6) Continue baking on the top oven rack for an additional 10 minutes or until the topping is golden brown.

7) Serve with vanilla ice cream while it's still warm.

129. HONEY PEANUT BUTTER BREAKFAST BANANA SPLITS

prep time: 5 MINUTES

total Time: 5 MINUTES

INGREDIENTS

- 1 banana
- 1 Tbsp peanut butter
- 1 tsp honey
- Pinch cinnamon
- 1/2 cup of your favorite Greek yogurt (I use plain or vanilla)
- 2 Tbsps honey roasted peanuts

INSTRUCTIONS

1. Using a knife, cut the banana in half lengthwise. In a small bowl, combine the peanut butter, honey, and a pinch of cinnamon. Microwave for 10-20 seconds, or until the mixture is pourable. In a bowl, layer the banana and yogurt. Over the top, pour the peanut butter mixture. On top, sprinkle with peanuts or honey nut granola. Serve.

Nutrition

CALORIES: 386TOTALFAT: 17gCHOLESTEROL: 6mgSODIUM: 167mgCARBOHYDRATES: 45gFIBER: 6gSUGAR: 27gPROTEIN: 21g

130. PINEAPPLE SHRIMP STIR FRY

yield: 4 SERVINGS

prep time: 10 MINS

cook time: 10 MINS

total Time: 20 MINS

INGREDIENTS

- 2 tbsps cornstarch
- 1 tbsp onion powder
- 1 tbsp garlic powder
- 1 ½ Pound shrimp, shells removed
- 2 tbsp cooking oil, divided
- 1 cup of snap peas, cut in half
- 1 red pepper, diced

- 2 cups of chopped pineapple, or canned pineapple chunks
- Sesame seeds for serving.
- Pineapple Stir Fry Sauce
- 1 tbsp cornstarch
- ½ cup of pineapple juice can sub orange juice
- ¼ cup of hoisin sauce, gluten-free, if needed
- ¼ cup of soy sauce, gluten-free, if needed
- 1 tbsp minced ginger
- ½ tsp sea salt
- 3 cloves garlic, minced

INSTRUCTIONS

1. If you're serving this with rice, start there.
2. Combine the cornstarch, onion powder, and garlic powder in a medium mixing basin. Coat the shrimp with the sauce. The batter will become quite sticky.
3. 2 tbsp cornstarch, 1 tbsp onion powder, 1 tbsp garlic powder
4. Next, make the stir fry sauce. Half-fill a measuring cup with cornstarch. Combine the cornstarch and a tiny amount of pineapple juice. Combine the remaining sauce ingredients with the residual juice.
5. 12 cup pineapple juice, 14 cup hoisin sauce, 14 cup soy sauce, 1 tbsp grated ginger, 12 tsp salt, 3 garlic cloves, 1 tbsp cornstarch 1 tsp sriracha sauce (optional) (more, to taste)
6. 1 tbsp oil, heated in a large nonstick frying pan over medium-high heat Place the shrimp on the pan in a single layer and spread them out evenly. Cook for 2 minutes on each side before removing them from the pan.
7. In the remaining 1 tbsp of oil, cook the snap peas, red pepper, and pineapple for 2-3 minutes, or until crisp-tender.
8. 1 red pepper, 2 cups chopped pineapple, 1 cup snap peas
9. Return the shrimp to the pan, swirl the sauce, and then pour it over the shrimp and veggies, mixing everything together. Allow 1 minute for the sauce to thicken before serving the stir fry with sesame seeds on top.

Nutrition

serving: 1 serving = ¼ of the recipe, calories: 370kcal, carbohydrates: 36g, protein: 39g, fat: 9g, cholesterol: 274mg, sodium: 1588mg, potassium: 798mg, fiber: 4g, sugar: 18g, calcium: 157mg, iron: 3mg

131. BRIOCHE FRENCH TOAST

Prep Time:5 minutes

Cook Time:20 minutes

Total Time:25 minutes

INGREDIENTS

- 4 eggs
- ¾ cup of whole milk
- 1 tbsp sugar
- 1 tsp vanilla extract
- 3 tbsps divided Butter
- 10 slices brioche
- ½ cup of pure maple syrup, warmed
- fresh berries for serving

INSTRUCTIONS

1. In a low shallow dish – a pie plate works well – whisk the eggs. If you want to cover numerous pieces of bread at once, use a 13- x 9-inch baking dish. Whisk together the milk, sugar, and vanilla extract until smooth.
2. Melt 1 tbsp butter in a 12-inch to 14-inch pan over MEDIUM heat. Meanwhile, slather one brioche slice with the egg mixture on both sides. Once the butter has melted and foamed, add the wrapped brioche. Dip and transfer as many brioche pieces as will fit without touching in the pan. Cook for 3 to 4 minutes, or until golden brown, then turn and cook for 3 to 4 minutes more.
3. Keep the French toast warm by placing it on a serving platter. If you don't have a warming tray, place the French toast on a baking sheet and cook it in the oven at 200 degrees until ready to serve.

4. Wipe the skillet clean with a paper towel and repeat with the remaining butter, bread, and egg mixture.
5. Serve immediately with warm maple syrup and fresh berries.

NUTRITION

Calories: 531 kcal · Carbohydrates: 58 g · Protein: 13 g · Fat: 27 g · Cholesterol: 272 mg · Sodium: 448 mg · Potassium: 169 mg · Sugar: 23 g · Calcium: 138 mg · Iron: 1.3 mg

132. SPICY BISQUICK SAUSAGE BALLS

Active:15 mins

Total:55 mins

Yield: Serves 15

Ingredients

- 3 cups of all-purpose baking mix (such as Bisquick Original Pancake & Baking Mix)
- 1 pound hot ground pork sausage
- 1 (8- Ounces) block of medium Cheddar cheese, shredded
- 1 (8- Ounces) shredded block pepper Jack cheese
- 6 tbsp whole milk
- 2 tbsps grated yellow onion
- 2 tbsps chopped fresh Cilantro
- Cooking spray

Directions

1) Set the oven's temperature to 350 degrees Fahrenheit (180 degrees Celsius). In a sizable mixing basin, add the baking mix, sausage, cheeses, milk, onion, and Cilantro. Press the ingredients together with your hands to thoroughly incorporate. Place 2 inches apart on baking sheets that have been gently oiled after forming 1-inch balls (with cooking spray).

2) Cook for 20 to 25 minutes, or until gently browned, in a preheated oven. Make the bowl warm before serving.

133. CROCK-POT PECAN PIE BREAD PUDDING RECIPE

Servings 8

Prep Time 20 mins

Cook Time 1-2 Hours

Ingredients

- 7 Cup of Stale Bread Cubed
- 2 Tbsps Melted Unsalted Butter
- 3 Large Eggs
- 1/3 Cup of Light Brown Sugar
- 1/4 Cup of Granulated Sugar
- 1 Cup of Light Corn Syrup
- 1 Tsp Pure Vanilla Extract
- 1/2 Tsp Kosher Salt
- 1 Tsp Ground Cinnamon
- 1 Cup of Chopped Pecans

Instructions

1. In a large mixing basin, toss the bread pieces in the melted butter.
2. In a medium mixing bowl, whisk together the eggs, brown sugar, granulated sugar, corn syrup, vanilla extract, salt, and cinnamon until fully incorporated.
3. Mix in the pecans well.
4. Stir the bread pieces into the egg mixture until they are thoroughly coated.
5. Coat a 6 quart or larger slow cooker with nonstick cooking spray.
6. The bread pudding mixture should fill the slow cooker halfway.
7. Cook on HIGH for 1 to 2 hours, or until the bread pudding is firm in the center.
8. Turn the slow cooker off before serving and ladle the warm bread pudding into bowls, if preferred, topped with a dollop of vanilla ice cream.

Nutrition

Calories: 960kcal, Total Fat: 32g, Cholesterol: 70mg, Sodium: 1574mg, Potassium: 206mg, Carbohydrates: 150g, Dietary Fiber: 9g, Sugars: 35g, Protein: 21g, Calcium: 32%, Iron: 50%

134. FRESH FRUIT WITH VANILLA CREAM

Prep/Total Time: 10 min.

6 servings

Ingredients

- 4 cups of fresh fruit (raspberries, blueberries, strawberries, and/or peaches)
- 3 ounces cream cheese, softened
- 1/4 cup of confectioners' sugar
- 2 to 3 tbsps half-and-half cream
- 1/2 tsp vanilla extract
- 1/4 tsp orange or almond extract

Directions

1. Arrange the fruit in a serving bowl or individual dessert bowls. In a mixing basin, whisk together the cream cheese and confectioners' sugar. Whisk in the cream and extract gradually until smooth. Over the fruit, pour the liquid.

Nutrition

1 serving: 126 calories, 6g fat 18mg cholesterol, 49mg sodium, 18g carbohydrate (16g sugars, 2g fiber), 2g protein.

135. APPLE PEACH PIE

Prep:25 mins

Cook:55 mins

Total:80 mins

Servings:8 servings

Ingredients

- The 2-crust pie crust recipe
- 1 cup of sugar
- 2 tbsps tapioca
- 1/2 tsp ground cinnamon
- 5 Granny Smith apples (peeled and sliced)
- 1 peach (peeled and sliced, or 1/2 cup of frOuncesen solid pack peaches)
- 1/2 cup of crushed corn flakes
- 2 tbsps dry lemon Jell-O

- 2 tbsps butter
- 1 tbsp sanding (decorator's) sugar

Make

1. Gather the required materials.
2. Preheat the oven to 400 degrees Fahrenheit (200 degrees Celsius). A 9-inch pie pan should be lined with one cold pie crust.
3. In a large mixing bowl, combine the sugar, tapioca, cinnamon, and apple and peach slices, and gently toss to cover the fruit.
4. Sprinkle corn flakes in the bottom of the pie crust, then fill with the apple-peach mixture.
5. Sprinkle dry lemon Jell-O over the fruit and dot with little chunks of butter.
6. Top with the top crust and flute it.
7. Slit the top crust in an artful manner, then dust with sanding sugar.
8. Bake at 400°F for 10 minutes, then lower to 350°F and bake for another 45–50 minutes, or until liquids are boiling and the crust is deep golden brown.
9. Allow the pie to cool on a wire rack for at least one hour before serving.

10. Serve and have a good time!

136. GRILLED POUND CAKE WITH BERRIES

Total Time

Prep/Total Time: 25 min.

6 servings

Ingredients

- 1 cup of sliced fresh strawberries
- 1 cup of fresh raspberries
- 1 cup of fresh blueberries
- 5 tbsp sugar, divided
- 1 tbsp minced fresh mint
- 1 cup of heavy whipping cream
- 1 tbsp lemon juice
- 1 tsp grated lemon zest
- 3 tbsp butter, softened
- 6 slices of pound cake (about 1 inch thick)

Directions

1. In a large mixing basin, combine the strawberries, raspberries, blueberries, 2 tbsp sugar, and mint.

2. Whisk the cream in a small mixing basin until it thickens. Mix in the remaining sugar well. Soft peaks should develop after adding the lemon juice and zest. Refrigerate until ready to serve.
3. Brush the cake slices on both sides with butter. Cover and grill for 1-2 minutes on each side, or until light golden brown, over indirect medium heat. Serve with berries and whipped cream.

Nutrition

1 piece: 377 calories, 27g fat 136mg cholesterol, 193mg sodium, 34g carbohydrate (24g sugars, 3g fiber), 3g protein.

137. COCONUT CHOCOLATE BROWNIES

Prep time20 mins

Cooking time30 mins

Serves30

Ingredients

- 125g butter
- 1/4 cup of cocoa
- 1 cup of Chelsea White Sugar
- 2 eggs
- 1 tsp vanilla essence
- 1/2 cup of coconut
- 1/2 cup of flour
- 1/2 tsp baking powder
- Chelsea Icing Sugar to dust

Method

1) Set the oven's temperature to 180 degrees Fahrenheit.

2) Prepare a little 20-cm square baking pan with grease and have it handy. Melted butter and cocoa powder are combined with a whisk.

3) After adding the eggs one at a time, thoroughly beat in the Chelsea White Sugar between additions.

4) Sift the flour, baking powder, and vanilla extract in a mixing bowl. Add the coconut and vanilla extract.

5) Set the oven to 350°F and bake the food for 30 minutes.

6) Permit the cake to completely cool before icing it with Chelsea sugar.

138. CINNAMON ROLL APPLE COBBLER

Prep Time: 10 MINUTES

Cook Time: 45 MINUTES

Total Time: 1 HOUR

INGREDIENTS

- 2 cans of Pillsbury Grands Cinnamon Rolls
- 5 large apples (3 granny smith, 2 sweeter variety)
- 1/3 cup of light brown sugar
- 2 Tbsps corn starch
- 1 Tbsp ground cinnamon
- 1/4 tsp ground nutmeg
- 1/8 tsp ground cloves
- pinch of salt

INSTRUCTIONS

1) Set the oven to 375 degrees Fahrenheit and butter or oil a skillet or 10-inch round baking dish that is oven-safe. Turn off the heat under the pan.

2) Combine the sugar, cornstarch, spices, and salt in a large mixing basin.

3) Before slicing the apples into tiny 1/8- to 1/4-inch pieces, peel and core them. Until the apples are well covered, toss them with the sugar mixture. You could use two big wooden spoons, but I like to use my hands. Place the apples in an equal layer in the greased dish.

4) Prebake the cinnamon buns in the oven for 20 minutes before adding them. As a result, the cinnamon rolls won't get soggy.

5) Put the apple mixture in the oven again and add the cinnamon buns on top. Bake the cinnamon rolls at 375°F for another 25 minutes, or until they are golden brown and the apple layer is bubbling. Remove it from the oven.

6) Drizzle or spoon the frosting from the cinnamon roll container over the cinnamon rolls. Serve immediately!

139. CINNAMON TOAST PUMPKIN SEEDS

Prep:10 mins

Cook:40 mins

Total: 50 mins

Servings:10

Ingredients

- 3 tbsp melted Butter
- 1 tsp ground cinnamon
- ¼ tsp salt
- 1 ½ cup of pumpkin seeds
- 2 tbsp white sugar

Directions

6. Preheat the oven to 300 degrees F. (150 degrees C).
7. Combine the butter, cinnamon, and salt in a mixing basin.
8. In a large mixing bowl, pour the butter mixture over the pumpkin seeds and toss to coat evenly. Place coated seeds in a single layer on a baking sheet.
9. In a preheated oven, cook, occasionally rotating, until seeds are softly browned, about 40 minutes. Remove the baking sheet from the oven and evenly sprinkle the seeds with sugar.

140. BLACKBERRY COBBLER RECIPE

PREP TIME: 10 minutes

COOK TIME: 45 minutes

TOTAL TIME: 55 minutes

SERVINGS: 8 SERVINGS

Ingredients

- 5 cups of fresh blackberries
- 1/2 cup of white granulated sugar
- 1 tsp vanilla extract

Topping

- 1/2 cup of (1 stick) unsalted butter, melted
- 1 cup of white granulated sugar
- 1 egg
- 1 cup of all-purpose flour
- 1 1/2 tsp baking powder
- 1/4 tsp salt

Instructions

1) Set the oven's temperature to 350 degrees Fahrenheit (180 degrees Celsius). A 13x9-inch baking dish with a cooking spray or butter coating, or a deep-dish pie plate, should be set aside.

2) In a large mixing basin, combine the blackberries, 1/2 cup sugar, and vanilla essence. Stir until the berries are thoroughly coated, and the sugar has been absorbed. Fill the baking dish with the mixture.

3) In a medium mixing bowl, combine the melted butter, sugar, and egg. In another bowl, mix the flour, baking soda, and salt. Using the back of a spoon or a rubber spatula, spread the batter evenly over the blackberries.

4) Bake the fruit and crust for 40 to 45 minutes, or until the fruit is bubbling and the crust is golden. It's still warm, yet, at the same time. Add some vanilla ice cream on top. Enjoy!

Nutrition

Calories: 353kcal | Carbohydrates: 59g | Protein: 4g | Fat: 13g | Fat: 7g | Cholesterol: 51mg | Sodium: 85mg | Potassium: 265mg | Fiber: 5g | Sugar: 42g | Calcium: 76mg | Iron: 1mg

141. MAPLE WALNUT ICE CREAM

Prep:30 mins

Cook:35 mins

Additional:3 hrs

Total:4 hrs 5 mins

Servings:8

Ingredients

- 1 ½ cup of heavy whipping cream
- 5 egg yolks
- 1 ½ cup of milk
- 2 tbsp white sugar
- 1 tbsp corn syrup
- ¾ cup of maple syrup
- ⅛ tsp coarse salt
- ¼ tsp vanilla extract

Wet Walnuts:

- 1 ½ cup of walnut halves
- ½ cup of maple syrup
- 1 tbsp maple syrup
- 1 pinch salt

Directions

1. Fill a large mixing bowl halfway with cream and strain it through a mesh sieve. Whisk the egg yolks together in a separate bowl.
2. Cook the milk, sugar, and corn syrup together in a saucepan over medium-low heat until the milk steam, about 5 minutes. Slowly pour roughly 1/2 cup of heated milk into the egg yolks with a whisk. Scrape the egg yolk mixture into the pot using a heatproof spatula.
3. Cook and stir the milk mixture constantly with the spatula for about 10 minutes, scraping the bottom of the pot often or until it thickens and coats the spatula. Remove the saucepan from the heat and pour the mixture through a mesh strainer into the cream.
4. Place the bowl over a larger bowl of cold water and whisk to cool, adding 3/4 cup maple syrup, coarse salt, and vanilla as required. Allow the mixture to chill for 2 hours.
5. Preheat the oven to 275 degrees Fahrenheit (190 degrees Celsius) (135 degrees C). Spread walnuts out on a baking sheet.
6. 15 minutes before serving, roast walnuts until golden brown and fragrant in a preheated oven. Allow for room temperature cooling of the nuts. Chop the nuts coarsely.
7. Heat 1/2 cup + 1 tbsp maple syrup in a pot until it boils. After adding the walnuts, return to a boil. After 10 seconds of stirring, remove from heat and set aside to cool completely. The nuts will be wet and sticky after they have cooled.
8. Take the cream mixture out of the fridge and pour it into your ice cream machine according to the manufacturer's instructions. During the last five minutes of churning, add the wet walnuts.

Nutrition

487 calories; protein 6.9g; carbohydrates 46.1g; fat 32.5g; cholesterol 192.8mg; sodium 77.3mg.

142. CINNAMON-SUGAR PUMPKIN SEEDS

YIELDS:8 - 10

PREP TIME:0 HOURS 5 MINS

TOTAL TIME:0 HOURS 30 MINS

INGREDIENTS

- 2 tbsp. butter
- 2 cups pumpkin seeds
- 1 tsp. cinnamon

- 2 tbsp. sugar

DIRECTIONS

1. Preheat the oven to 350 degrees Fahrenheit (180 degrees Celsius). As the oven heats up, microwave the butter in 20-second increments until thoroughly melted.
2. After coating pumpkin seeds in melted butter, toss them with cinnamon and sugar.
3. On a parchment-lined baking sheet, roast the seeds for 25 to 27 minutes or until lightly golden.

143. BACON-WRAPPED SCALLOPS

Prep Time20 minutes

Cook Time15 minutes

Total Time35 minutes

INGREDIENTS

- 2 pounds large sea scallops patted dry
- 1 pound bacon slices cut in half crosswise
- 1/4 cup of maple syrup
- 2 tbsps soy sauce
- 1/4 tsp garlic powder
- salt and pepper to taste
- 2 tbsp chopped Parsley
- cooking spray

INSTRUCTIONS

1. Preheat the broiler in the oven. Coat a sheet pan with cooking spray.
2. Wrap a strip of bacon around each scallop and fasten with a toothpick. Arrange the scallops in a single layer on the baking pan.
3. In a small bowl, combine the maple syrup, soy sauce, garlic powder, salt, and pepper. Brush the tops of each scallop with half of the mixture.
4. Broil for 10-15 minutes, or until scallops and bacon are cooked through. Brush the leftover sauce over the scallops halfway through the cooking time.
5. Serve with Parsley on top.

NUTRITION

Calories: 259kcal | Carbohydrates: 15g | Protein: 28g | Fat: 14g | Cholesterol: 86mg | Sodium: 729mg | Potassium: 502mg | Sugar: 8g Calcium: 27mg | Iron: 1mg

144. CHILI LIME BAKED COD

yield: 4 SERVINGS

prep time: 10 MINUTES

cook time: 20 MINUTES

marination time: 15 MINUTES

total time: 45 MINUTES

Ingredients

- 1.5 Pounds cod, cut into fillets
- 1/4 cup of avocado oil
- 1 tsp lime zest
- 2 Tbsp lime juice
- 1 large clove of garlic, minced
- 1 1/2 tsp chili powder
- 1 tsp ground paprika
- 1 1/2 tsp dried oregano
- 1/4 tsp black pepper
- 1/2 tsp sea salt

Instructions

1) In a measuring cup or mixing dish, whisk the marinade ingredients until well combined.

2) Pour the marinade over the cod fillets in a container or zip-top bag that can be sealed. Shake the sealed bag (or container) to distribute the marinade evenly.

3) Chill for at least 30 minutes and up to 10 hours before serving.

4) Set the oven to 400 degrees Fahrenheit when you are prepared to bake.

5) Place the fish in a large casserole dish with the marinade. On the oven rack at the top, bake the fish for 15 minutes or until it is thoroughly cooked.

6) Accompany with your preferred side dish. My lemon-garlic-rosemary rice is really well-liked.

145. EASY HONEY CHIPOTLE SALMON

Prep Time: 15 minutes

Cook Time: 15 minutes

Total Time: 30 minutes

Yield: serves 4

Ingredients

- 1/3 cup of (5 Tbsps) unsalted butter, melted
- 1/4 cup of (90g) honey
- 1 – 2 garlic cloves, minced (I use 2)
- 1 tsp ground chipotle chili pepper
- 1/2 tsp pepper
- 1/2 tsp salt
- 4 individual salmon filets (or a large 2 Pounds filet)

Instructions

1. In a medium mixing bowl, combine everything (except for the salmon, of course). Place the salmon in a zip-top bag, a Tupperware container, or a baking dish. Pour half of the marinade over the top. Give everything a thorough shake. The remainder can be saved for the fourth stage. Marinate for at least 15 minutes and as long as 8 hours.
2. Meanwhile, preheat the grill to medium-high heat or the oven to 375°F (191°C).
3. Grill the fish on foil or on a wood plank. Grill the salmon skin side down for 15 minutes, or until the thickest section reaches an internal temperature of 145°F (63°C) (approximately 10 minutes per 1-inch thickness measured from the thickest part of the filet).
4. Alternatively, bake the salmon for 15-20 minutes, depending on thickness, on a preheated baking sheet or until the thickest section reaches an internal temperature of 145°F (63°C).
5. Brush the heated fish with the remaining marinade before serving. Leftovers can be kept in the refrigerator for a few days. Reheat until the temperature you want is attained.

146. CRAB AND COD FISH CAKES WITH TOMATO SALSA

Preparation time

30 mins to 1 hour

Cooking time

30 mins to 1 hour

Serves 6

Ingredients

For the fishcakes

- 500g/1Pounds 2Ounces floury potatoes, peeled and diced
- 500g/1Pounds 2Ounces cod loin, skinned

- 6 spring onions, finely chopped
- 2 tbsp full-fat mayonnaise
- 2 tsp Dijon mustard
- 130g/4¾Ounces dressed crab or 100g/3½Ounces mixed fresh crabmeat (tinned is fine)
- 2 tbsp chopped fresh Parsley
- dash of hot pepper sauce, such as Tabasco
- 100g/3½Ounces Japanese panko breadcrumbs
- knob of butter, plus extra for greasing
- 1 tbsp oil
- Salt and freshly ground black pepper

For the salsa

- 6 firm tomatoes, deseeded, diced
- 1 small red onion, finely chopped
- 1 tbsp white wine vinegar
- 4 tbsp olive oil
- 2 tbsp chopped fresh Parsley

Method

1. Preheat the oven to 200 degrees Celsius/180 degrees Celsius, fan/Gas 6 degrees Celsius.
2. With the potatoes, bring a saucepan of salted water to a boil. Cook until the potatoes are tender, about 15 minutes. Drain and mash well. After seasoning with salt and pepper, set aside to chill.
3. To make a package, butter a sheet of foil and set the cod loin in the center, season with salt and pepper, then wrap the foil over it. On a baking sheet, heat for 20 minutes or until just cooked through. Before serving, allow cooling. When the fish has totally cooled, flake it into large pieces with care. Set aside the cooking juices.
4. Combine the cooled mash, spring onions, mayonnaise, and mustard in a mixing bowl. 2 tbsp of the fish cooking liquid, flaked cod, and crab meat. Combine the Parsley and hot pepper sauce in a large mixing bowl. Season to taste with salt and pepper.
5. Using moist palms, form the mixture into 8 fishcakes, each about 9cm/312 in diameter. After placing on a tray, chill for at least 15 minutes.
6. Place the breadcrumbs on a plate and coat each fishcake. Refrigerate for another 30 minutes after returning the tray to the fridge.
7. Meanwhile, combine all of the ingredients in a bowl and season with salt and pepper.
8. In a large, heavy-bottomed frying pan, melt the butter and oil over high heat, then cook the fishcakes for 4 minutes on each side, or until golden brown all over. It's vital not to crowd the pan during frying; if required, cook in two batches.
9. Serve alongside a simple salad and a spicy tomato salsa.

147. CAJUN BLACKENED TILAPIA

Prep: 5 mins

Cook: 8 mins

Total: 13 mins

Yield: Serves: 4

Ingredients

- 1 tsp pepper
- ½ tsp cayenne, or more to taste
- 1 ½ tsp celery salt
- 1 tbsp paprika
- 1 ½ tsp garlic powder
- 1 ½ tsp dried thyme
- 8 tilapia fillets, 2 to 4 Ounces each
- 4 tbsp melted unsalted butter

Directions

1. Combine pepper, cayenne, celery salt, paprika, garlic powder, and thyme in a small bowl and whisk well.
2. Heat a large cast-iron pan to a smoking temperature over high heat. Before covering the fillets in the spice mixture, brush both sides with butter.
3. Cook the fish in batches, turning once, for 3 to 4 minutes, until browned on both sides and flaky on the inside. Serve immediately.

Nutrition

338 calories; fat 17g; saturated fat 8g; protein 43g; carbohydrates 2g; fiber 1g; cholesterol 141mg; sodium 558mg.

148. GARLIC BAKED HADDOCK

Prep Time 15 mins

Cook Time 15 mins

Total Time 30 mins

Ingredients

- 1 1/2 Pounds of haddock fillets
- 4 tbsp. salted butter melted
- 3 garlic cloves finely minced
- 4 tbsp. white cooking wine
- 2 tbsp. fresh-squeezed lemon juice
- 15 Ritz crackers crumbled
- Fresh Parsley minced

Instructions

1) Set the oven's temperature to 350 degrees Fahrenheit (180 degrees Celsius). The fish fillets should be properly rinsed before being dried with a paper towel. Fill your ceramic or baking dish halfway with water.

2) Combine the melted butter with lemon juice, cooking wine, and garliCup A few tbsp should go in the baking dish's bottom.

3) Top the butter mixture in the baking dish with the fish fillets.

4) Douse the top with the remaining butter mixture. Place the Ritz crackers on top of the fish in an even layer. The Parsley should then be softly sprinkled on top.

5) Bake for 15 minutes, uncovered, or until the fish flakes easily.

6) To make the Ritz cracker crumbs crispier, I broil them for an additional five minutes. Find the settings that work best for you by inspecting your oven.

149. SWORDFISH WITH GREMOLATA

Prep:15 mins

Bake:15 mins

Total:30 mins

Servings:4

Ingredients

- 1 ½ cup of packed flat-leaf Parsley
- 1 lemon
- 2 tbsps chopped dill
- 3 cloves garlic, chopped
- 1 tsp lemon pepper
- 4 swordfish steaks (about 6 ounces each), 3/4 inch thick
- 2 cups of raw quick-cook brown rice
- 1 14.5 ounces can of chicken broth
- 1 cup of mixed sweet red and orange peppers, diced
- Lemon slices, for garnish

Directions

1. Preheat the oven to 450°F (230°C). Coat a glass baking dish with nonstick spray.

2. Parsley should be chopped; 3/4 cup is required. Grate 1 tbsp of lemon zest. Set aside 2 tbsp of lemon juice. In a mixing bowl, combine Parsley, grated lemon peel, dill, garlic, and 3/4 tsp lemon pepper. Set the gremolata aside.
3. Drizzle the lemon juice over the swordfish in the baking dish that has been prepared. To taste, add the remaining 1/4 tsp lemon pepper.
4. Preheat the oven to 450°F and bake the salmon for 15 minutes, or until it readily flakes.
5. Meanwhile, prepare the rice according to the package directions, but instead of water, use chicken broth. After adding the peppers and 2 tbsp gremolata, cover and set aside for 5 minutes.
6. Serve the swordfish with rice and the remaining gremolata on the side. Serve with a squeeze of lemon on top as a finishing touch.

Nutrition

407 calories; fat 8g; cholesterol 48mg; saturated fat 2g; carbohydrates 53g; insoluble fiber 4g; Protein 29g; sodium 680mg.

150. HALIBUT WITH LEMON, SPINACH, AND TOMATOES

Total: 20 min

Prep: 10 min

Cook: 10 min

Yield: 2 servings

Ingredients

- 1/4 cup of olive oil
- 2 (6-ounce) halibut fillets
- Salt and freshly ground pepper
- 1 lemon, juiced
- 1 tbsp butter
- 2 (10-ounce) bags of baby spinach
- 3 cloves crushed garlic
- 1/2 tsp salt
- 6 Roma diced tomatoes
- 1/2 cup of olive oil
- 1/2 cup of chopped kalamata olives

Directions

1. Fresh basil leaves as a garnish
2. In a large saute pan, heat the olive oil over medium-high heat. When the oil is hot, add the halibut steaks to the pan and cook for 3 to 4 minutes on each side, or until a fork easily slides

into the fish. To taste, season with salt, pepper, and lemon juice. To keep warm, remove from the heat and cover with a cloth.
3. In a large saute pan over medium heat, combine the olive oil and butter. Add the spinach, along with the crushed garlic and salt, gradually. Saute the spinach until it has softened.
4. Has begun to wither. To taste, season with lemon juice and pepper.
5. In a small saucepan, combine the tomatoes, olive oil, garlic, salt, and kalamata olives.
6. Olives. Cook the tomatoes on high heat right away to avoid them turning to mush.
7. Sauce.
8. Place spinach in the center of each bowl, followed by the halibut.
9. A leaf of spinach Serves the halibut with the sauce and fresh herbs on top.
10. Basil.

151. FOIL PACK LIME CILANTRO SALMON

prep time 5 MINUTES

cook time 8 MINUTES

total time 13 MINUTES

INGREDIENTS

- 6-ounce center-cut salmon fillet
- 1 medium lime, sliced thin for nestling under salmon
- 1/2 cup of red bell peppers (may be substituted with other peppers, zucchini, broccoli, etCup)
- 1 tbsp olive oil
- 1 lime, zested and juiced
- Kosher salt and freshly ground black pepper, to taste
- 1 to 2 tbsps fresh Cilantro, finely minced; plus more for garnishing if desired

INSTRUCTIONS

1. Outside, preheat the grill to medium-high heat. Preheat the oven to 425°F (200°C).
2. Place 1 large sheet of foil on the counter, arrange the salmon in the center, nestle the lime slices from 1 lime beneath the fish, drizzle with olive oil, and equally sprinkle with 1 tsp lime zest and the juice from the second lime.
3. Season with salt, pepper, and Cilantro, then fold the foil pack securely, place it on the grill, and cook for 8 to 10 minutes. The amount of time it takes to grill salmon depends on several aspects, including the type of grill, its size, the heat setting, and the thickness of the salmon. Check it after 15 minutes if baking it in the oven, and go from there.
4. If preferred, top with additional Cilantro and serve straight soon.

NUTRITION

CALORIES: 978TOTALFAT: 63gCHOLESTEROL: 250mgSODIUM: 542mgCARBOHYDRATES: 12gFIBER: 3gSUGAR: 4gPROTEIN: 89g

152. LEMON BUTTER SCALLOPS

yield:4 SERVINGS

prep time:5 MINUTES

cook time:10 MINUTES

total time:15 MINUTES

INGREDIENTS

- 1 tbsp unsalted butter
- 1 pound scallops
- Kosher salt and freshly ground black pepper, to taste
- FOR THE LEMON BUTTER SAUCE
- 2 tbsps unsalted butter
- 2 cloves garlic, minced
- Juice of 1 lemon
- Kosher salt and freshly ground black pepper, to taste
- 2 tbsps chopped fresh parsley leaves

DIRECTIONS

1) Melt 1 tbsp of butter in a large pan over medium-high heat.

2) Cut the scallop's side muscle out, give it a cold water rinse, and thoroughly pat it dry.

3) To taste, season the scallops with salt and pepper. Working in batches, cook the scallops in the skillet in a single layer until golden brown and transparent in the middle, approximately 1 to 2 minutes on each side. Take out of the oven, then place somewhere warm.

4) Melt 2 tbsp of butter in a pan to make the lemon butter sauce. Stirring often, cook for 1 minute, or until garlic is aromatiCup Add salt and pepper to taste after adding the lemon juice.

5) If wanted, garnish the scallops with Parsley and serve them right away with the lemon butter sauce.

153. BLACKENED RED SNAPPER

Prep30 mins

Cook30 mins

Total1 hr

INGREDIENTS

- 1/2 cup of black rice or brown rice
- 3/4 tsp table salt plus more for cooking rice
- 1/2 cup of plain yogurt
- 2 tsp grated lemon zest plus 1 tsp juice, preferably organic
- 3 tbsp garlic oil
- 1 1/2 tsp smoked paprika
- 1/2 tsp ground coriander
- 1/2 tsp ground fennel
- 1/4 tsp cayenne pepper
- 1/8 tsp ground cloves
- 1/4 tsp freshly ground black pepper
- 18 ounces (18 cups of) fresh baby spinach
- 4 (4 to 6 ounce) skin-on red snapper fillets or another firm white fish, 3/4 to 1 inch (18 to 24 mm) thick

DIRECTIONS

1. In a Dutch oven, bring 4 quarts of water to a boil over medium-high heat. Cook, stirring periodically, for 20 to 25 minutes, or until the rice is done. Add a few minutes to the cooking time if you're using brown rice.
2. Drain the rice and season to taste with salt and pepper in a bowl. Cover to keep warm.

3. In a small bowl, combine the yogurt, lemon zest, and juice, and season with salt and pepper to taste. Refrigerate the dish until ready to serve.
4. In a small microwave-safe dish, heat 1 tbsp oil, paprika, coriander, fennel, cayenne, cloves, pepper, and 1/2 tsp salt until fragrant, about 30 seconds. Allow for little chilling before serving.
5. In a large covered microwave-safe bowl, microwave spinach and 1/4 cup water for 3 to 4 minutes, stirring once, until spinach has wilted and decreased in volume by half. (Alternatively, you may do this in two batches, each with 2 tbsp of water and 2 minutes of cooking time in a smaller bowl.)
6. Remove the microwave bowl from the microwave and set it aside, covered, for 1 minute. Carefully remove the cover and drain the spinach onto a strainer. Use the back of a rubber spatula to gently press spinach against the colander to release excess liquid.
7. Move the oven rack 4 inches (10 cm) away from the element to heat the broiler. A rimmed baking pan should be lined with aluminum foil.
8. Using paper towels, dry the red snapper fillets before brushing the spice mixture evenly on the flesh side. Place the snapper skin side down on the prepared sheet. Broil for 4 minutes, or until snapper flakes apart and registers 130°F (54°C) when lightly probed with a paring knife. Serve the fish on individual dishes or on a large platter.
9. Meanwhile, in a 12-inch (30-cm) pan, heat the remaining 2 tbsp oil over medium heat until it shimmers, about 1 minute. Coat the spinach in the dressing. Toss with tongs for another 2 minutes, or until spinach is glossy green, then season with the remaining 1/4 tsp salt. Season with salt and pepper to taste.

10. In a serving bowl, combine the spinach, snapper, rice, and yogurt sauce.

154. COCONUT PINEAPPLE SHRIMP SKEWERS

PREP:20 mins

COOK:5 mins

TOTAL:1 hr 25 mins

Ingredients

- 1/2 cup of light coconut milk
- 4 tsp Tabasco Original Red Sauce or hot sauce of choice
- 2 tsp soy sauce
- 1/4 cup of freshly squeezed orange juice
- 1/4 cup of freshly squeezed lime juice from about 2 large limes
- 1 pound large shrimp 31-40 count, peeled and deveined (you can use fresh or frOuncesen, thawed shrimp)
- 3/4 pound pineapple chunks 1 inch-cut
- Canola oil for grilling
- Freshly chopped Cilantro and/or green onion for serving

Instructions

1. Combine the coconut milk, Tabasco sauce, soy sauce, lime juice, and orange juice in a medium mixing bowl. Apply the sauce to the shrimp. For 1-2 hours, marinate in the fridge with a cover on, tossing occasionally. While the shrimp marinates, soak the wooden skewers in warm water. If pineapple is required, prepare it now.
2. Set the grill's temperature to medium-high. Remove the shrimp from the marinade and place them in a separate area to cook. Alternately thread the pineapple and shrimp onto the skewers.
3. Lightly spray the shrimp with canola oil before grilling it. Grill the shrimp for 3 minutes, flip them over, and cook them for an additional 2 to 3 minutes, brushing them with marinade once more until they are just cooked through. On a serving platter, garnish with Cilantro and green onions. Serve immediately.

Nutrition

SERVING: 1(of 4)CALORIES: 165kcalCARBOHYDRATES: 12gPROTEIN: 24gFAT: 2gSODIUM: 597mgFIBER: 1gSUGAR: 7g

155. GRILLED LOBSTER SMOTHERED IN BASIL BUTTER

Total: 1 hr 5 min

Prep: 40 min

Cook: 25 min

Yield: 4 servings

Ingredients

- 1 pound unsalted butter
- 1/2 cup of basil chiffonade
- Salt and freshly ground pepper to taste
- 4 (2 1/2 pound) whole lobsters
- 2 tbsps olive oil

Directions

1. Pulse the butter, basil, salt, and pepper to taste in a food processor until smooth. Chill for at least 30 minutes after filling a medium ramekin halfway with the mixture and covering it with plastic wrap. Split the lobsters in half lengthwise. As you bring the knife down through the tail, only cut through the flesh, leaving the shell intact. Split the lobster in half and keep the two halves together. Remove the claws and legs of the lobsters and carefully break them with the knife handle. Over medium-low heat, place the claws and legs on the grill and cover with a pie dish. Cook each side for 5–7 minutes. After brushing the lobster bodies with the oil, season them with salt and pepper to taste. Place them meat side down on the grill over medium heat. Grill for 8 to 10 minutes
2. Remove the lobsters from their shells and apply the basil butter to them.

156. TUNA ZUCCHINI CAKES

Prep/Total Time: 25 min.

3 servings

Ingredients

- 1 tbsp butter
- 1/2 cup of finely chopped onion
- 1 pouch (6.4 ounces) of light tuna in water
- 1 cup of seasoned bread crumbs, divided
- 1 cup of shredded zucchini
- 2 large eggs, lightly beaten
- 1/3 cup of minced fresh Parsley
- 1 tsp lemon juice
- 1/2 tsp salt
- 1/8 tsp pepper
- 2 tbsps canola oil

Directions

1) Melt the butter in a large pot over medium-high heat. While cooking, toss the onion periodically until it softens. Turn off the heat under the pan.

2) Combine the tuna, 1/2 cup of bread crumbs, zucchini, eggs, Parsley, lemon juice, salt, and pepper in a bowl with the onion mixture. Six 1/2-inch thick patties should be placed on top of the remaining breadcrumbs.

3) Set a big skillet over medium heat and warm the oil. Cook for 3 minutes on each side, or until well cooked and browned.

Nutrition

2 fish cakes: 400 calories, 19g fat 170mg cholesterol, 1261mg sodium, 31g carbohydrate (4g sugars, 3g fiber), 26g protein.

157. HORSERADISH SAUCE FOR FISH

Prep:25 mins

Cook:25 mins

Total:50 mins

Ingredients

- 1 cup of plain low-fat or nonfat yogurt
- ¼ cup of fresh dill snipped
- 1 tbsp grated horseradish root
- 2 tsp fresh lemon juice
- ¼ tsp Dijon-style mustard

Instructions

1. In a medium mixing bowl, combine all of the ingredients.
2. Combine everything well.
3. Refrigerate after covering with plastic wrap.
4. Serve alongside poached, grilled, or baked fish and seafood.

Nutrition

Calcium: 36mgCalories: 22kcalCarbohydrates: 1gCholesterol: 2mgFat: 1gIron: 1mgPotassium: 11mgProtein: 3gSodium: 14mgSugar: 1g

158. HOMEMADE ENCHILADA SAUCE

Prep Time: 3 mins

Cook Time: 7 mins

Total Time: 10 minutes

INGREDIENTS

- 3 tbsps olive oil
- 3 tbsp flour (whole wheat flour, all-purpose flour, and gluten-free flour blend all work!)
- 1 tbsp ground chili powder (scale back if you're sensitive to spice or using particularly spicy chili powder)
- 1 tsp ground cumin
- ½ tsp garlic powder
- ¼ tsp dried oregano
- ¼ tsp salt, to taste
- Pinch of cinnamon
- 2 tbsps tomato paste
- 2 cups of vegetable broth
- 1 tsp apple cider vinegar or distilled white vinegar
- Freshly ground black pepper, to taste

INSTRUCTIONS

1) Combine the dry ingredients in a small bowl (flour, chili powder, cumin, garlic powder, oregano, salt, and optional cinnamon). Keep the broth and tomato paste close to the heat source.

2) In a medium saucepan, heat the oil until a little sprinkle of the flour/spice combination sizzles when it comes in touch with it. Be patient and keep an eye on the stove because this might take some time.

3) When it's finished, add the flour and spice mixture. Stirring periodically, cook for 1 minute, or until aromatic and darker in color. Add the tomato paste and continue whisking while gently adding the broth while avoiding lumps.

4) Increase the heat to medium-high and simmer the mixture, adjusting the heat as necessary to maintain the desired temperature. Cook for 5 to 7 minutes, whisking occasionally, or until the sauce has significantly thickened and is difficult to mix with a spoon. (As it cools, the sauce will thicken even more.)

5) Turn off the heat, add the vinegar, and add freshly ground black pepper to taste. If required, add extra salt to the bowl (I usually add another pinch or two). There are enchiladas wherever you look!

159. GRILLED SCALLOPS WITH MEYER LEMON SALSA VERDE

Prep Time:4 minutes

Cook Time:8 minutes

Total Time:12 minutes

Ingredients

- 3 tbsps extra-virgin olive oil
- 1 tsp finely grated lemon zest
- 1 ½ tbsps Meyer lemon juice
- ½ cup of beet greens
- 2 tbsp fresh parsley leaves
- 2 tbsp fresh cilantro
- 1 tbsp fresh basil
- 2 cloves garlic
- 12 large scallops tendons removed
- 1 tsp kosher salt
- 1 tsp freshly ground black pepper

Instructions

1. Using a paper towel, pat each scallop dry. Place everything on a baking sheet with a rack inside. Refrigerate the scallops until just before cooking.
2. In a food processor, puree the zest, juice, olive oil, garlic, greens, herbs, salt, and pepper. Take it out of the equation.

3. Preheat the grill to a high temperature. To guarantee that the grates become extremely hot, cover the grill. After opening the lid, clean the grates with a steel brush. Cover for another 2 to 3 minutes to return the grates to high heat.
4. Take the scallops out of the fridge, skewer them, and season with salt and pepper.
5. Wet a wad of paper towel with canola oil. Grab the wad with tongs and massage the towels along the grates to completely grease them.
6. Reduce to medium-high heat. Place the skewered scallops on one side of the grill at an angle to get diagonal grill marks.
7. Cook for 4 minutes before turning and cooking for another 2 minutes. Part of the glaze should be used to glaze the scallops. The scallops should be somewhat opaque in the center. Cut one in half if you need to double-check.

Nutrition

Serving: 0g | Carbohydrates: 0g | Protein: 0g | Fat: 0g | Cholesterol: 0mg | Sodium: 0mg | Potassium: 0mg | Fiber: 0g | Sugar: 0g | Calcium: 0mg | Iron: 0mg

160. BAKED HALIBUT RECIPE

prep time: 5 MINS

cook time: 12 MINS

INGREDIENTS

- 1 Pounds Halibut fillet
- 1/4 cup of olive oil
- 1/2 tsp Salt
- 1/4 tsp Black pepper
- 1/4 tsp Paprika
- 1/4 tsp smoked paprika
- 1/4 tsp Garlic powder
- Juice from one medium lemon

INSTRUCTIONS

1. Preheat the oven to 425°F (200°C).
2. Bake the fish in an oven-safe baking dish.
3. In a small mixing bowl, combine the salt, black pepper, paprika, smoked paprika, garlic powder, lemon juice, and olive oil.
4. Place the fish in a baking dish or on a baking sheet pan. Brush the mixture over the top.
5. Allow 10-12 minutes for the mixture to become opaque.
6. As the main meal, serve with quinoa, spaghetti, or couscous.

NUTRITION

Calories: 224, Fat: 15g, Cholesterol: 56mg, Sodium: 368mg, Potassium: 493mg, Carbohydrates: 1g, Sugar: 1g, Protein: 21g, Calcium: 8%, Iron: 1%

161. SPICY GRILLED SHRIMP

Prep:15 mins

Cook:6 mins

Total:21 mins

Servings:6

Ingredients

- 1 large clove of garlic
- 1 tsp coarse salt
- ½ tsp cayenne pepper
- 1 tsp paprika
- 2 tbsps olive oil
- 2 tsp lemon juice
- 2 pounds large shrimp, peeled and deveined
- 8 wedges of lemon for garnish

Directions

1. Set the grill to medium heat.
2. In a small bowl, crush the garlic with the salt. Combine the cayenne pepper and paprika, then add the olive oil and lemon juice to produce a paste. In a large mixing bowl, toss the shrimp with the garlic paste until thoroughly coated.

3. Lightly grease the grill grate. 2 to 3 minutes per side, or until shrimp are opaque. Serve immediately in a serving dish with lemon wedges on the side.

Nutrition

164 calories; protein 25.1g; carbohydrates 2.7g; fat 5.9g; cholesterol 230.4mg; sodium 585.7mg.

162. SPICY PEPPERED CRAB LEGS

Total: 40 min

Prep: 30 min

Cook: 10 min

Yield: 4 servings

Ingredients

- 3 pounds Alaskan king or snow crab legs, thawed if frOuncesen
- Freshly ground pepper
- 2 tbsps vegetable oil
- 1 stick unsalted butter, cubed
- 6 cloves garlic, chopped
- 10 thin slices of peeled ginger
- 8 scallions, cut into 2-inch pieces
- 4 red seeded and finely chopped jalapeno peppers
- 2 tsp sugar
- 2 tbsps oyster sauce
- 2 tbsps soy sauce

Directions

1) Use kitchen shears to cut the crab legs into 3-inch chunks. To make it simple to remove the meat from the shell after cooking, each piece should be cut along one of the shell's edges.

2) Position the remaining parts close to the heat source. In a small pan over medium-high heat, roast 2 tsps of pepper until fragrant, about 2 minutes; remove from heat.

3) In a big Dutch oven, heat the butter and vegetable oil until they start to sizzle (you can also set a roasting pan over two burners). Cook for one minute, stirring often, or until the sugar, scallions, jalapenos, ginger, and garlic are aromatiCup

4) Combine the crab pieces, oyster sauce, and soy sauce in a mixing bowl. Cook for approximately 5 minutes, stirring occasionally, or until well cooked. The roasted pepper is then added and cooked

for an additional minute while stirring often. In a mixing bowl, combine the crab and sauce. Rice should be served alongside.

163. EASY GARLIC HERB BUTTER BAKED SALMON.

Prep Time: 10 minutes

Cook Time: 15 minutes

Total Time: 25 minutes

Ingredients

- 2 kg (4Pounds) side of salmon (I always ask the fishmonger to pin-bone the fish for me but to leave the skin on)
- ½ cup of butter softened
- 4 garlic cloves minced
- 2 tbsp fresh dill finely chopped
- 1 tbsp parsley finely chopped
- 1 tbsp thyme finely chopped
- 2 tsp lemon zest
- 2 tsp salt
- 1 tsp pepper
- lemon wedges to serve

Instructions

1) Combine melted butter, minced garlic, finely chopped herbs, lemon zest, salt, and pepper in a mixing bowl.

2) Use paper towels to pat the surface of the fish dry. If the salmon's surface is not completely dry, the butter will not stick to it.

3) Arrange the salmon on a roasting pan or baking sheet lined with parchment paper and grease the flesh side completely.

4) Set the oven to 350°F and bake the salmon for 10 to 15 minutes, depending on how done you want it.

5) After taking the salmon out of the oven, let it for five minutes to rest.

6) Cut into slices and serve with a drizzle of butter and a squeeze of lemon.

Nutrition

Calories: 238kcal | Carbohydrates: 2g | Protein: 29g | Fat: 12g | Cholesterol: 79mg | Sodium: 397mg | Potassium: 706mg | Fiber: 1g | Sugar: 1g | Calcium: 23mg | Iron: 1mg

164. LEMON GARLIC BUTTER SHRIMP

PREP:10 MINS

COOK:10 MINS

TOTAL:20 MINS

INGREDIENTS

- 1/3 cup of divided butter
- 4 cloves garlic, minced (or 1 tbsp)
- 1 3/4 pounds (800 g) shrimp (or prawns), peeled and deveined, tails intact
- Kosher salt and freshly ground black pepper, to taste
- Juice half a lemon (about 2 tbsps -- add more if desired)
- 2 tbsps water
- Fresh chopped Parsley to garnish

INSTRUCTIONS

1) 2 tbsp of butter, heat over medium-high heat in a large pan. Cook the garlic until it is fragrant (about 1 minute).

2) To taste, season the shrimp with salt and pepper. Cook for two minutes on one side, stirring once or twice. Cook for an additional 2 minutes on the other side, or until the pink shows.

3) Combine the remaining butter, lemon juice, and water in a mixing bowl. Cook, often stirring, until the butter has melted and the shrimp are cooked through (do not overcook them). Turn off the heat. Taste the bowl and adjust the seasonings accordingly, adding extra lemon juice, salt, or pepper as desired.

4) Top rice or spaghetti with freshly cut parsley.

NUTRITION

Calories: 338kcal | Carbohydrates: 1g | Protein: 40g | Fat: 18g | Cholesterol: 540mg | Sodium: 1544mg | Potassium: 170mg | Calcium: 298mg | Iron: 4.3mg

165. HERB FISH

Prep/Total Time: 20 min.

4 servings

Ingredients

- 1/4 cup of finely chopped onion
- 2 tbsps butter
- 1/2 tsp minced garlic
- 1 tbsp lemon juice
- 2 tsp dried parsley flakes
- 1/4 to 1/2 tsp salt
- 1/4 tsp dried tarragon
- 1/8 tsp dried thyme
- 1 pound whitefish or sole fillets
- 1/4 cup of dry bread crumbs

Directions

1) Combine the onion, butter, and garlic in a small microwave-safe dish. When the onion is partially cooked, cover the container and microwave on high for 1–2 minutes. Combine the lemon juice, Parsley, salt, tarragon, and thyme in a mixing bowl.

2) Distribute the fillets halfway within a greased 2-quart round microwave-safe dish. Place half of it on top of the butter mixture. Bread crumbs and the remaining butter mixture should be mixed, then applied to the fillets.

3) Cook salmon in the microwave on high for 4–6 minutes, or until it flakes easily with a fork.

Nutrition

4 ounce-weight: 186 calories, 7g fat 69mg cholesterol, 330mg sodium, 6g carbohydrate (1g sugars, 1g fiber), 23g protein.

166. SUPER GROUPER

Prep:10 mins

Cook:10 mins

Total:20 mins

Servings:4

Ingredients

- ½ cup of butter, melted
- 2 tbsps lemon juice
- ¼ tsp garlic salt
- ½ tsp dried Parsley

- ⅛ tsp paprika
- ¼ tsp ground white pepper
- 2 pounds grouper fillets
- 2 tbsps mayonnaise
- ⅛ tsp paprika

Directions

1) Set the oven to 180 degrees Celsius or 350 degrees Fahrenheit (175 degrees C). Melted butter and lemon juice should be combined. A piece of foil that has been placed on the broiler pan should be covered with 2 tbsp of the mixture.

2) Combine garlic salt, Parsley, paprika, and white pepper in a mixing bowl. Apply the spice mixture to both sides of the fillets.

3) Cook the fillets in the oven for 10 minutes or until the flesh is readily flaked. Brush additional mayonnaise and lemon butter on the fillets. Paprika should be added immediately before serving.

Nutrition

465 calories; protein 44.4g; carbohydrates 1.1g; fat 30.8g; cholesterol 146.9mg; sodium 410.2mg.

167.FISH MAYONNAISE RECIPE

Total Cook Time30 mins

Prep Time10 mins

Cook Time20 mins

Recipe Servings4

Ingredients

- 650 gm fish fillets
- 1 Tbsp lemon juice
- 2 tsp salt or to taste
- 1 tbsp finely chopped celery
- 1 cup of mayonnaise
- Greens - to garnish

Method

- The fish fillets should be rubbed with lemon juice and 1 tsp of salt. Before rinsing, set aside for five minutes.

- Before the fish is tender but still has its shape, steam or boil it. Drain and set the water aside to cool.
- Once the fish has cooled and been well-drained, place it on a serving platter (or lightly wiped).
- Toss the celery in the mayonnaise with 1 tsp of salt.
- Cover the fish with mayonnaise and garnish with leaves before serving.

168. GARLIC BUTTERFISH RECIPE

PREP TIME10 minutes

COOK TIME10 minutes

TOTAL TIME20 minutes

INGREDIENTS

- 12 Ounces. (340 g) firm white fish fillet (halibut, cod, or pollock fillet)
- salt
- ground black pepper
- 3 dashes of cayenne pepper
- 2 tbsp corn starch
- 2 tbsps cooking oil
- lemon wedges

GARLIC BUTTER SAUCE

- 1/2 stick (4 tbsp) salted butter, melted
- 3 cloves garlic, minced
- 1/2 tbsp lemon juice
- 1 tbsp chopped parsley

INSTRUCTIONS

1. Cut the fish into not-too-thin pieces to make pan-frying simpler. The fish is seasoned with salt, black pepper, and cayenne pepper. The fish should be coated with corn starch. Take it out of the equation.

Fish with Garlic Butter

1. In a mixing bowl, combine all of the ingredients for the Garlic Butter Sauce. Take it out of the equation.
2. Preheat a skillet to medium-high heat (ideally nonstick). When the frying oil is heated, add the fish and fry it in a single layer until crispy and golden brown on both sides. With a wooden spatula or tongs, delicately flip the fish over. Make sure the fish isn't broken.

3. After removing the fish from the pan, drain it on paper towels. Toss the fish with the Garlic Butter Sauce and serve immediately with lemon wedges.

169. PINEAPPLE SHRIMP

YIELDS:4 SERVINGS

PREP TIME:0 HOURS 10 MINS

TOTAL TIME:0 HOURS 20 MINS

INGREDIENTS

FOR THE SAUCE

- 1/2 Cup pineapple juice
- 1/2 Cup low-sodium chicken broth
- 1/4 Cup low-sodium soy sauce
- 2 tbsp. Sriracha
- 2 tbsp. light brown sugar
- 2 tbsp. rice wine vinegar
- 1 tbsp. minced ginger
- 2 tsp. cornstarch

FOR SHRIMP

- 1 Pound. medium shrimp, peeled, deveined, and patted dry
- Kosher salt
- Freshly ground black pepper
- 4 tsp. extra-virgin olive oil
- 1 red bell pepper, chopped
- 2 Cup fresh pineapple cubes
- 2 green onions, sliced, for garnish

DIRECTIONS

1) In a pan over medium heat, combine the pineapple juice, chicken stock, soy sauce, Sriracha, brown sugar, vinegar, ginger, and cornstarch. Give the sauce 7 minutes to boil, or until it has thickened and reduced by a third.

2) Use salt and pepper to season the shrimp. 3 tbsp of olive oil, heated in a big pan over medium heat. Cook the shrimp for about 2 minutes total, turning once until they are pink. Place a plate for cooling.

3) Fill the same pan with the final tsp of oil. Cook the bell pepper for 3 minutes, or until it is transparent and soft. Add the sauce and pineapple after turning the heat up to high. Add the shrimp once the mixture has reached a simmer. Serve immediately and top with green onions.

170. RED SNAPPER CEVICHE

Total:55 mins

Yield:4

Ingredients

- 1 pound skinless red snapper fillets, cut into 1/4-inch dice
- 3/4 cup of fresh lime juice
- 1/4 cup of fresh lemon juice
- 1 jalapeño, seeded and minced
- 1/2 cup of finely diced red bell peppers
- 1/2 cup of finely diced yellow bell peppers
- 1/2 thinly sliced small red onion
- 1 minced small garlic clove
- Pinch of ground cumin
- Pinch of crushed red pepper
- Salt
- 1 tbsp minced Cilantro
- 1 tbsp extra-virgin olive oil

Directions

1. In a large mixing bowl, combine the chopped fish, lime, lemon, jalapeno, red and yellow bell peppers, red onion, garlic, cumin, crushed red pepper, and salt. Allow the ceviche to cool for 30 minutes. Serve with Cilantro and a sprinkle of extra-virgin olive oil.

171. PERUVIAN RED SNAPPER CEVICHE

Prep Time:10 minutes

Cook Time:20 minutes

Aji Sauce:30 minutes

Total Time:1 hour

Ingredients

- Aji Verde Sauce (Peruvian Green Sauce)
- 60 g Jalapenos (about 2 peppers)

- 4 Ounces Ricotta Cheese
- 15 g Fresh Garlic (about 3 cloves)
- 1 tsp White Wine Vinegar
- 2 tsp Extra Virgin Olive Oil
- 1 Lime juiced
- 90 g Mayo (about ¾ cup of)
- 2 tbsp Cilantro chopped, stems and leaves
- Peruvian Red Snapper Ceviche
- 16 Ounces Red Snapper
- 6 Ounces Lime Juice freshly squeezed (about 4 limes)
- 3 Ounces Lemon Juice freshly squeezed (about 2 lemons)
- 2 Ounces Orange Juice freshly squeezed (about 1 orange)
- 1 dash Salt
- ¼ tsp Black Pepper
- 30 g Red Onion shaved (about ¼ onion)
- 15 g Jalapeno or Habanero sliced (about 1 pepper)
- 1 tsp Cilantro chopped
- 2 tbsp Above Aji Verde Sauce

Instructions

1. Aji Verge Aji Verge Aji Verge Aji Verge Aji Verge Aji Verge (Peruvian Green Sauce)
2. Combine all of the aforementioned items in a blender.
3. Begin by blending on the lowest setting for 20 seconds, then gradually increase the speed to the next level every 20 seconds. You've made it to the summit. Blend until all of the ingredients are thoroughly incorporated and no large cilantro bits remain.
4. Season the sauce to taste with:
5. Add additional jalapenos if you want it hot.
6. Add additional ricotta if it's a little too hot.
7. Allow at least 30 minutes for the sauce to thicken in the refrigerator. The sauce will continue to develop flavor while it sits in the fridge. In the fridge, the sauce will last 7-10 days.
8. Peruvian Red Snapper Ceviche
9. Cut the red snapper into little bite-size pieces. Place the snapper in a large mixing basin.

10. Squeeze the lime, lemon, and oranges into a small basin.
11. I prefer to juice with a juicing machine since it gets the most juice from the fruit. On the other hand, a hand-held juicer will suffice. Because you won't be able to extract all of the juice, you may need more fruit.
12. Once all of the fruit has been juiced, pour the juice over the sliced fish, season with salt and pepper, 2 tbsp aji Verde sauce, and the shaved onions. After that, combine the fish, lemon juice, spices, and onions in a mixing bowl. After everything is well blended, cover with a lid or plastic wrap and keep in the refrigerator. The circus will take around 20 minutes to finish cooking the fish.
13. After 20 minutes, remove from the fridge and top with sliced jalapeno and Cilantro.
14. This dish is often accompanied by tortilla chips, plantain chips, roasted sweet potato, or crispy choclo. Choose anything you choose or what is most convenient for you!

172. LINGUINE WITH CLAMS AND FENNEL

Total:40 mins

Yield:4

Ingredients

- ½ cup of extra-virgin olive oil (plus more for drizzling)
- 3 leeks (cup of white and light green parts only, thinly sliced crosswise)
- ¾ pound linguine
- ½ fennel bounds (medium, 1/2 cup of cored and thinly sliced)
- 2 cloves garlic (minced)
- 4 pounds Manila clams (scrubbed)
- 1 cup of dry white wine
- 1 cup of fish stock (or low-sodium chicken broth)
- 4 tsp neonatal (see Note sambal or other chunky chile paste)
- 1 tbsp lemon juice (fresh)
- 2 tbsp parsley (chopped)
- Kosher salt
- Pepper
- basil leaves (Torn for garnish)

Directions

1) 2 tbsp hot oil in a saucepan. The leeks should be cooked for about 8 minutes over medium heat, often turning, until they are soft and just starting to brown. Pour into a basin for mixing.

2) Cook the linguine in a large pot of salted boiling water until it is just al dente; then drain.

3) In the meantime, warm 2 tbsp of olive oil in a pan. Cook for about 3 minutes, stirring periodically, over moderate heat to soften the fennel. The clams, white wine, and stock should all be combined before being gently boiled. Clams should be covered and cooked for 3 to 5 minutes, or until they open. Once they do, transfer them to a sizable mixing bowl. Any unopened clams should be taken out of the stew and thrown away. The remaining claims should be shelled; 12 should be retained intact in their shells.

4) Bring the liquids to a boil in a pot before adding the linguine, neonatal, mussels, and leeks. When the pasta is thoroughly covered, and the sauce has thickened, add the last 1/4 cup of olive oil and continue tossing. Salt and pepper to taste, then incorporate the lemon juice and half of the Parsley. With basil, Parsley, and a drizzle of olive oil on top, serve the spaghetti in small bowls.

173. CHILLED CORN SOUP OVER LOBSTER SALAD

PREP TIME1 hour 30 minutes

Ingredients

- chilled corn soup
- 3 tbsps extra virgin olive oil
- 3 tbsps salted butter
- 2 garlic cloves, minced
- 1 bunch scallions, divided use- white part minced, dark greens sliced
- 1/2 shallot, minced
- 1/2 white onion, minced
- 1 handful of fresh dill, chopped
- 6 ears of corn, kernels removed, cobs saved
- 13.66 ounces can coconut milk
- 4 cups of water
- lobster salad
- 2 pounds lobster claw and tail meat
- 1/2 cup of butter
- 1/2 cup of chardonnay
- 1 tbsp dried dill
- 1 small shallot, minced
- 1/4 cup of celery leaves, chopped
- juice of 1 lemon
- 2 tsp dijon
- 1 tbsp extra virgin olive oil
- 1/2 English cucumber, peeled, seeded, and diced
- 8 cherry tomatoes, halved
- 1/4 jalapeno, seeded and thinly sliced
- 1/8 red bell pepper, seeded and thinly sliced
- 1 pinch salt

Directions

1. soup made from maize that has been chilled
2. Melt the butter and EVOO in a heavy-bottomed stock pan or dutch oven.
3. Sauté until the onion, shallot, the white half of the scallions, and garlic are clear.
4. After adding the corn kernels, cook for 3 minutes.
5. After adding the dill and coconut milk can, let for 5 minutes of cooking time.
6. In a large mixing basin, combine the water and corn cobs. Heat the water to a rolling boil.
7. Cook for 20 minutes on a low heat setting.
8. With an immersion blender, puree the soup until it is thick but not lumpy.
9. Cool the soup fully before serving (30-60 minutes in the freezer if planning on serving immediately).

10. Salad de langoustines
11. While the soup is simmering, prepare the lobster. Melt the butter in a big saucepan. Combine the chardonnay and dill in a mixing bowl.
12. After the lobster meat has warmed up, reduce the heat to low and add it. Cook for 3-5 minutes per side on each side, rotating once the lobster is opaque.
13. Drain the lobster and place it in a freezer bag or in a bowl of cold water to chill.
14. In a small bowl, combine the dijon, lemon, and salt. With a fork, whisk in the EVOO. In the same pan, add the shallots and celery leaves.
15. Place chilled lobster in a basin and slice it into bite-size pieces. Combine everything in a large mixing bowl.
16. To assemble, place a spoonful of lobster mixture on each of the four bowls. The cucumber, tomato, jalapeño, and red bell pepper are evenly distributed among the bowls.
17. Cover the lobster salad with chilled corn soup, but not totally. Serve with chopped scallions on top.

174. GARLIC HONEY-LIME SHRIMP RECIPE

PREP TIME10 minutes

COOK TIME5 minutes

ADDITIONAL TIME7 minutes

TOTAL TIME22 minutes

INGREDIENTS

- 1 Pound. (0.4 kg) shelled and deveined shrimp
- 1 tbsp olive oil
- 1 tbsp melted unsalted butter
- 4 cloves minced garlic
- 3 tbsps honey
- 1 1/2 tbsp lime juice
- 1/4 tsp salt
- 3 dashes of cayenne pepper
- chopped Parsley

INSTRUCTIONS

1. Rinse the shrimp in cool water. Drain and set aside the water.
2. In a pan, heat the olive oil and butter (cast-iron recommended). Cook until the garlic begins to brown slightly, then add the shrimp. Stir and boil the shrimp a few times before adding the

honey, lime juice, salt, and cayenne pepper. Cook, constantly stirring, until the honey lime sauce has thickened. Serve immediately with a garnish of chopped Parsley.

175. SPICY RED SNAPPER WITH MANGO SALSA

Prep:25 mins

Ingredients

- 1 pound fresh or frOuncesen red snapper fillets
- 1 tbsp lime juice
- 1 tbsp water
- 1 tsp paprika
- ½ tsp salt
- ¼ tsp ground ginger
- ¼ tsp ground allspice
- ¼ tsp ground black pepper
- 1 recipe Mango Salsa (see recipe below)
- 1 medium lime, cut into wedges
- Fresh cilantro or parsley sprigs

Directions

1) If the fish is frOuncesen, it must first be thawed. Rinse well before blotting with paper towels to dry. Four serving-sized pieces should be cut out of each piece. Determine the thickness of the fish. Brush fish with a mixture of lime juice and water from a small bowl. Season the fish with paprika, salt, ginger, allspice, and black pepper in a separate small dish.

2) Put the fish in a baking dish that is not too deep. Cook salmon in an uncovered 450°F oven until it flakes easily when checked with a fork. (Allocate 4–6 minutes for each thickness of 1/2 inch.)

3) Brush the fish with the pan juices just before serving. Serve mango salsa on the side. Lime wedges and cilantro or parsley stems can be used as a garnish if preferred. Four people are fed by this bowl.

176. LIME-CILANTRO TILAPIA

Prep/Total Time: 25 min.

4 servings

Ingredients

- 1/3 cup of all-purpose flour
- 3/4 tsp salt
- 1/2 tsp pepper
- 1/2 tsp ground cumin, divided
- 4 tilapia fillets (6 ounces each)
- 1 tbsp olive oil
- 1/2 cup of reduced-sodium chicken broth
- 2 tbsps minced fresh Cilantro
- 1 tsp grated lime zest
- 2 tbsps lime juice

Directions

1. In a small bowl, combine flour, salt, pepper, and 1/4 tsp of cumin. Brush off excess flour mixture from both sides of the fillets.
2. In a large nonstick skillet, heat the oil over medium heat. Cook, uncovered, for 3-4 minutes on each side or until salmon flakes easily with a fork. Remove from oven and set aside to keep warm.
3. In the same pan, bring the broth, Cilantro, lime zest, lime juice, and remaining cumin to a boil. Reduce heat to low and simmer for another 2-3 minutes, uncovered, or until slightly thickened. Serve with tilapia.

Nutrition

1 fillet with 2 tbsps sauce: 198 calories, 5g fat 83mg cholesterol, 398mg sodium, 6g carbohydrate (1g sugars, 0 fiber), 33g protein.

177. GRILLED SWORDFISH SKEWERS WITH ITALIAN SALSA VERDE

Prep Time20 MINS

Cook Time6 MINS

Preheating Grill10 MINS

Total Time36 MINS

Ingredients

For the swordfish

- 3 swordfish steaks about ~1 ¾-2 Pounds total
- 2 large lemons thinly sliced, plus more for serving
- For the Italian salsa verde
- 2 cups of finely chopped Parsley
- 2 anchovies
- 1 large garlic clove
- 1 Tbsp capers drained
- ½ lemon zested and juiced

pinch of red pepper flakes

- ½ tsp Kosher salt
- ¼ cup of extra virgin olive oil

Instructions

1) Get the sauce ready. All of the components for the Italian salsa verde should be coarsely chopped before being placed in a medium mixing basin.

2) Combine the lemon juice and olive oil in a whisk. Next, add the olive oil and blend by stirring. Add salt and pepper to taste and make any necessary adjustments.

3. Bring the grill's temperature up. Grills should be preheated to 450–475 degrees Fahrenheit with the lid off.

4) Prepare the swordfish in advance. Take off the swordfish's skin and throw it away. The remaining swordfish steaks should be taken out of the pan and divided into pieces that are 2" broad. Season the meat with Kosher salt and freshly ground black pepper on all sides.

5) Set the skewers in a circular pattern. Alternate slices of seasoned swordfish cubes with folded-over lemon segments on metal skewers. Three to four swordfish chunks should be used per skewer. Before assembling, soak wooden or bamboo skewers for an hour.

6) Swordfish on the grill is advised. Brush some grill spray or olive oil on the grates once the grill is heated. The swordfish should be cooked for 2 to 3 minutes on the first side or until it readily peels away from the grill grate. Skewers should be flipped (grill gloves are necessary!) Cook the swordfish for an additional 2 to 3 minutes, or until the internal temperature reaches 130 to 135 degrees Fahrenheit. Serve immediately with salsa verde after being taken off the grill!

Nutrition

Calories: 270kcal | Carbohydrates: 7g | Protein: 22g | Fat: 18g | Cholesterol: 68mg | Sodium: 376mg | Potassium: 643mg | Fiber: 2g | Sugar: 2g | Calcium: 57mg | Iron: 2mg

178. GARLIC BUTTER LOBSTER TAILS

PREP TIME10 minutes

COOK TIME10 minutes

TOTAL TIME20 minutes

INGREDIENTS

- 1 Pound. shell-on lobster tails (4 lobster tails)
- cayenne pepper
- 1/2 stick melted (4 tbsp) salted butter
- 4 cloves minced garlic
- 1 tbsp chopped Italian parsley leaves
- 1 tsp lemon juice
- lemon slices

INSTRUCTIONS

1) Set your oven's broiler to high.

2) If the lobster tails are frOuncesen, defrost them. Cut through the top half of the lobster's shell in the direction of the tail with a pair of kitchen shears. Cut once more into a rectangle of one inch.

3) Take the lobster's shell off to reveal the flesh. Place the lobsters in a skillet or on a baking sheet and set them aside. Spice up the lobster meat with a dash of cayenne.

4) Microwave the butter in a basin for 30 seconds to melt it. Melted butter should be combined with lemon juice, Parsley, and garliCup The ingredients have to be thoroughly blended.

5) Distribute the garlic butter evenly throughout the lobster. Lay some out for dipping.

6) In the oven, broil the lobster tails for 5-8 minutes, or until they are opaque and well cooked. Lemon wedges and the leftover garlic butter should be served right away.

179. GARLIC PARSLEY BUTTER SHRIMP

Prep: 5 mins

Cook: 10 mins

Total: 15 mins

INGREDIENTS

- 1 pound jumbo shrimp deveined, shells off except the tail
- 1/4 cup of butter unsalted
- 3 cloves garlic
- 1/4 cup of Parsley
- 1/2 tsp salt
- 1/2 tsp pepper
- 1 lemon juiced

INSTRUCTIONS

1. Preheat the oven to 425°F (200°C).
2. Follow these steps to produce compound butter: In a food processor, pulse the butter, garlic, Parsley, salt, and pepper until they form a paste.
3. To butter the shrimp, do the following: Half of the butter paste should be put in portions on the bottom of a pan. Place the shrimp in the skillet over the butter, then top with the remaining butter paste, making sure that each shrimp is well covered.
4. Bake for about 10 minutes, or until the shrimp is slightly pink and the skillet is hot and bubbling.
5. With a squeeze of lemon juice on top.

Nutrition

Calories: 228kcal (11%)Carbohydrates: 3g (1%)Protein: 23g (46%)Fat: 13g (20%) Cholesterol: 316mg (105%)Sodium: 1176mg (51%)Potassium: 157mg (4%) Calcium: 184mg (18%)Iron: 2.8mg (16%)

180. COCONUT PINEAPPLE SHRIMP SKEWERS

PREP:20 mins

COOK:5 mins

TOTAL:1 hr 25 mins

Ingredients

- 1/2 cup of light coconut milk
- 4 tsps Tabasco Original Red Sauce
- 2 tsp soy sauce
- 1/4 cup of freshly squeezed orange juice
- 1/4 cup of freshly squeezed lime juice
- 1 pound large shrimp
- 3/4 pound pineapple chunks
- Canola oil Freshly chopped Cilantro and/or green onion

Instructions

1. In a medium mixing bowl, combine the coconut milk, Tabasco sauce, soy sauce, orange juice, and lime juice. Coat the shrimp with the sauce. Cover and marinate in the refrigerator for 1-2 hours, stirring occasionally. Soak wooden skewers in warm water while the shrimp marinates. Meanwhile, if a pineapple is needed, get it ready.
2. Preheat the grill to medium-high temperature. Take the shrimp out of the marinade and set them aside to cook. Thread the shrimp and pineapple onto skewers alternately.
3. Before placing the shrimp on the grill, gently brush it with canola oil. Brush the shrimp with the marinade and grill for 3 minutes, then turn and cook for another 2-3 minutes, coating the shrimp with the marinade once more, until just cooked through. Garnish with Cilantro and green onions on a serving plate. Serve right away.

Nutrition

1(of4)CALORIES: 165kcalCARBOHYDRATES: 12gPROTEIN: 24gFAT: 2gSODIUM: 597mgFIBER: 1gSUGAR: 7g

181. GRILLED BBQ CHICKEN

COOK TIME45 minutes

TOTAL TIME45 minutes

SERVINGS6 servings

Ingredients

- 1 whole chicken cut into pieces (3-4 pounds)
- 2 tbsps olive oil
- salt & pepper to taste
- 2 cups of barbecue sauce

Instructions

1) Turn the grill's heat to medium.

2) Season the chicken with salt and pepper to taste after rubbing it with olive oil.

3) Cook with the skin-side down for 15 minutes on an oiled grate.

4) Apply barbecue sauce to the meat's reverse side. For another 20 to 30 minutes (the breasts and thighs should reach 165 and 175 degrees, respectively), brush the sauce over.

5) Give yourself a 5-minute break before serving.

NUTRITION

Calories: 478, Carbohydrates: 39g, Protein: 24g, Fat: 24g, Cholesterol: 95mg, Sodium: 1068mg, Potassium: 461mg, Fiber: 1g, Sugar: 32g, Calcium: 45mg, Iron: 1.7mg

182. KETO GRILLED CALIFORNIA AVOCADO CHICKEN

Prep Time: 10 minutes

Cook Time: 20 minutes

Servings: 4 people

Ingredients

- 4 boneless skinless chicken breasts
- 2-3 cloves garlic minced
- 2 tbsps balsamic vinegar
- 2 Tbsps olive oil
- 1 tbsp Italian seasoning
- 1/2 tsp salt
- 1/4 tsp pepper
- Avocado Tomato Topping
- 4 slices of fresh mOunceszarella cheese
- 1 cup of plum or grape tomato cut in half*
- 2 avocados diced
- 1/4 cup of fresh chopped basil chopped
- 1 tsp olive oil

- Juice of ½ lemon
- Dash of salt and pepper

Instructions

1. Combine the chicken, garlic, balsamic vinegar, and spices in a large mixing basin. Stir until all of the chicken is coated. Cover and marinate in the fridge for 30 minutes or up to 24 hours.
2. Follow these steps to cook chicken: In a large heavy-duty pan or skillet over medium-high heat, grill chicken for 8-10 minutes on each side or until cooked through. Top with mOunceszarella cheese and avocado tomato mixture right away.
3. Follow these instructions to make Avocado Tomato Salsa: While the chicken is cooking, combine the diced avocado, diced tomato, chopped basil, olive oil, 12 lemon juice, and a tsp of salt and pepper in a medium mixing bowl. Whisk everything together slowly to mix. Cover and place in the refrigerator until ready to use.

Nutrition

Serving: 1serving | Calories: 457kcal | Carbohydrates: 13g | Protein: 33g | Fat: 31g | Cholesterol: 95mg | Sodium: 614mg | Potassium: 1034mg | Fiber: 8g | Sugar: 3g Calcium: 190mg | Iron: 2mg

183. SWEET CHILI CHICKEN

PREP TIME15 minutes

COOK TIME10 minutes

TOTAL TIME25 minutes

INGREDIENTS

- 12 Ounces. (340 g) skinless boneless chicken breast/thigh, cut into small pieces
- oil, for deep-frying
- 1 tbsp oil
- 2 cloves minced garlic
- 4 tbsps bottled Thai sweet chili sauce
- 1 tsp lime juice
- 1 pinch salt
- 1/2 tsp white sesame
- 1/2 tbsp chopped cilantro leaves

FRYING BATTER:

- 1 egg white
- 1/2 cup of all-purpose flour

- 1/4 cup of corn starch
- 1/2 tsp baking powder
- 1/2 cup of water, ice-cold
- 1 tbsp cooking oil
- 1 pinch salt

INSTRUCTIONS

1. To prepare the batter, combine all of the ingredients in a mixing bowl and whisk until smooth. Combine the chicken with the batter in a separate bowl.
2. In a wok/skillet, heat about two inches of oil. As soon as the oil is heated enough, deep-fry the chicken till golden brown. Place the chicken on a platter lined with paper towels to absorb any excess oil.
3. After cleaning the wok/skillet, heat it over medium heat. Garlic and oil should be stirred together until aromatic Toss the fried chicken with the sweet chili sauce, lime juice, and salt in the pan. Stir to coat the chicken in the sweet chili sauce completely.
4. Serve with white sesame seeds and cilantro leaves on top. Serve immediately.

184. LEMON GARLIC CHICKEN THIGHS

yield:6 SERVINGS

prep time:2 HOURS 15 MINUTES

cook time:20 MINUTES

total time:2 HOURS 35 MINUTES

INGREDIENTS

- 1/2 cup of chicken stock
- 2 tbsps olive oil
- 3 tbsps freshly squeezed lemon juice
- 1 tbsp lemon zest
- 2 cloves garlic, minced
- 2 tsp Dijon mustard
- 1 tsp dried oregano
- 1/2 tsp dried thyme
- Kosher salt and freshly ground black pepper, to taste
- 2 pounds boneless, skinless chicken thighs
- 1 1/2 tbsp canola oil

DIRECTIONS

1. In a medium mixing bowl, combine the chicken stock, olive oil, lemon juice, lemon zest, garlic, Dijon mustard, oregano, thyme, 1 1/2 tsp salt, and 1 1/2 tsp pepper.

2. In a gallon Ziploc bag or a large mixing bowl, combine the chicken and chicken stock mixture; marinate for at least 2 hours overnight, turning the bag occasionally. Remove the chicken from the marinade.
3. Heat canola oil in a cast-iron grill pan over medium-high heat.
4. Place the chicken in a single layer on the grill pan, working in batches, and cook until golden brown and cooked through, about 4-5 minutes on each side, or until an internal temperature of 165 degrees F is achieved.
5. Serve immediately.

185. GRILLED SALSA VERDE CHICKEN

YIELDS:4

PREP TIME:0 HOURS 20 MINS

TOTAL TIME:0 HOURS 40 MINS

INGREDIENTS

- 1 jar divided salsa verde
- 2 tbsp. Extra-virgin olive oil
- Juice of 1/2 a lime
- 2 cloves minced garlic
- 1/2 tsp. chili powder
- 1/2 tsp. ground cumin
- 1 pound boneless skinless chicken breasts
- 4 slices of Monterey jack
- 1 jalapeño, thinly sliced
- 1/2 red onion, finely chopped
- 2 tbsp. Freshly chopped Cilantro
- Lime wedges for serving.

DIRECTIONS

1. In a large mixing bowl, combine 12 cups of salsa verde, olive oil, lime juice, garlic, chili powder, and cumin (Save 12 cups of salsa verde for basting the chicken and another 12 cups for serving.) Toss the chicken into the mixture until it is well coated. Allow 20 minutes for marinating.
2. Cook the chicken for 6 minutes on a medium-high grill. After rotating the chicken and covering each breast with more salsa verde, cook for another 6 minutes.
3. Cover and cook for an additional 4 minutes, or until the cheese has melted and the chicken is cooked through, topping each piece of chicken with a slice of Monterey Jack, a jalapeño, and a red onion.

186. HONEY SPICED GLAZED CHICKEN THIGHS

yield: 4 servings

prep time: 10 minutes

cook time: 15 minutes

total time: 25 minutes

Ingredients

- 8 boneless skinless chicken thighs
- 2 tsp chili powder
- 2 tsp smoked paprika
- 2 tsp garlic powder
- 1 tsp cumin
- 1 tsp kosher salt
- 1 tsp fresh cracked pepper
- 1 tsp red pepper flakes
- 1/2 tsp dried oregano
- 1/2 cup of honey
- 2 tbsps apple cider vinegar

Instructions

1. Untuck chicken thighs to flatten them.
2. In a small mixing bowl, combine chili powder, smoked paprika, garlic powder, cumin, kosher salt, black pepper, red pepper flakes, and dried oregano.
3. Season both sides with salt and pepper and put flat on a sheet pan.
4. Set your oven's broiler on low and place the oven rack in the top position.
5. Cook the chicken for 5-7 minutes in the oven before turning it.
6. Cook for 5-7 minutes on the other side.
7. Turn the chicken over and baste it with the honey apple cider vinegar mixture.
8. Return the chicken to the oven and broil for a few minutes, or until the honey has thickened and glazes the chicken. It may smoke a little, but that's to be expected.
9. Before serving, remove the chicken from the oven and lay it aside to cool for a few minutes.

10. Roast the chicken for 15 to 20 minutes at 400 degrees in a gas oven with the broiler on the bottom.

Nutrition

Calories: 515TotalFat: Cholesterol: 273mgSodium: 969mgCarbohydrates: 38gFiber: 1gSugar: 35gProtein: 55g

187. SPICY GRILLED CHICKEN TACOS WITH AVOCADO CREMA

Prep Time: 10 minutes

Servings: 4 -6 servings

Ingredients

- 2 boneless skinless chicken breasts (approximately one pound)
- 8-10 corn tortillas

MARINADE

- 2 chipotles in adobo sauce (2 of the actual peppers)
- 2 tbsp adobo sauce (from the chipotles in adobo)
- 1/2 cup of olive oil
- 1 clove of garlic, minced
- 1/4 tsp salt
- juice of 1/2 a lime

AVOCADO CREMA

- 1/2 cup of Mexican crema (or sour cream)
- 1/2 an avocado
- 1 tbsp shallots, diced
- 1 clove garlic
- juice of 1/2 a lime
- 1/4 tsp salt

Instructions

FOR THE MARINADE AND CHICKEN PREP

1. On a chopping board, cover the chicken with plastic wrap. After crushing the chicken to a uniform thickness, place it in a plastic bag. Refrigerate the remaining marinade ingredients for at least 30 minutes and up to 24 hours in a plastic bag.

FOR GRILLING

1. Remove the chicken from the marinade and heat up the grill to high. Before cooking, pour any remaining marinade over the chicken.
2. Before turning the chicken, cook it for six minutes over direct heat. When the internal temperature of the chicken reaches 165 degrees F on an instant-read thermometer, remove it from the oven.
3. Allow 10 minutes to settle before shredding with a fork.

MAKING THE AVOCADO CREMA

1. Add all ingredients to a food processor and pulse until thoroughly combined. It may be prepared in advance and stored in the refrigerator for up to five days.

MAKING THE TACOS

1. Add a couple of tbsp of shredded chicken and a dollop of crema to your corn tortilla. Cotija cheese, Cilantro, white onions, or tomatoes can be added as toppings.

188. HAWAIIAN CHICKEN KABOBS

Prep:10 mins

Cook:20 mins

Additional:2 hrs

Total:2 hrs 30 mins

Servings:8

Ingredients

- 3 tbsps soy sauce
- 3 tbsps brown sugar
- 2 tbsp sherry
- 1 tbsp sesame oil
- ¼ tsp ground ginger
- ¼ tsp garlic powder
- 8 skinless, boneless chicken breast halves - cut into 2-inch pieces
- 1 (20 ounces) can of pineapple chunks, drained
- Skewers

Directions

1. In a shallow glass dish, combine the soy sauce, brown sugar, sherry, sesame oil, ginger, and garlic powder. Toss the chicken pieces and pineapple with the marinade in a large mixing bowl until evenly coated. Refrigerate for at least 2 hours after covering and marinating.
2. Preheat the grill to medium-high temperature.
3. Lightly grease the grill grate. Thread chicken and pineapple alternately on skewers. Grill for 15 to 20 minutes, turning once or twice, or until the chicken and juices run clear.

Nutrition

203 calories; protein 23.6g; carbohydrates 17.1g; fat 4.2g; cholesterol 60.8mg; sodium 412.6mg.

189. CHEESY GARLIC STUFFED CHICKEN RECIPE

PREP:15 minutes

COOK:30 minutes

TOTAL TIME:45 minutes

INGREDIENTS

- 4 chicken breasts
- 4 cloves of garlic sliced
- ½ cup of grated mOunceszarella cheese
- ½ cup of grated parmesan cheese divided
- 4 tbsps unsalted butter room temperature
- 2 tsp Italian seasoning divided
- 1 cup of all-purpose flour
- 3 eggs beaten
- 2 cups of Panko breadcrumbs
- Salt and pepper to taste
- Oil

INSTRUCTIONS

1. Preheat the oven to 375 degrees Fahrenheit (190 degrees Celsius).
2. In a small mixing bowl, thoroughly combine the garlic, mOunceszarella, 14 cups parmesan, butter, and 1 tsp Italian spice.
3. 4 tbsp unsalted butter, 2 tsp Italian spice, 4 garlic cloves, 12 cups shredded mOunceszarella cheese, 12 cups grated parmesan cheese
4. Combine the cheese and garlic filling ingredients in a glass bowl.
5. A 3-inch wide pocket should be carved into the thick side of each chicken breast (almost to the other side, but do not cut all the way through).
6. four chicken breasts
7. Fill a quarter of the cheese filling into each chicken breast and secure with toothpicks. Take it out of the equation.
8. Raw chicken breasts are split open on a wood cutting board and stuffed with a garlic cheese mixture.
9. Prepare three shallow bowls for the breading station. In a separate bowl, combine the flour with a pinch of salt and pepper. Crack the eggs in the second bowl. Combine the breadcrumbs, 14 cups parmesan, 1 tsp Italian seasoning, salt, and pepper in the third bowl.

10. 1 cup all-purpose flour, 2 cups Panko breadcrumbs, 3 eggs, salt, and pepper
11. Three white bowls: one for flour, another for beaten eggs, and a third for breadcrumbs and parmesan cheese
12. Preheat a cast-iron skillet over medium-high heat. Fill the skillet with enough oil to thoroughly cover the bottom.
13. Oil
14. Flour each side of the chicken, then dip it in the egg, and then in the breadcrumb mixture. Repeat with the remaining chicken breasts until they are all breaded and ready to fry.
15. Chicken breast with a breadcrumb and parmesan crust
16. Cook the chicken for 3-4 minutes on each side, or until golden brown. Bake for 20 minutes, or until the chicken reaches a temperature of 165°F at its thickest point in the oven.
17. Breaded cheesy garlic chicken breasts in a pan before cooking
18. Before serving, remove the bowl from the oven and put it aside for 5 minutes.

190. BEER CHICKEN RECIPE

PREP:10 minutes

COOK:15 minutes

TOTAL TIME:25 minutes

INGREDIENTS

- 8 chicken thighs bone-in/skin on
- Sea salt and black pepper to season

FOR THE MARINADE

- 12 ounces of Corona beer
- 5 garlic cloves crushed
- 1 tbsp fresh thyme
- 1 tbsp vegetable or chicken stock powder
- 1 tbsp honey
- 2 tbsps olive oil

INSTRUCTIONS

1) The thigh cutlets must be washed and dried. The chicken should be put in a large mixing dish. To taste, add salt and pepper to the food.

2) Use a skewer to stab the chicken all the way through. Add the beer, garlic, thyme, stock powder, and honey after that. Refrigerator marinating takes four hours. Cover with foil.

3) After two hours, turn the chicken over to make sure the marinade is distributed evenly.

4) When it's time to cook, warm the olive oil in a large pan over medium-high heat.

5) Sear the chicken skin down until golden and crisp when the grill begins to smoke. Reduce heat to low after flipping, then sear the other side until golden.

6) Boil the beer marinade in a skillet over high-medium heat until it has been cut in half. Pour over the chicken after turning the heat up to high. Once the sauce has thickened, further reduce it. To keep the skin of the chicken wet, periodically brush it with beer sauce.

7) Remove the pan from the heat and serve over mashed potatoes.

191. BAKED CHICKEN AND ZUCCHINI

Cook:30 mins

Total:50 mins

Servings:4

Ingredients

- 1 egg
- 1 tbsp water
- ½ tsp salt
- ⅛ tsp ground black pepper
- 1 cup of dry bread crumbs
- 2 tbsps olive oil
- 4 skinless, boneless chicken breast halves
- 1 tbsp minced garlic
- 2 tbsps olive oil
- 5 zucchinis, sliced
- 4 tomatoes, sliced
- ⅔ cup of shredded mOunceszarella cheese
- 2 tsp chopped fresh basil
- ⅓ cup of shredded mOunceszarella cheese

Directions

1) Set the oven to 200 degrees Celsius (400 degrees Fahrenheit) (205 degrees C). Grease a 9x13-inch baking dish very lightly.

2) In a small bowl, stir the egg, water, salt, and pepper. The remaining bread crumbs are placed in a large, resealable plastic bag, with 2 tbsp set aside. After dipping the chicken in the egg mixture and coating it with a shake, put it in the bag.

3) 2 tbsp of olive oil heated over medium heat in a large pan. Cook the chicken in a pan for two to three minutes on each side, or until both sides are browned. The chicken should be taken out of the pan. Cook and toss the zucchini and garlic in the remaining 2 tbsp of oil in a pan over medium heat for approximately 2 minutes, or until the zucchini is just beginning to soften. Transfer to the baking pan that was previously ready.

4) 2 tbsp breadcrumbs (scatter over zucchini). Basil, tomato slices, and 2/3 cup mOunceszarella cheese are the toppings. On top of the zucchini layer, put the chicken. The aluminum foil must be placed over the baking dish.

5) Bake the chicken for about 25 minutes in a preheated oven or until the juices run clear and the meat is no longer pink in the center. In the middle, an instant-read thermometer should register at least 165 degrees Fahrenheit (74 degrees C). Add the remaining mOunceszarella cheese to the top after removing the lid. Until the cheese is completely melted, bake for 5 minutes.

Nutrition

506 calories; protein 39.8g; carbohydrates 34.1g; fat 24.1g; cholesterol 129.2mg; sodium 768.4mg.

192. EASY CHIPOTLE CHICKEN RECIPE

PREP:5 minutes

COOK:20 minutes

TOTAL:25 minutes

INGREDIENTS

- 1/2 medium yellow onion, chopped
- 1/4 cup of water
- 4 cloves garlic
- 2 tbsps olive oil
- 1 tbsp vinegar (white or apple cider vinegar both work)
- 2 chipotle chiles in adobo sauce
- 1 tbsp adobo sauce (from canned chipotle chiles)
- 1 tbsp ancho chili powder (or regular chili powder if that's all you have)
- 2 tsp ground cumin
- 2 tsp dried oregano
- 2 tsp coarse kosher salt
- 3 pounds boneless skinless chicken breasts or thighs
- cooking spray

INSTRUCTIONS

1. Chicken should be marinated.
2. In the bowl of a food processor or blender, combine all of the ingredients except the chicken. Blend until everything is perfectly smooth.
3. In a large resealable storage bag, pour the marinade over the chicken. Close the bag and massage the chicken all over until it is evenly coated.
4. Refrigerate for 30 minutes or up to 8 hours before serving.
5. Cooking the chicken (best method for chicken breasts)
6. Preheat the oven to 425°F and spray a large baking dish with nonstick cooking spray (or grease with olive oil). Remove the chicken breasts from the marinade and stack them in the baking dish in a single layer.
7. Bake for 20-30 minutes, or until the chicken reaches an internal temperature of 160°F. I highly recommend using an in-oven thermometer like this one to detect when the chicken is done (affiliate link).
8. Remove the chicken from the oven and place it in a baking dish covered with aluminum foil. Allow 10 minutes for the chicken to rest before rechecking the temperature, which should now be 165°F.
9. Chicken can be chopped or sliced. Season to taste with a dash of salt.

10. On the stovetop, saute the chicken (great for chicken thighs)
11. 2 tbsp olive oil, heated in a large nonstick pan over medium-high heat Transfer the marinated chicken to the skillet with tongs and cook for 5-7 minutes per side, or until fully done. Remove and discard the used marinade.
12. Place the chicken on a cutting board and set it aside to rest for 5 minutes.
13. Chicken can be chopped or sliced. Season to taste with a dash of salt.
14. Cooking the chicken on the grill
15. Preheat the grill to 375 degrees Fahrenheit over medium-high heat. Remove the chicken from the marinade using nonstick frying spray or olive oil.
16. Place chicken on the grill, cover, and cook for 10-15 minutes, or until completely cooked through and internal temperature reaches 165°F, depending on the thickness of the chicken.
17. Place the steaks on a cutting board after removing them from the grill. Allow yourself a 5-minute break.
18. Chicken can be chopped or sliced. Season to taste with a dash of salt.

193. SPICY CHICKEN KEBABS

Prep:30 mins

Cook:15 mins

Makes 20

Prep:30 mins

Cook:15 mins

Ingredients

- 3 garlic cloves, roughly chopped
- knob of fresh ginger, roughly chopped, plus extra to serve
- 1 orange, grated zest, and juice
- 3 spring onions, roughly chopped
- 2 tbsp clear honey
- 1 tbsp light soy sauce
- 2 tbsp vegetable oil
- 4 small skinless, boneless chicken breast fillets, cut into cubes
- 20 button mushrooms
- 20 cherry tomatoes
- 2 large red peppers, seeded and each cut into 10

Method

1) In a food processor, combine the spring onions, ginger, orange zest, and garlic to create a paste. Add the honey, orange juice, soy sauce, and oil before blending. The diced chicken should be marinaded for at least an hour, preferable overnight. Add the mushrooms in the final 30 minutes so they can take on some of the flavors.

2) Thread the chicken, tomatoes, mushrooms, and peppers onto 20 wooden skewers, and cook the chicken for 7-8 minutes on each side on a griddle pan, or until the chicken is cooked through and golden brown. As they cook evenly, turn the kebabs often and baste them as needed with the marinade. Eat with your fingers after arranging on a platter studded with chopped spring onions.

194. GRILLED THAI CURRY CHICKEN SKEWERS WITH COCONUT-PEANUT SAUCE

Servings: 5

Total Time: 40 Minutes

INGREDIENTS

FOR THE CHICKEN

- 1/4 cup of soy sauce
- 3 tbsps dark brown sugar, packed
- Zest of one lime
- 2 tbsps vegetable oil
- 3 garlic cloves, minced
- 1 tbsp curry powder
- 1/2 tsp ground ginger
- 1/4 tsp ground cardamom
- 1/2 tsp salt
- 2-1/2 - 3 pounds boneless, skinless chicken breasts

FOR THE COCONUT-PEANUT SAUCE

- 1 (13-Ounces) can of coconut milk (do not use low fat)
- 1/4 cup of peanut butter
- 1/3 cup of dark brown sugar, packed
- 1-1/2 tbsp soy sauce
- 1 tbsp red curry paste
- 3 tbsps fresh lime juice, from 2 limes

FOR SERVING

- 1 lime, cut into wedges

INSTRUCTIONS

1. Pound the chicken breasts to an even 1/2-inch thickness between two pieces of wax or parchment paper. Remove the breasts from the pan and chop them into 1-1/2" pieces.
2. Combine the soy sauce, dark brown sugar, lime zest, vegetable oil, garlic, curry powder, ginger, cardamom, and salt in a large mixing bowl. Toss the chicken pieces about in the basin until they are evenly coated. Cover the bowl with plastic wrap and refrigerate for at least 4 hours or overnight.
3. To create the sauce, mix together the coconut milk, peanut butter, brown sugar, soy sauce, and red curry paste in a medium pot. Bring to a boil, then reduce to low heat and simmer for 3 minutes, stirring occasionally. Lime juice should be squeezed directly from the lime. Take it out of the equation.
4. Preheat the grill to high heat. Meanwhile, thread the chicken pieces onto skewers. Spray the grill with nonstick cooking spray. Cook the skewers for 10 minutes on the grill, turning once, or until the chicken is cooked through. Serve the chicken skewers with the Coconut-Peanut Sauce and lime wedges, if desired.

195. GRILLED GARLIC CHICKEN SKEWERS

Prep Time: 1 hour 30 minutes

Cook Time: 15 minutes

Total Time: 1 hour 45 minutes

Ingredients

- 2 Chicken Breasts, cut into 1-inch pieces
- 1 bell pepper, optional, cut into 1-inch pieces
- 1 medium onion, optional, cut into 1-inch pieces
- 1 zucchini, optional, cut into 1-inch rings
- 8 bamboo skewers
- 2 Tbsp mayo
- 4 Tbsp ranch

- 4 garlic cloves, finely chopped
- Dash of Johny's Seasoning, or paprika

Instructions

1) Combine all of the marinade ingredients in a medium mixing basin. Blend everything thoroughly.

2) In a mixing bowl, combine the chicken breasts and marinate. Before serving, place in the fridge for at least one hour.

3) Before using, soak wooden skewers in a casserole dish half-filled with water. By doing this, they won't burn on the grill.

4) When the marinating of the chicken is complete, preheat the grill to medium heat.

5) Skewer chicken and vegetables all at once.

6) Grill chicken skewers for about 15 minutes, or until the meat is well cooked, over medium heat. Turn the chicken three times to guarantee even cooking on all four sides of the skewer.

196. HONEY SRIRACHA GRILLED CHICKEN THIGHS

Prep Time5 mins

Cook Time35 mins

Total Time40 mins

Ingredients

- 2.5 Pounds. Just BARE Chicken Thighs
- 3 Tbsps unsalted butter
- 1 Tbsp minced fresh ginger
- 2 garlic cloves, minced
- 1/4 tsp smoked paprika
- 1/4 tsp ground cloves
- 4 Tbsps honey
- 6 Tbsps Sriracha
- 1 Tbsp lime juice

Instructions

1) Set the grill to medium-high heat and preheat it to 400 degrees.

2) Melt the butter in a little pot. When the butter has melted, add the fresh ginger and garliCup Stir the mixture for one minute or until it begins to smell.

3) Next, include the lime juice, honey, Sriracha, ground cloves, and smoky paprika. Cook on low heat for 4-5 minutes after stirring to mix.

4) Pat the chicken thighs dry with a paper towel. On both sides, season with salt and pepper.

5) The grill grates have to be coated with cooking spray or a cloth dipped in olive oil.

6) Lay the chicken thighs skin side down before placing them on the grill. Cook on the grill for four to five minutes. On the opposite side, cook the chicken for a further 4-5 minutes.

7) Cook the chicken for a total of 165 minutes, turning it over every 3 to 4 minutes to prevent burning. (About 25 to 30 minutes)

8) Brush the glaze over the chicken's top and bottom during the final five minutes of cooking.

9) Turn off the grill's heat.

10) Serve

197. BAKED STICKY HONEY GARLIC BUFFALO WINGS

PREP TIME5 MINUTES

COOK TIME45 MINUTES

TOTAL TIME50 MINUTES

Ingredients

- 4 pounds of wings patted dry with a paper towel
- 1 Tbsp Baking Powder
- 1 tsp garlic powder
- 1 tsp salt
- 1/4 tsp pepper
- Honey Garlic Buffalo Sauce:
- 1 cup of buffalo sauce like Franks Red Hot Sauce
- 3/4 cup of honey
- 1/4 cup of brown sugar
- 1 Tbsp Worcestershire sauce
- 1 Tbsp Cornstarch

Instructions

1. Preheat the oven to 400 degrees Fahrenheit (200 degrees Celsius). Line a baking sheet with parchment paper or aluminum foil and coat it with cooking spray. Fill a ziplock bag with the

wings. Shake the baking powder, garlic powder, salt, and pepper together to coat them evenly. Place them on the prepared baking sheet.

2. In a preheated oven, bake for 45-50 minutes, or until crispy and no longer pink.
3. In a mixing bowl, combine the following ingredients to make the Honey Garlic Buffalo Sauce. Just before the wings are done, mix the buffalo sauce, honey, brown sugar, Worcestershire sauce, and cornstarch in a medium saucepan. Over medium-high heat, whisk for 3-4 minutes, or until it has thickened. Apply a glue coat to the wings.

198. CHICKEN FAJITA COBB

PREP TIME 15 mins

COOK TIME 15 mins

TOTAL TIME 30 mins

INGREDIENTS

For the Chicken

- 1 tbsp vegetable oil
- 2 chipotle peppers in adobo finely chopped
- 1 tsp garlic powder
- 1 tsp ground cumin
- 1/2 tsp dried oregano
- 1/2 tsp black pepper
- 4 boneless skinless chicken thighs (or 3 boneless, skinless chicken breasts)

For the Salad

- 3-4 cups of market greens
- 2 corn on the cob kernels removed
- 1 cup of cherry tomatoes halved
- 1 cup of sautéed bell peppers
- 1-2 avocados sliced
- ½ cup of feta
- Kosher salt and freshly cracked black pepper to taste

For the Vinaigrette

- 1 lemon juiced
- 2 cloves garlic minced
- 1 shallot finely chopped
- 2 tsp red wine vinegar
- 1/3 cup of olive oil
- kosher salt to taste

INSTRUCTIONS

1) In a small bowl, mix the black pepper, cumin, dried oregano, garlic powder, and chipotle peppers in adobo. The marinade should be combined with the chicken in a large zip-top plastic bag. Combine the chicken and marinate in a zip-top bag. Put it in the fridge to marinate for at least an hour.

2) Whether cooking inside or outside, heat the grill to 400 degrees Fahrenheit (medium-high heat). On the grill, cook the chicken for 5 to 6 minutes per side, or until done. Allow the chicken to rest for 10 minutes after removing it from the grill. You may use it as required by slicing the chicken crosswise.

3) Arrange the greens on a large platter, then sprinkle with all the garnishes.

4) Combine all of the vinaigrette's components in a mixing bowl. Before serving, toss the salad with the vinaigrette.

199. GREEK CHICKEN BITES

Prep Time: 10 minutes

Cook Time: 10 minutes

Marinating Time: 20 minutes

Total Time: 20 minutes

Ingredients

- 1 Pound. Chicken breasts cut into 1" pieces (about 2 breasts)
- 2 tbsps extra-virgin olive oil
- juice and zest of 1 lemon (about 2 tbsp juice and 1 tsp zest)
- 2 cloves garlic minced (about 1 tsp)
- 2 tsp dried oregano
- 1 tsp kosher salt
- 1/2 tsp black pepper
- 1/4 cup of white wine or chicken broth, or water in a pinch

Instructions

1. Combine the olive oil (2 tbsp), lemon juice and zest (1 lemon), minced garlic (2 cloves), dried oregano (2 tsp), kosher salt (1 tsp), and black pepper (1/2 tsp) in a small bowl or glass measuring cup.
2. In a plastic bag or a closed container, place the cut-up chicken breasts. Toss the chicken in the marinade to coat it (or smush around in the plastic bag). Allow at least 20 minutes for marinating, but preferably 2-24 hours (you may skip this step if you're in a hurry or didn't plan ahead).

3. Over medium-high heat, heat a large, heavy pan until it is blazing hot (this may take a few minutes if you are using cast iron or only about 30 seconds to a minute if using another material).
4. In the skillet, arrange the chicken in an even layer. Cook for about 5 minutes, stirring occasionally. Cook for a further 5 minutes on the other side, or until the chicken is thoroughly cooked (internal temperature should be 165 degrees F, or cut into a piece to ensure it is no longer pink).
5. While bathing the chicken in the white wine (1/4 cup), deglaze the bottom of the skillet with it, using a spatula or wooden spoon to loosen all the stuck-on browned chunks. Cook until the wine has mostly evaporated and the deglazed drippings have coated the chicken. Serve.

Nutrition

Calories: 195kcal | Carbohydrates: 1g | Protein: 24g | Fat: 10g | Cholesterol: 73mg | Sodium: 713mg | Potassium: 420mg | Fiber: 1g | Sugar: 1g | Calcium: 12mg | Iron: 1mg

200. HONEY GARLIC CHICKEN DRUMSTICKS

Prep Time10 mins

Cook Time1 hr

Total Time1 hr 10 mins

INGREDIENTS

- 10 (4 Ounces) chicken drumsticks skin on
- 2 tbsp butter melted
- 2 tbsps honey
- 2 tbsps Dijon mustard
- 1 tsp Diamond Crystal kosher salt
- ¼ tsp black pepper
- 1 tsp garlic powder

INSTRUCTIONS

1) Set the oven's temperature to 350 degrees Fahrenheit (180 degrees Celsius). A big baking sheet with a rim should be lined with foil and lightly buttered (this will save you some significant cleanup later as the honey caramelizes).

2) Position the drumsticks in the pan in any way you choose. Melted butter, honey, mustard, salt, black pepper, and garlic powder should all be combined in a bowl. Brush the chicken with the mixture all over to coat it evenly.

3) Bake the chicken for 30 minutes, basting with a fresh pastry brush every 15 minutes, or until the juices run clear. It took 75 minutes, all told, in my old oven. It takes 60 minutes in the new one, which I feel is more realistiCup Cup

NUTRITION

Serving: 2drumsticks | Calories: 340kcal | Carbohydrates: 7g | Protein: 46g | Fat: 12g | Sodium: 566mg | Sugar: 7g

201. VEGGIE-PACKED CHICKEN FRIED RICE

Prep:20 mins

Cook:25 mins

Total:45 mins

Servings:4

Ingredients

- 9 tsp divided vegetable oil
- 1 red bell pepper, cut into strips
- ½ medium onion, sliced
- 1 (6 ounces) skinless, boneless chicken breast half, cut into cubes
- 2 cups of chopped zucchini
- 2 cups of chopped carrots
- 1 cup of chopped cabbage
- 1 cup of chopped sugar snap peas
- ⅓ cup of low-sodium chicken or vegetable broth
- 1 ½ tbsps minced garlic
- 1 tbsp minced fresh ginger
- 2 cups of cooked short-grain brown rice
- 2 tbsp low-sodium soy sauce
- 2 tsp sesame oil
- ¼ cup of sliced green onions
- ½ tsp salt

Directions

1) 2 tbsp vegetable oil heated to shimmering condition over medium-high heat in a large covered pan or wok. While cooking, occasionally toss until the pepper and onion are crisp-tender, about 5 minutes. Pour into a basin for mixing.

2) Heat the remaining 2 tbsp of oil in the same skillet until it shimmers. Cook the chicken for 5 minutes, periodically turning, or until no longer pink. In a bowl, combine with the veggies. (Skip this step if you're using precooked chicken.)

3). Heat the final 2 tbsp of oil until shimmering. Along with the diced zucchini, carrots, cabbage, and sugar snap peas, cook for 2 minutes, stirring periodically. Cook the veggies for a further 3 minutes with the lid on, or until they are tender-crisp. Place in a basin for mixing.

4) Heat the remaining 3 tbsp of oil in the same skillet until it shimmers. Cook the garlic and ginger for 15 seconds, stirring once or twice. Rice should be heated for two minutes while being periodically stirred, and clumps are broken up (and precooked chicken, if using). The bowl's contents should be seasoned with salt, soy sauce, sesame oil, green onions, and green onions. Cook well combined and cooked for a further 5 minutes, turning and periodically stirring.

Nutrition

360 calories; protein 16.3g; carbohydrates 41.8g; fat 14.4g; cholesterol 25mg; sodium 652.2mg.

202. BUFFALO CHICKEN & BLUE CHEESE SLAW

Prep:30 mins

Cook:1 hr

Serves 4

Ingredients

- 8 skin-on, bone-in chicken thighs
- 100ml hot sauce
- 2tsp smoked paprika
- 1tbsp light brown soft sugar
- 1tbsp white wine vinegar
- 1tsp garlic powder
- 30g butter, cubed
- For the slaw
- 120g blue cheese, crumbled
- 150g soured cream
- 4tbsp mayonnaise
- 1tbsp finely chopped chives
- 1 lemon, juiced
- Granny smith apple, cored and cut into matchsticks
- celery, finely chopped
- ¼ medium finely chopped white cabbage
- pointed spring cabbage, finely chopped

Method

1. Preheat the oven to 180°C/160°F fan/gas mark 4 4 Place the chicken skin-side up in a roasting pan. After slicing the skin with a sharp knife, season the chicken and roast for 35 minutes.
2. STEP 2 Whisk together the spicy sauce, paprika, sugar, vinegar, garlic powder, and butter in a saucepan. Stir until the butter has melted over low heat, then lower to low heat and simmer for 1 minute. Season. After draining any excess juices and fat, pour half of the sauce into the roasting tray. Return the chicken to the oven for another 20 minutes, or until thoroughly done. Preheat the oven to its maximum temperature and add the remaining sauce. Cook for 5 minutes in total.
3. Crumble the cheese in a mixing bowl and add the soured cream, mayonnaise, chives, and lemon juice. Toss together the apple, celery, cabbage, and cheese sauce. Serve the chicken with a side of slaw.

203. CHICKEN BROCCOLI STIR FRY RECIPE

Prep Time: 15 minutes

Cook Time: 15 minutes

Total Time: 30 minutes

Ingredients

Chicken and Broccoli:

- 1 Pound chicken breast (boneless skinless), cut into 3/4" pieces
- 2 Tbsp divided cooking oil (I used extra light olive oil)
- 1Pounds broccoli, cut into florets (about 5 cups of)
- 1 small yellow onion, sliced into strips
- 1/2 Pounds white button mushrooms, thickly sliced

Stir Fry Sauce Ingredients:

- 2/3 cup of low sodium chicken broth
- 3 Tbsp low sodium soy sauce (use Tamari for gluten-free), or added to taste
- 2 Tbsp light brown sugar, packed (or honey to taste)
- 1 Tbsp corn starch
- 1 Tbsp sesame oil
- 1 tsp fresh ginger, peeled and grated (lightly packed)
- 1 tsp grated garlic (2 small cloves)
- 1/4 tsp black pepper, plus more to season chicken

Instructions

1) In a small bowl, mix together all of the sauce's components until the sugar and corn starch are dissolved (warm broth will help dissolve the sugar faster). The sauce is set apart.

2) Lightly season the chicken, then slice it into bite-sized pieces that are no thicker than 3/4". A sizable, heavy pan or wok should be heated over medium-high heat. Extra virgin olive oil, 1 tbsp Transfer to a basin and loosely cover to keep warm after stirring for a further 5 minutes, or until golden brown and thoroughly cooked.

3) Add broccoli florets, sliced onions, and sliced mushrooms to the same skillet along with one tbsp of oil. Reduce heat to medium or low after 3 minutes, or until mushrooms are cooked, and broccoli is crisp-tender.

4) Pour the sauce on top of the veggies after giving them a brief spin to break up any starch clumps. Cook the sauce for 3–4 minutes, or until it has thickened and the flavors of the ginger and garlic have diminished. Add a tsp of water at a time to the sauce to thin it down.

5) Add the chicken back to the pan and stir for an additional 30 seconds, or until thoroughly heated. Serve over hot rice and add more soy sauce to taste.

204. EASY CHICKEN STIR FRY RECIPE

Prep Time: 15 minutes

Cook Time: 15 minutes

Total Time: 30 minutes

INGREDIENTS

- 1 Pounds chicken breast, boneless skinless (or chicken thighs)
- 1/2 zucchini, sliced or cubed
- 3 Tbsp divided oil
- 2 Tbsp unsalted butter
- 1 cup of broccoli, cut into florets
- 1 small carrot, julienned or cubed
- 8 Ounces mushrooms, sliced
- 1/2 red pepper, cubed
- 4 garlic cloves, minced
- 1 tsp minced fresh ginger,
- 1/2 onion, cubed
- 1/2 cup of cashews

Stir fry sauce-

- 1/2 cup of chicken broth

- 1/4 cup of water
- 1/4 cup of soy sauce
- 2 Tbsp honey
- 1 Tbsp cornstarch

INSTRUCTIONS

1) Combine all of the ingredients for the stir fry sauce in a mixing dish. Remove it from the equation.

2) Trim the thighs of any extra fat before slicing them into bite-sized pieces that are 1/2 inch thick. To make the veggies the same size as the chicken, cut them into even-sized pieces.

3) In a big skillet over medium-high heat, warm 1 tbsp oil. Add the chicken when the oil has warmed up. Cook the chicken while occasionally stirring until it is browned. Take the cooked chicken out of the pan, cover it, and set it aside.

4) Fill the same skillet with the remaining oil and butter. Combine the zucchini, broccoli, onions, mushrooms, red peppers, and carrots in a large mixing bowl. While cooking, toss the veggies periodically until they are tender.

5) Replace the chicken in the same pan. Cook the garlic and ginger for one minute after adding them.

6) In the same pan as the cashews, slowly bring the sauce to a boil.

7) Lower the heat to low and toss the stir fry often until the sauce thickens and is well incorporated.

8) Just before serving, garnish with green onions and sesame seeds.

NUTRITION

Calories: 445kcalCarbohydrates: 25gProtein: 18gFat: 32gCholesterol: 56mgSodium: 984mgPotassium: 691mgFiber: 3gSugar: 13gCalcium: 43mgIron: 2.7mg

205. CHEESY CHICKEN FRITTERS

Prep Time: 10 minutes

Cook Time: 20 minutes

Total Time: 30 minutes

Ingredients

Ingredients for Chicken Fritters:

- 1 1/2 Pounds of chicken breasts (3 large)

- 2 large eggs
- 1/3 cup of mayonnaise
- 1/3 cup of all-purpose flour, cornstarch, or potato starch for gluten-free
- 4 Ounces mOunceszarella cheese (1 1/3 cup of shredded)
- 1 1/2 Tbsp chopped fresh dill
- 1/2 tsp salt, or to taste
- 1/8 tsp black pepper
- 2 Tbsp Extra light olive oil to saute (or any high heat cooking oil)
- Ingredients for Garlic Aioli Dip (Optional)
- 1/3 cup of mayonnaise
- 1 garlic clove, pressed
- 1/2 Tbsp lemon juice
- 1/4 tsp salt
- 1/8 tsp black pepper

Instructions

1) Place the chicken in a large mixing bowl after slicing it into pieces that are 1/3" thick using a sharp knife. Having a slightly chilled chicken breast will make slicing it simpler.

2) Add the remaining ingredients for the batter to the mixing bowl: 1 1/2 tbsp dill, 1/2 tsp salt, 1/8 tsp black pepper, or to taste; 2 eggs; 1/3 cup mayonnaise; 1/3 cup flour; 1 1/3 cups shredded mOunceszarella after thoroughly combining all the ingredients, cover and refrigerate for two hours or overnight.

3) In a large nonstick pan, heat 2 tbsp of oil to medium heat. The heated oil will get one heaping Tbsp of the chicken mixture at a time. Cook the chicken for a further 3 minutes after turning it over, or until the exterior is golden brown and the bird is well cooked. Use additional oil as necessary while you continue making the remaining fritters.

4) Combine all of the components for the aioli (if needed) in a small bowl or measuring cup and stir until well combined.

206. BAKED GARLIC LEMON WINGS

PREP TIME 10 minutes

COOK TIME 30 minutes

MARINATE TIME 15 minutes

TOTAL TIME 55 minutes

INGREDIENTS

- 1 1/2 pounds (0.6 kg) of chicken wings
- 4 clove minced garlic
- 1 1/2 tbsp soy sauce
- 1 tbsp lemon juice
- 2 1/2 tbsp honey
- 3 dashes of black pepper powder
- 1 pinch of cayenne pepper
- Lemon wedges

INSTRUCTIONS

1. Preheat the oven to 400 degrees Fahrenheit (200 degrees Celsius) (207 degrees Celsius).
2. Cleaning and rinsing chicken wings are necessary. Pat dry with paper towels.
3. The chicken wings are marinated in garlic, soy sauce, lemon juice, honey, black pepper, and cayenne pepper. Everything should be completely combined. Allow 15 minutes for this to happen.
4. Place the chicken wings on a baking sheet lined with parchment paper. Preheat the oven to 350°F and bake for 30 minutes, or until the top is golden brown. Serve immediately with lemon wedges, ranch dressing, or Asian chili sauce. Squeeze a little lemon juice on top before serving.

207. CHICKEN FAJITAS WITH BELL PEPPERS

Total:25 mins

Yield:4

Ingredients

- 1/4 cup of divided vegetable oil
- 3 medium minced cloves garlic,
- 1/4 tsp kosher or sea salt, plus more for seasoning
- 1/2 tsp chile powder
- 1/4 tsp ground cumin
- 1/2 tsp paprika
- 1/4 tsp sugar
- 2 tsp fresh lime juice
- 1 pound boneless, skinless chicken breasts, sliced into strips
- 1 medium onion, sliced
- 1 red bell pepper, seeded and sliced
- 1 green bell pepper, seeded and sliced
- 1 orange bell pepper, seeded and sliced
- Fresh cracked black pepper
- Flour or corn tortillas for serving
- Shredded cheese and sour cream for serving
- Chopped avocado, chopped Cilantro, and salsa or chopped tomatoes for serving

Directions

1) Combine 3 tbsp of vegetable oil, garlic, salt, chili powder, cumin powder, paprika, sugar, and fresh lime juice in a small mixing bowl. Remove it from the equation.

2) In a big skillet over medium-high heat, warm the oil. Stir in the chicken after adding the oil. Cook the chicken for a further 2 minutes, or until it is lightly browned. Cook the veggies for 3 to 5 minutes, or until they are tender, after adding the onion and bell pepper.

3) Continue cooking for an additional 2 minutes, or until everything is well cooked, and the spice combination is incorporated. To taste, add salt and pepper to the food. If preferred, serve with tortillas and extra toppings.

208. CHICKEN TAGINE WITH APRICOTS AND ALMONDS

Active Time30 min

Total Time1 1/2 hr

Ingredients

- 1 tsp ground cinnamon
- 1 tsp ground ginger
- 1/2 tsp turmeric
- 1/2 tsp black pepper
- 1 1/4 tsp salt
- 3 tbsp plus 1/4 cup of olive oil
- 1 (3-Pounds) chicken, cut into 6 pieces, wings and backbone discarded
- 1 tbsp unsalted butter
- 1 medium red onion, halved, then sliced 1/4 inch thick
- 4 garlic cloves, finely chopped
- 5 fresh cilantro
- 5 sprigs of fresh flat-leaf Parsley
- 1 1/2 cup of water
- 2 tbsps mild honey
- 1 (3-inch) cinnamon stick
- 1/2 cup of dried Turkish apricots, separated into halves
- 1/3 cup of whole blanched almonds
- Special Equipment
- a 10- to a 12-inch tagine or heavy skillet; kitchen string

Method

1) In a large mixing bowl, combine the ground cinnamon, ginger, turmeric, pepper, 1 tsp salt, and 2 tbsp oil. Add the chicken and thoroughly coat.

2) In the base of the tagine (or a pan), heat the butter and 1 tbsp oil over medium heat until hot but not smoking. Then, brown the chicken for 8 to 12 minutes, turning once, skin side down. Place a plate for cooling. In the same way, brown the remaining chicken, adding any leftover spice mixture from the dish.

3) Add the onion and the final 1/4 tsp of salt, and simmer, covered, for 8 minutes. Cook the garlic for three minutes, stirring now and again. Combine Cilantro and Parsley in a kitchen string bundle; add to tagine along with 1/2 cup water, poultry, and any juices that have gathered atop the bowl. Cook for 30 minutes with a lid on low heat.

4) While the chicken cooks, in a 1- to 2-quart heavy saucepan, bring the honey, remaining cup of water, cinnamon stick, and apricots to a boil. Then, lower the heat and simmer the mixture uncovered until the apricots are very soft (add more water if necessary). Cook for 10 to 15 minutes, stirring occasionally, or until the apricots are mushy and the liquid has thickened into a glaze.

5) Prepare the remaining 1/4 cup of oil in a small pan over medium heat. Saute the almonds for 1 to 2 minutes, stirring periodically while the apricots are cooking. A slotted spoon should be used to transfer to paper towels to drain.

6) Add the apricot mixture to the tagine ten minutes before the chicken is finished cooking. Spread the almonds over the chicken after removing the herbs and cinnamon stick.

209. HERB AND GARLIC TURKEY BURGERS

Total Time: 40 mins

Yield: 2

INGREDIENTS

- ½ pound turkey cutlets or white meat ground turkey breast (free-range, hormone-free, antibiotic-free)
- 3 celery stalks, cut into chunks (1¼ cup of)
- 1/2 yellow onion, coarsely chopped (3/4 cup of)
- 2 garlic cloves, coarsely chopped
- 2 tbsp fresh sage leaves (about 8 to 10 leaves)
- 1 tbsp fresh marjoram or oregano
- ½ tsp Celtic sea salt
- 1 egg (fresh organic, free-range)
- ¼ tsp fresh pepper
- 2 tbsps coconut oil
- Optional toppings for serving:
- 3 tsp avocado mayonnaise
- 3 tbsps Dijon mustard
- 1 large tomato, thinly sliced
- 1 avocado, thinly sliced

INSTRUCTIONS

1) Break up the turkey cutlets into little bits and process them in a food processor.

2) In a large mixing bowl, combine all the ingredients.

3) Combine celery, onion, garlic, sage, marjoram, and salt in the same food processor bowl. Onion and celery should be finely chopped—not mushy.

4) Combine the turkey, egg, and freshly ground pepper in a mixing bowl.

5) Ensure that the celery mixture is distributed throughout the turkey.

6) Form six patties from the turkey.

7) Place a big skillet over medium heat and warm the oil.

8) Cook the turkey patties for 5 minutes on each side, or until they are well heated through.

9) Take the patties out of the skillet.

10) Offer slices of tomato and avocado on the side. Distribute Dijon mustard and avocado mayonnaise as a garnish.

210. EASY GREEK LEMON CHICKEN

PREP TIME 5 MINUTES

COOK TIME 40 MINUTES

TOTAL TIME 45 MINUTES

Ingredients

- 5 chicken thighs bone-in and skin on
- 1/4 cup of olive oil
- 3 garlic cloves minced
- 1/2 tsp Kosher salt
- 1/4 tsp black pepper
- 1 tsp dried oregano
- 1/4 tsp crushed red pepper
- 1 tsp dried thyme
- 2 lemons, one cut into wedges and one juiced and zested

Instructions

1. Preheat the oven to 375 degrees Fahrenheit (190 degrees Celsius).
2. Combine the chicken thighs, olive oil, garlic, salt, pepper, oregano, crushed red pepper, thyme, lemon juice, and zest in a large mixing basin.
3. In a cast-iron pan, place the chicken thighs skin side up.
4. Toss the lemon wedges in the leftover marinade and arrange them in the pan between the chicken pieces.
5. Roast for 35-40 minutes, or until golden brown and crispy.

211. SESAME GINGER CHICKEN

Total: 1 hr 30 min

Prep: 15 min

Inactive: 1 hr

Cook: 15 min

Yield: 4 servings

Ingredients

Chicken Marinade:

- 2 1/2 pounds boneless, skinless chicken thighs, cut into 1-inch cubes
- 6 tbsp sesame oil
- 2 1/2 tbsps sugar
- 2 tbsps soy sauce
- 1 tsp cracked black pepper

Stir-Fry:

- 1 cup of plus 2 tbsps cornstarch
- Vegetable or peanut oil
- 2 tbsps minced garlic
- 1 tbsp minced ginger
- 4 tbsps Chinese Shaoxing rice wine
- 2 tbsp hoisin sauce
- 2 tbsps oyster sauce
- 2 tbsp low-sodium soy sauce
- 1 1/2 tbsp honey
- 1 tbsp sambal chili sauce
- 1 tbsp Thai chili sauce
- 1 lemon, zest, and juice
- Toasted sesame seeds for Garnish
- Scallions, thinly sliced at an angle, for Garnish
- Rice, for serving

Directions

1) To make the chicken marinade, combine the chicken, sesame oil, sugar, soy sauce, and pepper in a mixing dish. Stir to evenly coat, cover, and put in the fridge for a half-hour.

2) Combine all of the stirred ingredients fry's in a large mixing bowl. Take the chicken out of the refrigerator. Each piece of chicken should be coated with 1 cup of cornstarch in a shallow baking dish. Extra should be scraped off.

3) Pour enough oil into a Dutch oven or high-sided saute pan to thoroughly cover the chicken pieces. The mixture should be heated over a high flame until it is smooth and reaches 375°F. The chicken was deep-fried for three minutes, or until golden brown. Add the chicken in stages to prevent crowding and to prevent the temperature of the oil from falling too low. Transfer to a platter covered with paper towels.

4) In a large saute pan, heat 1 tbsp of oil to medium-high heat. Cook garlic and ginger for 30 seconds, or until they are aromatic and golden colored. Rice wine, hoisin, oyster, soy, honey, and chili sauces are all brought to a low boil.

5) To avoid lumps, make sure the water is extremely cold before adding the remaining 2 tbsp of cornstarch to the 1/4 cup of cold water in a glass measuring cup. Before adding the mixture to the sauce, Cook for an additional minute or until the sauce has thickened. Use salt and pepper to taste to season.

6) Pour enough sauce over the fried chicken to coat it completely. Lemon juice and zest should be combined in a mixing bowl. Add toasted sesame seeds and scallions just before serving.

7) Serve immediately over rice.

212. GRILLED LEMON-GARLIC CHICKEN WITH PEACH SALSA

6Servings

20minPrep

1hr8minTotal

Ingredients

- ⅔ Cup fresh lemon juice
- Add Hy-Vee Select olive oil
- ⅓ Cup Hy-Vee Select olive oil
- Add minced garlic
- 6 clove(s) minced garlic
- Add Hy-Vee dried oregano leaves
- 1 tbsp. Hy-Vee dried oregano leaves
- Add kosher salt
- 2 tsp. kosher salt
- Add Hy-Vee black pepper
- 2 tsp. Hy-Vee black pepper
- Add chicken quarters (about 4 pounds)
- 6 chicken quarters (about 4 pounds)
- Add ripe Colorado peaches, peeled, pitted, and chopped
- 3 ripe Colorado peaches, peeled, pitted, and chopped
- Add red bell pepper, seeded and finely chopped
- 1 red bell pepper, seeded and finely chopped
- Add jalapeno peppers, seeded and finely chopped
- 2 jalapeno peppers, seeded and finely chopped
- Add finely chopped yellow onion
- 2 tbsp. finely chopped yellow onion
- Add chopped fresh cilantro

- 1 tbsp. chopped fresh cilantro
- Add lime peel
- 1 tsp. lime peel
- Add fresh lime juice
- 2 tbsp. fresh lime juice
- Add rice wine vinegar
- 1 tbsp. rice wine vinegar
- Add packed Hy-Vee brown sugar
- 1 tsp. packed Hy-Vee brown sugar
- Add Hy-Vee unsalted butter, melted
- 2 tbsp. Hy-Vee unsalted butter, melted
- Add (12 Ounces) jar of Hy-Vee peach preserves
- 1 (12 Ounces) jar of Hy-Vee peach preserves

Directions

1) In a medium mixing bowl, combine the olive oil, oregano, garlic, lemon juice, salt, and black pepper to make the marinade. Place the mixture in a large bowl and close the bag with plastic wrap. Put the chicken into the bag, zip it up, and shake it around to coat the inside. For at least 4 hours, the chicken should be chilled. Flip the bag occasionally.

2) To make salsa, add peaches, bell pepper, jalapenos, onion, cilantro, lime juice, lime peel, and rice wine vinegar in a medium mixing bowl. Keep chilled until you're ready to serve.

3) A charcoal or gas grill should have one side set up for medium-heat direct grilling and the other for indirect cooking.

4) Melt the butter for the peach glaze in a small pot. Cook the preserves while often stirring until they become the consistency of a glaze. Ensure your own warmth.

5) The grates on the grill need to be oiled. Remove the chicken from the marinade and discard it. Over the direct fire, grill the chicken for 8 minutes, flipping once. A thermometer placed into the thickest part of the chicken should read 165 degrees after another 35 to 40 minutes of cooking on the indirect heat side of the grill. During the final 10 minutes of cooking, baste the chicken with the peach glaze. Salsa should be served alongside the chicken.

213. LIGHT HONEY-GLAZED CORNISH HENS

Prep:10 mins

Cook:50 mins

Total:60 mins

Servings:4 servings

Ingredients

- 2 Cornish game hens (about 1 1/2 pounds each)
- 1 tsp (grated) fresh orange peel
- 1/4 cup of orange juice concentrate (thawed, undiluted)
- 3 tbsps lemon juice
- 2 tbsps soy sauce
- 2 cloves garlic (crushed and minced)
- 1 tbsp honey
- 1/2 tsp onion powder
- 1/4 tsp dried thyme
- 2 tsp. oil or nonstick cooking spray
- 1/2 cup of onion (chopped)
- Optional Garnish: fresh orange wedges
- 1 tsp cornstarch mixed with 1 tsp water (cold)

Make

1. Gather the required materials. Preheat the oven to 350 degrees Fahrenheit (180 degrees Celsius).
2. Place the game birds breast-side down on a chopping board and cut in half along the backbone. Extra skin and fat should be eliminated.
3. In a small microwave-safe dish, combine orange peel, lemon juice, orange juice concentrate, soy sauce, honey, garlic, onion powder, and thyme. Bring to a boil in a microwave oven; leave aside.
4. Coat a baking dish in cooking spray or grease it gently.
5. Divide the chopped onion into four pieces on a baking dish and place the bird's bone side down on the onions.
6. Pour the orange juice mixture over the birds.
7. In a warm oven, bake birds for 45 minutes, basting with cooking fluids every 10 to 15 minutes. If they brown too quickly, cover them loosely with aluminum foil.
8. When the birds are done, remove them from the oven dish, onions and all, and place them on hot dinner plates.
9. If desired, garnish with orange slices. Remove the fat from the baking dish's juices. If necessary, thicken pan juices with 1 tsp cornstarch and 1 tsp cold water. Juices should be served separately.

10. Serve with freshly cooked rice and a green vegetable. Enjoy!

214. GRILLED CORNISH HENS

Prep: 15 min. Grill: 50 min.

4 servings

Ingredients

- 1/4 cup of butter, softened
- 2 green onions, finely chopped
- 2 tbsps minced fresh parsley
- 2 tbsps grated fresh ginger root
- 3 minced garlic cloves
- 1 tsp divided salt
- 1/2 tsp divided pepper
- 4 Cornish game hens (20 to 24 ounces each)

Directions

1) Combine the butter, onions, parsley, ginger, garlic, 1/2 tsp salt, and 1/4 tsp pepper in a small bowl.

2) Each game hen should have the mixture spread over its top and under its skin. Fill the chickens' remaining salt and pepper compartments.

3) Lightly cover the grill rack with cooking oil on a paper towel using long-handled tongs. With a drip pan, get the grill ready for indirect heat.

4) Cook the birds in an indirect oven over medium heat for 45–60 minutes, covered, or until an instant-read thermometer registers 180° and the meat juices flow clear.

Nutrition

1 each: 803 calories, 60g fat 381mg cholesterol, 855mg sodium, 2g carbohydrate (0 sugars, 0 fiber), 60g protein.

215. CLASSIC BARBECUE CHICKEN

Hands-On:30 mins

Total:45 mins

Yield: Serves 8

Ingredients

- canola oil for the grill
- 12 bone-in, skin-on chicken pieces (such as thighs, breasts, and drumsticks; about 4 pounds total)
- kosher salt and black pepper
- ¾ cup of barbecue sauce

Directions

1. Preheat the grill to medium-high heat and set it up for indirect cooking. Once the grill is hot, clean the grate with a wire brush before you begin cooking, lightly oil the grill grate.
2. 1 tsp salt and 1 tsp pepper on the chicken Cover and grill for 30 to 40 minutes over indirect heat, or until an instant-read thermometer inserted in the thickest portion (avoiding the bone) registers 165° F.
3. Preheat the oven to high and place the chicken on top. 3–5 minutes, basting and occasionally turning until thoroughly browned and crispy. (Remove the chicken from the flames if the edges start to burn.)

Nutrition

305 calories; fat 13g; cholesterol 109mg; sodium 631mg; protein 35g; carbohydrates 10g; sugars 7g; iron 2mg; calcium 20mg.

216. HOW TO SMOKE A TURKEY ON THE GRILL

Prep:30 mins

Cook:3 hrs 30 mins

Brine:24 hrs

Total:28 hrs

Ingredients

- 2 quarts (1.9 liters) of apple juice
- 1 pound (450 grams) of brown sugar
- 1 cup of (240 milliliters) kosher salt
- 3 quarts water
- 3 large oranges, quartered
- 4 ounces (115 grams) of fresh ginger, thinly sliced
- 15 whole cloves
- 6 large bay leaves
- 6 cloves garlic
- 1 (12 to 14 pound) turkey
- 1 package of hickory chips
- Vegetable oil for brushing on turkey

Make

1. Gather the required materials.
2. Combine apple juice, brown sugar, and salt in a big pot. Bring to a boil and simmer until all of the sugar and salt have dissolved.
3. Remove any foam that forms on top and allow it to cool.
4. In a large (5-gallon or larger) stockpot or equivalent container, combine the apple juice mixture, 3 quarts of water, oranges, ginger, cloves, bay leaves, and garliCup

5. Remove any fatty deposits from the skin of the turkey as well as anything from the cavity.
6. Place the turkey in the refrigerator for 24 hours after bringing it. Ensure that the turkey is completely submerged at all times.
7. Soak the hickory chips in water and prepare your grill for indirect grilling on medium heat.
8. After taking the turkey from the brine, blot it dry with paper towels.
9. Legs should be twined together, and the turkey should be rubbed lightly with vegetable oil.

10. Preheat the grill to 325 degrees F (165 degrees C). Place the turkey on a roasting rack in a foil pan. On the grill, place away from direct heat.
11. After 30 to 40 minutes, wrap the wings with foil to prevent them from burning.
12. Regularly brush your teeth with vegetable oil. If the breasts start to brown too much, cover them with foil. The smoked turkey is done when the internal temperature in the thigh reaches 175 degrees Fahrenheit (80 degrees Celsius) and the internal temperature in the breast reaches 165 degrees Fahrenheit (75 degrees Celsius). Per pound, it should take 12 to 14 minutes.
13. Remove the steaks from the grill and leave them aside for 15 minutes to rest.
14. Carve and serve the meat.

217. HAPPY ORANGE TURKEY

Prep: 30 min. Bake: 3-3/4 hours + standing

24 servings

Ingredients

- 3 medium oranges
- 1/2 cup of butter, softened
- 1 turkey (14 to 16 pounds)
- 1 tbsp garlic powder
- 1 tsp salt
- 1/2 tsp pepper
- 2 tbsps butter, melted
- 1 small onion, cut into wedges
- 4 fresh rosemary sprigs
- 2 fresh thyme sprigs
- 2 tbsps all-purpose flour
- Turkey-size oven roasting bag
- 1-1/2 cup of Champagne
- 1/2 cup of orange juice

Directions

1) Orange zest should be finely grated. Fruit should be cut into wedges. Orange zest and softened butter are combined in a mixing basin. Gently remove the turkey's skin with your hands, then rub the butter mixture under the skin.

2) Dry the turkey with a paper towel. Garlic powder, salt, and pepper should be used to season the turkeys outside and inside. Over the top, drizzle the melted butter. Fill the cavity with the oranges, onion, rosemary, and thyme. Turkey holes should be impaled, and drumsticks should be tied together.

3) Shake the oven bag to cover the flour inside. In a roasting pan, place the oven bag. Put the turkey in the bag with the breast facing up. Over the bird, pour Champagne and orange juice. Make six 1/2-inch slits on the top of the bag, and then close it with the supplied knot.

4) Set the oven to 325 degrees Fahrenheit, and bake the meat for 3-3/4 to 4-1/4 hours, or until a thermometer inserted in the thickest part of the thigh reads 170°–175°F. To keep warm, put the turkey on a serving plate and wrap it with foil. Give yourself 20 minutes to relax before cutting. Gravy pan drippings can be thickened if necessary.

Nutrition

6 ounces cooked turkey: 374 calories, 19g fat 156mg cholesterol, 238mg sodium, 3g carbohydrate (2g sugars, 0 fiber), 43g protein.

218. SPATCHCOCK SMOKED TURKEY

PREP TIME: 20 mins

COOK TIME: 4 hrs 30 mins

TOTAL TIME: 4 hrs 50 mins

SERVINGS: 10 people

INGREDIENTS

- 1 15-pound turkey (spatchcocked)
- 8 Tbsps salted butter (softened)
- 4 Tbsps olive oil
- 1 tbsp coarse kosher salt
- 1 tbsp coarse black pepper

INSTRUCTIONS

1. Heat up the grill. Preheat your smoker to 275 degrees F with your chosen hardwood. I like to smoke turkeys with pecan, maple, apple, or alder wood. On this turkey, I used almond wood for the first time, and it was amazing!
2. The turkey should be spatchcocked before cooking. Before spatchcocking your turkey, remove any giblets, neck, or other internal components. Flip it from the breast side down and remove the backbone by cutting up both sides with kitchen shears. Snip the inside of the breast bone to flip the turkey. Press the center of the breast down when you hear a break, and the breast is flat on your work surface. The tips of the wings should be tucked under them.
3. Spread butter under the bird's skin. Using your fingertips, separate the skin from the breast and thigh flesh. 2 tbsp. Softened butter, put between the first breast and the skin Press on the outside of the skin to evenly spread the butter throughout the breast. Repeat with the remaining breasts and thighs until the skin of the turkey is thoroughly coated with butter.
4. To taste, add oil, salt, and pepper. Place the turkey breast side down on your work surface. 2 tbsp olive oil drizzled over the top. After spreading the oil all over with your hands, season with salt and black pepper. Turn the turkey over and drizzle with the remaining olive oil. To taste, season the top with salt and black pepper.
5. Cook the spatchcocked turkey in the smoker. Carefully transfer the turkey to the smoker grates, making sure the wings are tucked in, the thighs are turned out, and the turkey is sitting level. Close the cover and smoke for 4 to 4.5 hours, or until an internal thermometer in the thickest part of the breast reads 165°F. Temperatures in the thighs will most likely be higher, about 175-185 degrees Fahrenheit, which is good.
6. Allow the turkey to rest before serving. After gently taking the turkey from the smoker, place it on a wide cutting board. Allow the turkey to rest for 10-15 minutes before slicing.
7. Carve and serve the meat. Remove the thighs and legs first. Remove the limb from the remainder of the body and discard it. Remove the skin of the thighs and tear the meat. Before combining the thigh flesh with the skin, chop it into small pieces. Split and remove the wings with care, then cut them apart at the joints into separate pieces. Cut along the central breast line until you reach the ribs, then turn your knife and cut against the ribs to completely remove the breast. As desired, slice the breast into thick or thin slices. Arrange the carved turkey on the serving platter and garnish it with herbs, if desired. Enjoy!

219. ROASTED THANKSGIVING TURKEY

YIELDS:16 servings

PREP TIME:0 hours 10 mins

COOK TIME:5 hours 0 mins

TOTAL TIME:5 hours 10 mins

Ingredients

- 1 whole turkey (I used a 20-pounder), brined if desired
- 1/2 Cup (1 stick) butter, softened
- 1 whole orange
- 2 whole fresh rosemary sprigs, leaves stripped and minced

- 1 tsp. salt
- 1 tsp. black pepper

Directions

1. Preheat the oven to 275 degrees Fahrenheit (190 degrees Celsius).
2. If your turkey has been brined, rinse it under cold water well. Fill the sink with cold water and soak the turkey for 15 to 20 minutes to remove any saltiness. Set the turkey breast side up on a roasting rack after drying it. Cross the legs and knot them together with kitchen thread. Cover the entire pan with heavy aluminum foil, tucking it beneath the pan. Roast for 10 minutes per pound for the first stage (approximately 3 1/2 hours for a 20-pound turkey).
3. With a vegetable peeler, shave off large chunks of orange peel and slice them very thinly. In a mixing bowl, combine the butter, rosemary, salt, and pepper.
4. When the first stage of cooking is finished, take the turkey from the oven and remove the foil (the turkey will still be pale.) To fully cover the skin, smear the butter mixture all over it, including crevices. Insert a meat thermometer into the thigh and return the bird to the oven, basting every 30 minutes. Preheat the oven to 350 degrees Fahrenheit. Remove the turkey from the oven after it has reached an internal temperature of 165 to 168 degrees Fahrenheit. Cover loosely with clean aluminum foil until ready to cut.

220. ROASTED TURKEY BREAST

yield:8 SERVINGS

prep time:20 MINUTES

cook time:1 HOUR 30 MINUTES

total time:1 HOUR 50 MINUTES

DIRECTIONS:

1. Allow the turkey to come to room temperature for 30 minutes.
2. Preheat the oven to 325 degrees Fahrenheit. Spray or gently oil a 9 x 13 baking dish with nonstick spray. In the baking dish that has been prepared, place lemon slices.
3. In a small bowl, combine the butter, garlic, thyme, sage, and rosemary.
4. Dry the turkey well with paper towels. With your fingertips, gently remove the skin from the breast meat, then pour half of the butter mixture under the skin. Secure the skin over the butter with wooden picks.
5. Place the turkey breast side up on top of the lemon slices. Season the turkey with salt and pepper and the remaining butter mixture to taste.
6. Place the turkey in the oven and bake for 1 hour and 30 minutes, or until it reaches 165 degrees F on the inside.
7. Allow 20 minutes for resting before cutting; if desired, serve warm with gravy.

221. CLASSIC ROAST TURKEY

Prep:20 mins

Cook:3 hrs - 3 hrs and 30 mins

Serves 8 – 10

Ingredients

- 1 onion, quartered
- fresh bay leaves to flavor and serve
- 4.5-5.6kg/10-12 Pounds Bronze turkey, giblets removed
- 1 quantity of stuffing
- 85g butter, softened
- 1 whole nutmeg
- 10 rashers streaky bacon
- glass red wine, such as Merlot
- To serve
- pigs-in-blankets

Method

1. Preheat the oven to 190 degrees Celsius/fan 170 degrees Celsius/gas mark 5 5. Place the onion and a large sprig of a bay in the gap between the legs. Stuff half of the filling into the neck end, pressing it towards the breast. Use skewers to keep the neck skin in place and tie the turkey legs together at the top of the drumsticks to produce a neat shape.
2. Add 20 minutes per kilogram of turkey to the overall cooking time. (You might need to use the bathroom scales.)
3. In a big roasting tray, place the turkey on top of a massive sheet of extra-wide foil. Smear half of the nutmeg over the breast with the butter and season well. Wrap the bacon over the breast, pour the wine over it, and then firmly wrap the foil around it to make a bundle.

4. Roast for 90 minutes, then remove the foil, discard the bacon, and drain any leftover fat from the tin. Return the turkey to the oven with the foil open to brown, basting several times with the juices. 30 minutes before the turkey is done cooking, place pigs-in-blankets and your choice of stuffing around the turkey, or cook in a separate, lightly oiled skillet.
5. To check if the turkey is done, insert a spear into the thickest part of the thigh; the juices should run clear. If they are reddish, cook for another 15 minutes and then test again.
6. Cover the turkey, stuffings, and pigs-in-blankets with foil, then a couple of tea towels, and put aside for up to 30 minutes before carving. This allows the juices to settle back into the turkey, resulting in a juicy bird. Bay springs for Garnish.

222. PERFECT NEW YORK STRIP STEAK

Prep Time5 mins

Cook Time10 mins

Rest time5 mins

Total Time20 mins

INGREDIENTS

- 1 (8 Ounces) New York strip steak 1-inch thick
- ¼ tsp Diamond Crystal kosher salt
- ¼ tsp freshly ground black pepper
- ½ tbsp butter

INSTRUCTIONS

1. Preheat the oven to 500 degrees F.
2. Cook for 5-7 minutes, or until a well-seasoned cast iron pan is blazing hot.
3. Meanwhile, season both sides of the steak with kosher salt and black pepper.
4. Place the meat in a hot skillet. Cook without moving for 2 minutes on each side. This will produce a delectable crust. Cook the flat strip for another 30 seconds.
5. Using oven mitts, transfer the pan to the preheated oven. Cook the steak to medium-rare in 3-4 minutes. Before medium, roast for 4-5 minutes.
6. Remove the steak from the pan and set it aside in a bowl. Wrap it with foil loosely. Allow for 5 minutes of resting time before serving with butter on top.

NUTRITION

Serving: 1steak | Calories: 488kcal | Protein: 66g | Fat: 24g | Sodium: 414mg

223. HOW TO COOK STRIP STEAK

Cook Time15 minutes

Total Time15 minutes

Yield4 servings

Ingredients

- 2 Pounds strip steak (2 steaks about 1 1/2 inches thick)
- olive oil
- sea salt and fresh cracked black pepper
- 4 cloves garlic, peeled and smashed
- 3 Tbsp butter
- pan sauce
- 1/2 cup of red wine (drinking wine, not cooking wine)
- fresh rosemary, minced

Instructions

1) Before cooking, let the steaks rest on the counter for 30 minutes. The meat cooks more evenly when its internal temperature is raised gradually.

2) Olive oil should be used to massage the steaks, and both sides should be seasoned with salt and pepper. Heat up your skillet on high. This method allows you to achieve that gorgeous outside grill sear right on the burner.

3) Put the meat in a hot skillet and let it brown beautifully on its own. Cook the meat for 3–4 minutes on each side, or until it reaches the desired doneness. For a rare steak, cook it to 125 degrees Fahrenheit; for a medium-rare steak, 135 degrees Fahrenheit; for a medium steak, 145 degrees; for a medium-well steak, 155 degrees; and for a well-done steak, 160 degrees.

4) In the same pan, melt the butter and garlic, then baste the meat many times.

5) Place the meat on a dish and cover with foil to rest for 5–10 minutes while you prepare the pan sauce.

6) Slice the meat thinly across the grain.

7) in a saucepan

8) Use wine to deglaze the pan after removing the meat. If you don't want to use alcohol, you may substitute stock or even water, but I find the alcohol to have the nicest flavor. In any case, a significant amount of the alcohol will be burned off while the sauce is simmering.

9) When the sauce has thickened and decreased, stir in the minced rosemary. Before cooking, garlic cloves should be removed. Add salt and pepper to taste, then pour over the steak slices.

Nutrition

Calories: 613kcal | Carbohydrates: 2g | Protein: 47g | Fat: 43g | Cholesterol: 204mg | Sodium: 195mg | Potassium: 763mg | Fiber: 1g | Sugar: 1g | Calcium: 63mg | Iron: 4mg

224. SKILLET BEEF STEW

Prep Time: 15 minutes

Cook Time: 45 minutes

Total Time: 1 hour 5 minutes

Servings: 8

Ingredients

- 1 1/2 Pounds beef stew or beef tips
- 2 carrots
- 6-8 baby potatoes
- 1/2 cup of red wine
- 1 1/2 cup of beef stock
- 2 cloves garlic
- 2 tbsp butter
- 3 tbsp flour
- 1/2 tsp salt
- 1/4 tsp pepper
- olive oil
- 1 tbsp parsley

Instructions

1. Preheat the oven to 425°F (200°C).
2. Carrots should be cleaned, peeled, and finely chopped before being used. Wash the potatoes and cut them in half.
3. Layer carrots and potatoes in a baking pan. To coat, drizzle with olive oil and season with salt and pepper. Roast for about 20 minutes, or until fork-tender. Remove the dish from the oven and place it on a plate to cool.
4. 1 tbsp olive oil and 1 tbsp butter in a large pan (I use cast iron). In the pan, make sure the meat is in a single layer. Season with salt and pepper to taste.
5. The meat should be browned on both sides. When the meat is done, remove it from the pan and set it aside.
6. Reduce the heat to low and melt 1 tbsp of butter in the skillet.
7. There should be around 3 tbsp of fat in the bottom of the pan. Sift the flour and lard together in a large mixing bowl, scraping out any brown pieces from the bottom of the pan.
8. Using a Microplane, grate the garlic into the pan. Cook for 1 minute over low heat, occasionally stirring, with the flour mixture and garliCup
9. Slowly whisk in the wine until it is completely incorporated into the flour mixture. Bring the beef stock to a low boil, stirring constantly.

10. Combine the meat and vegetables in a large mixing basin. Cook, occasionally stirring, until the sauce thickens and all of the ingredients are well cooked.
11. Season with salt, pepper, and parsley, and gently mix to combine. Season to taste with salt and pepper.
12. Serve with a green salad and warm toast.

225. BEEF TEPPANYAKI MADE EASY.

Prep Time: 1 hr

Cook Time: 15 mins

Total Time: 1 hr 15 mins

INGREDIENTS

MARINADE

- 3 tbsps soy sauce
- 2 tbsps sweet cooking wine (Sherry, Marsala) - brandy can also be used
- 1 tbsp garlic powder
- ½ tsp sugar
- 1 tsp ground pepper

FOR FRYING

- 3 tbsp oil
- 1-2 tbsp cooking sweet wine (Sherry, Marsala) - brandy can also be used
- STIR-FRY VEGETABLES
- 2 tbsp oil
- 1 big bell pepper - julienned
- 1 medium carrot - julienned
- 3 stalks of green onions - julienned
- 1 big onion - sliced
- 1 cup of mushroom
- 1 tbsp soy sauce
- 1 tbsp sweet cooking wine -Mirin
- ground pepper

INSTRUCTIONS

1. Make extremely thin slices of the steak, no more than half a centimeter thick.
2. In a mixing bowl, combine all of the marinade ingredients. Combine the meat pieces well. Allow at least an hour for the marinating process.
3. Heat the oil in a frying pan or skillet over medium-high heat. In a skillet, brown the meat pieces. Place the cooked pieces on a plate to serve.

4. Cook for 1-2 minutes, or until the sauce has thickened, in the same pan with the remaining marinade and 1 tbsp wine after the meat has been cooked.
5. Pour the sauce over the cooked meat.

STIR-FRY VEGETABLES

1. 2 tbsp oil, heated over high heat in the same skillet Cook the carrots until they are almost soft. Mix together the remaining vegetables. At this stage, add the soy sauce and cooking wine. Salt & pepper to taste. Along with the meat, serve.

NUTRITION

CALORIES: 268KCALCARBOHYDRATES: 7GPROTEIN: 26GFAT: 14GCHOLESTEROL: 62MGSODIUM: 887MGPOTASSIUM: 435MGFIBER: 1GSUGAR: 3GCALCIUM: 25MGIRON: 2.5MG

---

226. GRILLED TUSCAN STEAK

Cook Time: 10 minutes

Total Time: 12 hours 35 minutes

Yield: serves 2

INGREDIENTS

- 2 1-inch thick steaks of choice (ribeye, strip, sirloin, etCup), about 1 1/2 pounds
- 3 tbsps olive oil
- 1 lemon, zested
- 8 cloves garlic, grated or crushed
- 4 sprigs of fresh rosemary, broken in half
- 1 tbsp dried oregano
- 2 tsp crushed red pepper flake
- 1 tsp ground black pepper
- 2 tsp Kosher salt

INSTRUCTIONS

1. To marinate the steaks, place them in an airtight container or baking dish. Over the top is a mixture of olive oil, lemon zest, garlic, fresh rosemary sprigs, dried oregano, crushed red pepper flake, and powdered black pepper. (Do not season the steaks with salt at this point!) Herbs and spices should be applied to all surfaces of the steaks. Cover with plastic wrap and refrigerate. Marinate for at least 12 hours and as long as two days.
2. Preheat the grill by doing the following: Preheat the grill at roughly 450 degrees Fahrenheit on medium heat. For this dish, I utilized my Weber 22-inch Original Kettle Grill from The Home Depot. Step-by-step directions for lighting a charcoal grill may be found on this page.
3. To cook the steaks, do the following: 30 minutes before grilling, remove the steaks from the refrigerator to allow them to come to room temperature. I normally remove them from the

fridge just before turning on the grill. Allowing time for the steak to warm up is essential since it cooks more evenly at room temperature rather than cold. Before putting the steaks on the grill, wipe them dry with a paper towel and season generously with Kosher salt.

4. Grill the steaks over direct medium heat on a grill. Grill for 2-3 minutes per side for an excellent medium-rare, or until a meat thermometer inserted in the middle of the steak reads 140 degrees F. (Add roughly 1 minute to the grill time on each side for each extra degree of doneness – for example, 3-4 minutes per side for medium, 4-5 minutes per side for medium-well, etCup)

5. Allow for 5-10 minutes of resting time before slicing and serving: Allow 5-10 minutes for the steak to rest before slicing and serving. Enjoy!

227. CAPRESE STEAK

YIELDS:4

PREP TIME:0 HOURS 15 MINS

TOTAL TIME:0 HOURS 30 MINS

INGREDIENTS

- 3/4 Cup balsamic vinegar
- 3 cloves garlic, minced
- 2 tbsp. honey
- 2 tbsp. Extra-virgin olive oil
- 1 tbsp. dried thyme
- 1 tbsp. dried oregano
- 4 (6-Ounces.) filet mignon, or 4 large pieces of sirloin
- 2 beefsteak tomatoes, sliced
- kosher salt4
- slices mOunceszarella
- Fresh basil leaves for serving

DIRECTIONS

1. In a small bowl, combine balsamic vinegar, garlic, honey, olive oil, dried thyme, and dried oregano.
2. Allow 20 minutes for the meat to marinate.
3. Salted and peppered tomatoes are recommended.
4. Preheat your grill to high. Grill the steaks for 4 to 5 minutes on each side, then top with mOunceszarella and tomatoes, then cover for 2 minutes, or until the cheese melts.
5. Sprinkle with basil just before serving.

228. GRILLED RIBEYES WITH HERB BUTTER

Prep: 25 min. + marinating Grill: 10 min.

4 servings

Ingredients

- 1/4 cup of olive oil
- 1/4 cup of dry red wine
- 1 tbsp minced fresh rosemary or 1 tsp dried rosemary, crushed
- 1 tbsp red wine vinegar
- 1 tbsp Dijon mustard
- 1 tsp coarsely ground pepper
- 1 tsp Worcestershire sauce
- 2 garlic cloves, minced
- 4 beef ribeye steaks (3/4 pound each)

Steak seasonings:

- 2 tsp kosher salt
- 1 tsp sugar
- 1 tsp herbes de Provence
- 1 tsp coarsely ground pepper

Herb butter:

- 1/4 cup of butter, softened
- 1 tbsp minced fresh parsley
- 1 tsp prepared horseradish

Directions

1) Combine the first 8 ingredients in a small bowl. To apply sauce, flip the steaks over. Overnight refrigerate covered.

2) Empty the marinade into the trash. Season the steaks with the combined steak spices.

3) Broil 3–4 inches from the flame for 7–10 minutes on each side, covered, over medium heat, or cook until the meat reaches the desired degree of doneness (a thermometer should register 135° for medium-rare, 140° for medium, and 145° for medium-well).

4) To prepare the herb butter, place the butter, parsley, and horseradish in a small mixing basin. On each steak, place 1 tbsp of herb butter.

229. CHILE-SPICED SKIRT STEAK TACOS

Total:35 mins

Yield: Makes 12 tacos

Ingredients

- 2 tsp sweet paprika
- 1 tsp ancho chile powder
- 1 tsp garlic powder
- 1 tsp onion powder
- 1 tsp light brown sugar
- 1/2 tsp chipotle chile powder
- 1/4 tsp ground cumin
- 1/4 tsp ground coriander
- 1 tsp salt
- 1/4 tsp freshly ground pepper
- 1/4 cup of plus 2 tbsps fresh lime juice
- 1 tbsp vegetable oil
- 1 1/2 pounds skirt steak, cut into 5-inch strips
- 12 corn tortillas, warmed
- Pico de Gallo, Avocado Salsa, and shredded cabbage for serving

Directions

1. In a large resealable plastic bag, combine the paprika, ancho powder, garlic powder, onion powder, sugar, chipotle, cumin, coriander, salt, and pepper. To integrate the lime juice and oil, shake the bag. After adding the meat, seal the bag. Allow the steak to come to room temperature for 2 hours.
2. Preheat the grill pan or the grill. Grill the steak for about 10 minutes over moderately high heat, flipping twice, or until lightly browned on the outside and medium-rare within. Allow 10 minutes for the steak to rest on a work surface. After thinly slicing the steak, serve with tortillas, Pico de Gallo, Avocado Salsa, and cabbage.

230. HEIRLOOM TOMATO AND STEAK CAPRESE

YIELDServes 4 to 6

PREP TIME10 minutes

COOK TIME8 minutes to 12 minutes

INGREDIENTS

- For the basil vinaigrette (makes about 1 cup of):
- 1 medium shallot, roughly chopped
- 2 cups of tightly packed fresh basil leaves (stems removed)
- 1 clove garlic
- 1/2 tsp
- red pepper flakes
- 1/2 cup of
- olive oil

- 2 tbsps
- red wine vinegar
- 1 tsp
- kosher salt, plus more as needed
- Freshly cracked black pepper
- For the case:
- 1/4 cup of olive oil
- 1/4 cup of red wine vinegar
- 2 cloves garlic, chopped
- 1 tsp dried basil
- 1 tsp
- dried thyme
- 1 tsp
- dried oregano
- 1 pound hanger or skirt steak
- 2 pounds of heirloom tomatoes, both regular and cherry, halved and quartered
- 1/4 medium red onion, thinly sliced
- 6 ounces of fresh mOunceszarella cheese, torn into bite-size pieces
- Kosher salt and freshly cracked black pepper

INSTRUCTIONS

1) To make the basil vinaigrette, place the shallot, basil, garlic, red pepper flakes, olive oil, red wine vinegar, and salt in a powerful blender. Blend completely smooth for one minute. Add salt and pepper to taste, and then cover and store in the fridge for up to 3 days.

2) Combine the tomatoes, basil, and olive oil in a large mixing basin. Combine the olive oil, vinegar, garlic, basil, thyme, and oregano in a large, nonreactive mixing basin. Pour half of the marinade into another bowl. Place the steak in a bowl and marinate for at least two hours in the fridge. Red onion and tomatoes are combined in the second bowl in the meantime. Remove it from the equation.

3) Set a grill to medium-high heat and get ready to cook. After removing the meat from the marinade, generously season it with salt and pepper. Depending on whether you like your steak medium-rare or medium, place the steak on the grill and cook for 4 to 6 minutes on each side. Ten minutes should be given for the meat to rest on the chopping board.

4) Arrange the tomatoes, red onion, unused marinade, and shredded cheese on a serving plate. Cut the steak against the grain and arrange it in the tomato salad. Drizzle the basil vinaigrette over the dish, and then add salt and pepper as desired. Serve right away.

229. FLANK STEAK WITH GARLIC BUTTER SAUCE

yield: SERVES 6

prep time: 10 MINUTES

cook time: 12 MINUTES

additional time: 3 HOURS 30 MINUTES

total time: 3 HOURS 52 MINUTES

Ingredients

- Flank steak (or skirt, or really whatever cut you like)
- olive oil
- salt and pepper
- 3 garlic cloves
- fresh thyme sprigs
- fresh rosemary sprigs
- Garlic Butter Sauce //
- 1/2 cup of butter
- 4 cloves garlic
- salt
- 1/4 cup of flat-leaf parsley, chopped

Instructions

- Begin marinating your steak a few hours before cooking it. Season to taste with salt and pepper. Drizzle some olive oil over the top and rub the garlic cloves in. Fresh herbs should be used on both the bottom and top of the steak. After covering in plastic wrap, chill for a few hours.
- 30 minutes before cooking, remove the meat from the refrigerator. Over high heat, cook for 4 to 6 minutes on each side.
- After covering the cooked steak in aluminum foil, let it rest for 10 minutes.
- While the steak is resting, start creating the butter sauce. Combine 1/2 cup butter, 4 minced garlic cloves, and a generous pinch of salt in a saucepan. Melt the chocolate over a low heat setting. The garlic will slowly sauté in the butter. Cut the flank steak against the grain as thinly as possible.
- Garnish the steak with garlic butter and chopped parsley.

230. HERB-CRUSTED PORK TENDERLOIN

Prep15 Min

Total1 Hr 5 Min

Servings6

Ingredients

- 2pork tenderloins (about 3/4 Pounds each)

- 1cup of soft bread crumbs (about 1 1/2 slices of bread)
- 1/4cup of chopped fresh parsley
- 2tbsps chopped fresh or 1/2 tsp dried thyme leaves
- 1tbsp olive or vegetable oil
- 1/2tsp salt
- 1/2tsp fennel seed
- 1/4tsp coarsely ground pepper
- 2cloves garlic, finely chopped

Method

- Preheat the oven to 450°F (230°C). Spray the shallow roasting pan and the rack with cooking spray. Place the pork tenderloins on a rack in a pan.
- In a small mixing bowl, combine the remaining ingredients. Evenly spread the herb mixture over the meat. In the thickest part of the pork, insert the tip of an ovenproof meat thermometer. Wrap the pork in foil loosely.
- After 20 minutes of baking, remove the foil. Cover and bake for another 10 to 15 minutes, or until a thermometer registers 155°F. Set aside for 10 to 15 minutes, or until an instant-read thermometer reaches 160°F, covered loosely with foil. (The temperature will rise by about 5°F, making slicing pork easier.)

Nutrition

230 Calories, 8g Total Fat, 28g Protein, 13g Total Carbohydrate, 1g Sugars

231. GRILLED FLANK STEAK GYROS

Hands-On:30 mins

Total:30 mins

Yield: Serves 4

Ingredients

- 1 (1-pound) flank steak
- ½ tsp kosher salt, divided
- ½ tsp garlic powder, divided
- ½ tsp freshly ground black pepper, divided
- Cooking spray
- ½ cup of peeled, shredded cucumber
- 1 (7-ounce) container plain 2% reduced-fat Greek yogurt
- ⅓ cup of vertically sliced red onion
- ⅓ cup of coarsely chopped fresh dill
- 1 tbsp extra-virgin olive oil
- 2 tbsps fresh lemon juice

- 4 (1.5-ounce) flatbread pockets (such as Toufayan SmartPockets)
- 4 (1/4-inch-thick) tomato slices, halved

Directions

1. Preheat the grill or grill pan to medium-high temperature.
2. Sprinkle 1/4 tsp salt, 1/4 tsp garlic powder, and 1/4 tsp pepper evenly over the meat. Cook for 10 minutes, turning after 6 minutes, or until the desired degree of doneness is attained, on a grill rack coated with cooking spray. Allow yourself a 5-minute break. Cut the steak diagonally into thin slices.
3. To remove any extra liquid, wrap the shredded cucumber in paper towels and softly compress. Combine the cucumber, remaining 1/4 tsp salt, remaining 1/4 tsp garlic powder, and remaining 1/4 tsp pepper in a small mixing dish.
4. Toss the onion, dill, oil, and juice in a mixing bowl to coat.
5. Serve with 2 tbsp yogurt mixture, 1/4 cup onion combination, and 1 halved tomato slice in each flatbread pocket.

Nutrition

335 calories; fat 12.2g; protein 34g; carbohydrates 21g; fiber 3g; cholesterol 68mg; iron 2mg; sodium 395mg; calcium 56mg.

232. EASY BEEF AND BROCCOLI

PREP TIME10 mins

COOK TIME10 mins

TOTAL TIME20 mins

Ingredients

- 3 Tbsps cornstarch, divided
- 1 pound flank steak, cut into thin 1-inch pieces
- 1/2 cup of low sodium soy sauce
- 3 Tbsps packed with light brown sugar
- 1 Tbsp minced garlic
- 2 tsp grated fresh ginger
- 2 Tbsps vegetable oil, divided
- 4 cups of small broccoli florets
- 1/2 cup of sliced white onions

Instructions

1) Combine 2 tbsp of cornstarch and 3 tbsp of water in a large mixing dish. Mix the meat in the basin by tossing it in there.

2) Combine the remaining 1 tbsp of cornstarch, soy sauce, brown sugar, garlic, and ginger in another small dish. The sauce is set apart.

3) Set a large sauté pan that is nonstick to medium heat. When the vegetable oil is heated, add 1 tbsp of the steak and fry, often tossing, until the beef is almost cooked through. Transfer the meat to a dish and set it aside using a slotted spoon.

4) Add the broccoli florets and thinly sliced onions to the pan with the remaining 1 tbsp of vegetable oil. Cook for 4 minutes, or until the broccoli is tender, stirring periodically. (For more information, see Kelly's Notes.)

5) Put the meat back in the pan and add the prepared sauce. Stirring regularly, bring the mixture to a boil, then reduce the heat to low and simmer for one minute, or until the sauce has substantially thickened. Serve this recipe with rice or noodles as a side dish.

233. HERB-CRUSTED BEEF TENDERLOIN

Active:10 mins

Stand:1 hr

Bake:50 mins

Rest:30 mins

Total:2 hrs 30 mins

Ingredients

- 1 (4-Pounds.) beef tenderloin, trimmed and tied
- ¼ cup of Dijon mustard
- 2 tbsps mayonnaise
- 1 cup of dry breadcrumbs
- 2 tbsps finely chopped fresh rosemary
- 1 tbsp chopped fresh thyme
- 1 ½ tsp kosher salt
- 1 tsp black pepper
- ½ tsp garlic powder
- 2 tbsps olive oil

Directions

1) Insert a baking sheet coated with aluminum foil inside of an oven-safe wire rack. To dry the meat, pat it with a paper towel. Place on a wire rack and let stand for an hour at room temperature.

2) Set the oven's temperature to 375 degrees Fahrenheit (190 degrees Celsius). Put mayonnaise and mustard in a small mixing basin. In a medium mixing bowl, combine breadcrumbs, rosemary, thyme, salt, pepper, and garlic powder; toss in oil. Apply the mustard concoction to the meat. To completely cover the meat, gently press the breadcrumb mixture onto it.

3) Cook for 45 to 50 minutes in a preheated oven, or until a thermometer placed into the center of the thickest section of the meat reads 120°F. The bowl should be taken out of the oven and set aside for 30 minutes. (While resting, the meat will continue to cook.) Serve beef slices that are 34 to 1 inch thick.

234. THE PERFECT STEAK WITH GARLIC BUTTER

yield:8 SERVINGS

prep time:20 MINUTES

cook time:10 MINUTES

total time:30 MINUTES

INGREDIENTS

- 4 (12-ounce) ribeye steaks*, 1 1/4-inch-thick, at room temperature
- 4 tbsps olive oil
- Kosher salt and freshly ground black pepper, to taste

FOR THE GARLIC COMPOUND BUTTER

- 1/2 cup of unsalted butter, at room temperature
- 1/4 cup of chopped fresh parsley leaves
- 3 cloves garlic, minced
- Zest of 1 lemon
- 1 tsp thyme, chopped
- 1 tsp rosemary, chopped
- 1 tsp basil, chopped
- 1/2 tsp kosher salt
- 1/4 tsp ground black pepper
- Pinch of cayenne pepper

DIRECTIONS

1. To prepare the garlic compound butter, combine butter, parsley, garlic, lemon zest, thyme, rosemary, basil, salt, pepper, and cayenne pepper in a medium mixing bowl. Form a log out of the mixture using parchment paper. Roll out the parchment to a 1 1/2-inch diameter, twisting the ends to seal them. Refrigerate for up to a week before using.

2. In the oven, preheat the broiler. Preheat the oven to 350 degrees Fahrenheit and insert an oven-safe skillet.
3. Using paper towels, dry both sides of the steak. Season with salt and pepper to taste and drizzle with olive oil. After removing the skillet from the oven, heat it over medium-high heat.
4. Heat the steak in the skillet for 1 minute or until a brown crust develops around it. After turning with tongs, cook for another 60 seconds.
5. Cook, flipping once, in the oven until the desired doneness is achieved, about 4-5 minutes for medium-rare. Allow three minutes for relaxation.
6. Serve immediately with garlic compound butter.

235. HOW TO COOK PORK SHOULDER STEAK

prep time:10 MINS

cook time:10 MINS

total time:50 MINS

INGREDIENTS

- 4 12 Ounces pork shoulder steaks
- 1/3 cup of olive oil
- 1 tbsp apple cider vinegar
- 1 tsp salt — could use less if desired
- 1/2 tsp black pepper
- 1 onion — sliced
- 2 tbsp fresh parsley
- 1/2 tsp fresh thyme — optional
- 1 tsp ground cumin
- 1 tsp paprika
- 1.2 tsp oregano

INSTRUCTIONS

1. On a chopping board, cover the steaks in plastic wrap. Pound the flesh with a meat mallet to tenderize and flatten the steaks, being careful not to strike the bones. Trim the fatty regions on the outsides of the steaks.
2. Place in a large zip-top bag or a mixing bowl. In a mixing dish, combine the olive oil, vinegar, and spices. After covering, chill for at least 30 minutes and up to 24 hours.
3. Preheat a gas grill from 450°F to 500°F. Clean the grates by removing them.
4. Cook for 5-6 minutes on each side, or until browned and internal temperature reaches 145 degrees Fahrenheit. I cook it at a higher temperature for a few minutes longer.
5. Allow 3-5 minutes for the meat to rest before serving. Serve.

NUTRITION

Calories: 384, Fat: 27g, Cholesterol: 89mg, Sodium: 649mg, Potassium: 572mg, Carbohydrates: 3g, Sugar: 1g, Protein: 29g, Vitamin A: 445%, Calcium: 28%, Iron: 1.5%

236. GLAZED COUNTRY RIBS

Prep:15 mins

Cook:45 mins

Additional:8 hrs

Total:9 hrs

Servings:6

Yield:6 servings

Ingredients

- ¾ cup of pineapple juice
- ½ cup of vegetable oil
- ½ cup of white wine
- ¼ cup of packed brown sugar
- 1 tbsp Worcestershire sauce
- 6 cloves garlic, minced
- 1 tsp salt
- 1 tsp ground black pepper
- 1 tsp dried rosemary
- 3 pounds of country-style pork ribs

Directions

1. In a medium mixing bowl, combine pineapple juice, vegetable oil, white wine, brown sugar, Worcestershire sauce, garlic, salt, crushed black pepper, and rosemary.
2. Puncture the ribs with a fork many times in a large, shallow dish. Half of the marinade should be poured over the ribs, and the remainder kept aside. Cover and marinate in the refrigerator for 8 hours or overnight, turning once.
3. Preheat an outdoor grill to medium indirect heat and lightly oil the grate.
4. Place the ribs on the prepared grill. Cook for 10 minutes per side, often basting with the remaining marinade. Cook for another 20 minutes, or until the desired doneness is achieved, turning halfway through.

237. TANGY PORK TENDERLOIN

Prep: 10 min. + marinating Grill: 20 min.

6 servings

Ingredients

- 2 pork tenderloins (1 pound each)
- 2/3 cup of honey
- 1/2 cup of Dijon mustard
- 1/4 to 1/2 tsp chili powder
- 1/4 tsp salt

Directions

- Place pork tenderloins in a large resealable plastic bag or a shallow glass container. In a mixing bowl, combine the remaining ingredients; put aside 2/3 cup. Toss the meat with the remaining marinade to coat it. After sealing or covering, chill for at least 4 hours, rotating occasionally.
- Drain the marinade and discard it. Cover and grill pork for 8-9 minutes on each side over indirect medium heat, or until meat juices run clear and a thermometer registers 160°-170°.
- Warm the sauce in a saucepan and serve it alongside the pork.

238. HONEY MUSTARD PORK CHOPS

Prep:10 mins

Cook:20 mins

Total:30 mins

Servings:4

Yield:4 servings

Ingredients

- ¼ cup of honey
- 2 tbsp prepared yellow mustard
- 1 tbsp butter
- 1 ½ pound center-cut boneless pork chops - 1/2-inch thick
- garlic powder, or to taste

Directions

1. Whisk together the honey and mustard in a mixing bowl until smooth.
2. Melt butter in a skillet over medium-high heat and add pork chops. Heat for 3 minutes, or until browned, with half of the garlic powder sprinkled over the chops. Cook for another 3 minutes after flipping the chops and seasoning with the remaining garlic powder.
3. Spray the chops with honey mustard sauce, flip them, and cook for another 5 minutes; turn the chops over and brush the other side with honey mustard sauce. Cook for 5 minutes more, or until chops are no longer pink on the interior and a meat thermometer inserted into the thickest portion of a chop registers 165 degrees F. (75 degrees C).

239. BONELESS PORK CHOPS RECIPE

PREP TIME3 minutes

COOK TIME12 minutes

TOTAL TIME15 minutes

INGREDIENTS

- 15 Ounces. (430 g) center-cut boneless pork chops (3 pork chops)
- salt
- ground black pepper
- 1 tbsp vegetable oil
- 2 tbsp unsalted butter, melted
- 3 cloves garlic, minced
- 1 tsp chopped Italian parsley, for garnishing

HONEY SAUCE:

- 2 1/2 tbsp honey
- 2 tbsp warm water
- 1/4 tsp salt
- 1/2 tsp apple cider vinegar
- 3 dashes of cayenne pepper

INSTRUCTIONS

1) Sprinkle salt and freshly ground black pepper over the pork chops on both sides. Combine all of the components for the honey garlic sauce in a mixing bowl. The ingredients have to be thoroughly blended.

2) Set a cast-iron frying pan over high heat (recommended). 1 tbsp each of butter and vegetable oil. In the same pan as the pork chops, cook for 3–4 minutes on each side or until the surface is browned. Repeat the process when you get to the opposite side.

3) Move the pork chops to the pan's outside edge, then melt the remaining butter in the middle. Cook for 10 seconds, or until the color of the garlic lightens to brown. Cook the honey garlic sauce until it has developed a thicker consistency or an amber-brown hue. Put the pork chops in a bowl and pour the sauce over them. Serve right after being taken off the heat and garnished with parsley.

240. EASY HONEY GARLIC PORK CHOPS RECIPE

PREP:10 MINS

COOK:12 MINS

TOTAL:22 MINS

INGREDIENTS

- 4 pork chops bone-in or out
- Salt and pepper to season
- 1 tsp garlic powder
- 2 tbsps olive oil
- 1 tbsp unsalted butter
- 6 cloves garlic, minced
- 1/4 cup of honey
- 1/4 cup of water (or chicken broth)
- 2 tbsps rice wine vinegar (or apple cider vinegar, or any white vinegar)

INSTRUCTIONS

1) Set the broiler (or grill) on medium-high in the oven. Just before cooking, season the chops with salt, pepper, and garlic powder.

2) In a pan or skillet, heat the oil over medium-high heat until it is hot. The chops should be seared until golden brown and done on both sides (about 4-5 minutes on each side). Put on a mixing bowl.

3. Lower the heat to the medium position. In the same pan, melt butter while scraping out any browned pieces. You should sauté garlic until it is fragrant (about 30 seconds). Honey, water, and vinegar should all be mixed together in a container. Turn up the heat to medium-high and simmer,

stirring regularly, until the sauce has considerably thickened and diminished (approximately 3-4 minutes).

4) Add the pork back to the pan, baste with sauce, and cook for an additional one to two minutes, or until the edges are just starting to brown.

5) Serve over rice, pasta, salad, or vegetables garnished with parsley.

NUTRITION

Calories: 332kcal | Carbohydrates: 15g | Protein: 29g | Fat: 12g | Cholesterol: 104mg | Sodium: 68mg | Potassium: 337mg | Sugar: 14g | Calcium: 18mg | Iron: 0.8mg

241. SLOW COOKER PORK CHILE VERDE

Prep Time10 mins

Cook Time6 hrs

Total Time6 hrs

Ingredients

For the Pork

- 3 tbsps vegetable oil
- 3 pounds boneless pork loin roast, cut into cubes
- 3 carrots, sliced into coins or shredded
- 1 yellow onion, diced
- 6 cloves garlic, minced
- 1 28-Ounces can think of green enchilada sauce
- 1 cup of salsa verde
- 1 4-Ounces can chop green chiles
- ½ tsp salt, or to taste
- fresh ground black pepper, to taste

For Serving

- Prepared rice
- Flour Tortillas, warmed
- Jalapenos, seeded and thinly sliced, for Garnish
- Chopped fresh cilantro to Garnish
- Sour cream, for Garnish
- Lime wedges

Instructions

1) In a large skillet, heat the oil.

2) In the heated oil, cook the pork, carrots, onions, and garlic until golden brown on each side.

3) After removing the pork mixture from the pan, place it in a 6-quart or bigger slow cooker.

4) In a slow cooker, combine the green chiles, enchilada sauce, salsa verde, salt, and pepper. Cover the slow cooker and simmer on LOW for 6 hours, or until the beef is soft and the internal temperature reaches 145°F. Use an instant-read thermometer to check for doneness at the 4-hour mark.

5) Take off the lid, give everything a thorough stir, and add salt and pepper to taste.

6) Allocate 8 to 10 minutes for relaxation time.

7) Garnish with cilantro and jalapenos before serving.

8) Top with sour cream and lime wedges and serve with cooked rice or tortillas.

242. LEMON-OREGANO LAMB CHOPS

Prep:40 mins

Total:40 mins

Ingredients

- 2 tbsps fresh lemon juice
- 1 tsp extra-virgin olive oil
- ½ tsp dried oregano
- 1 garlic clove, minced
- 8 (4-ounce) lamb loin chops, trimmed
- ½ tsp salt
- ¼ tsp freshly ground black pepper
- Cooking spray

Directions

1. Combine the lemon juice, olive oil, oregano, and garlic in a large zip-top plastic bag. To coat the lamb, turn it in the bag. Seal and marinate at room temperature for 15 minutes, turning halfway through.
2. Preheat a grill pan over high heat. Take the lamb out of the marinade and throw it away. Season the lamb to taste with salt and pepper. Using nonstick frying spray, coat the pan. Cook for 3 minutes on each side, or until the desired doneness is achieved.
3. 2 cups orzo, 1/4 cup feta cheese crumbles, 1/4 cup finely chopped red onion, 1/4 cup finely chopped carrot, 3 tbsp chopped fresh flat-leaf parsley, 1 tbsp red wine vinegar, 1 tbsp extra-virgin olive oil, 1/4 tsp salt, and 1/8 tsp black pepper

Nutrition

220 calories; fat 10.4g; protein 28.7g; carbohydrates 1.1g; fiber 0.2g; cholesterol 90mg; iron 2.1mg; sodium 375mg; calcium 23mg.

243. GREEK-STYLE LAMB BURGERS

Servings: Makes 6 burgers

Total Time: 20 Minutes

INGREDIENTS

FOR THE LAMB BURGERS

- 1 slice white bread, crust removed and cut into 1/4-inch pieces
- 2 tbsps milk
- 1/4 cup of finely chopped shallots, from 1 to 2 shallots
- 2 cloves garlic, minced
- 3 tbsps finely chopped fresh mint
- 1 tsp dried oregano
- 3/4 tsp salt
- 1/2 tsp freshly ground black pepper
- 1-1/2 pounds ground lamb (not lean; 80/20 beef may be substituted)
- 6 pita bread rounds (hamburger buns may be substituted)

FOR THE TOPPINGS

- 1 small head of iceberg lettuce, shredded
- 2 tomatoes, thinly sliced
- 1 red onion, thinly sliced
- 6 ounces crumbled feta cheese

INSTRUCTIONS

1. Preheat the grill to high heat.
2. Combine the bread pieces and milk in a medium mixing basin. Mash the ingredients together with a fork until paste forms. Combine the shallots, garlic, mint, oregano, salt, and pepper in a large mixing bowl. Mix in the lamb with your hands until it is evenly distributed. Make 6 oval-shaped beef patties, each approximately 12 inches thick, out of the beef mixture.
3. Grates for grilling should be greased. Cover and Cook for 2 to 4 minutes on the first side, or until well browned. Cook for a few minutes longer on the other side until the burgers are cooked through. Place the burgers in a bowl and cover them with foil while the pita rounds are warming on the grill. Assemble the burgers and serve with the tzatziki sauce and toppings.

244. PAN-FRIED PORK CHOPS WITH HONEY LIME GLAZE

PREP TIME10 mins

COOK TIME20 mins

TOTAL TIME30 mins

Ingredients

Pan-Fried Pork Chops

- 2 Pounds pork loin chops boneless (3 or 4 pork chops)
- ½ tsp salt
- ¼ tsp pepper
- 2 tbsps olive oil
- Honey-Lime Glaze
- 1 lime, freshly squeezed
- ¼ cup of honey
- 3 tbsps balsamic vinegar

Garnish

- 4 thyme sprigs, leaves only
- 1 lime sliced

Instructions

1. Browning pork chops in a pan
2. Season the pork chops on both sides with salt and pepper.
3. Heat the olive oil in a big skillet. Cook the pork chops for 4 minutes on each side over medium-high heat or until golden brown on both sides. Make certain they're completely done. Cook for a few minutes more if they aren't thoroughly cooked. Arrange a serving dish.
4. How to make a honey-lime glaze that's thick and syrupy
5. In the same skillet, combine 1 lime's freshly squeezed juice, honey, and balsamic vinegar. Bring to a boil, continually stirring.
6. Cook for a few minutes, or until the liquid has been reduced by a third or half and a thick glaze has formed.
7. Remove the skillet from the heat. Return the pork chops to the pan once they've been cooked.
8. While the pork chops are still cooking, let the glaze cool in the pan. As the glaze cools, it will thicken, and you can pour it over the pork chops.
9. Serve pork chops with fresh herbs and sliced lime.

245. GRILLED SPICE-RUBBED PORK CHOPS WITH SCALLION-LIME RICE RECIPE

Active:25 mins

Total:25 mins

Yield: Serves 4

Ingredients

- 4 (6-Ounces.) boneless center-cut pork loin chops (about 3/4 inch thick)
- 2 tbsps olive oil, divided
- Spicy Rub, Smoky Rub, or Herb Rub (recipes below)
- 1 ear of fresh corn, shucked
- 1 bunch scallions (6 to 8 scallions), root ends trimmed
- 1 (8.8-Ounces.) pouch pre-cooked microwavable brown rice
- 1 cup of halved multicolored cherry tomatoes
- 2 tbsps fresh lime juice (from 2 limes)
- 1/2 tsp kosher salt
- 1/2 tsp black pepper

Directions

1) Turn the grill's heat to medium-high (400 to 450 degrees Fahrenheit).

2) Spread 1 tbsp of the oil over the pork chops and place them on a baking sheet with a rim or in a shallow dish. Choose a rub and apply it liberally, pushing it into the chops to ensure adhesion. Place the corn and pork chops on a grill grate that has been coated with cooking spray. The pork should be cooked on the grill, covered, for 3 minutes on each side or until a thermometer placed into the center of the meat registers 140°F (the temperature will rise to 145°F while the meat rests off the heat). Turning occasionally, grill corn for 6 to 8 minutes, or until browned and cooked. Remove the chops and corn from the grill.

3) Place the onions on the grate after lightly spraying them with frying spray. Grill, often turning, for 90 seconds or until slightly softened and seared.

4) Cook brown rice according to the instructions on the package. After removing the corn kernels from the cob, place them in a large mixing bowl. To the corn, add scallions that have been thinly chopped into 1-inch pieces. In a mixing dish, combine the rice, tomatoes, lime juice, salt, pepper, and the last tbsp of oil. Alongside the pork chops, serve the rice combination.

246. LAMB CHOPS WITH ROSEMARY AND GARLIC

PREP TIME10 mins

COOK TIME10 mins

MARINATING30 mins

Ingredients

- 1 pound lamb rib chops
- 2 tbsps minced fresh rosemary
- 2 tsp salt
- 1 tsp freshly ground black pepper
- 1 garlic clove, minced
- 4 tbsps extra virgin olive oil, divided

Method

Marinate the lamb chops

1. In a small bowl, combine the rosemary, salt, pepper, garlic, and 2 tbsp of olive oil. With your fingers, coat the lamb chops with the marinade and massage it into the meat. If using double rib chops, cover and put aside at room temperature for 30 to 45 minutes.
2. If you're working with single rib chops and want a unique result, keep them in the rub in the fridge. The thin ribs may quickly overcook if you let them come to room temperature before searing them.
3. The chops can be marinated for up to 24 hours in the fridge. (Let the double rib chops come to room temperature for 30 to 40 minutes before cooking.)

Sear the lamb chops as follows

1. Heat the remaining 2 tbsp of olive oil in an oven-safe sauté pan over high heat. When the oil is shimmering hot, sear the chops. Sear the double rib chops on all sides for 2 to 3 minutes. If you want a rare or medium-rare result, only sear the single rib chops on two sides and for a minute (or less) on each side.

Check for doneness

1. If you want your lamb chops rare, remove them from the pan now.
2. Place the chops in a 400°F oven for 3 to 5 minutes if you want them more cooked, or keep them in the hot pan, bring the heat down to warm, and cover for a few minutes.
3. It's impossible to use a thermometer to verify the inner temperature of rib chops since they're so little and cook so quickly. As a result, I use the finger test to assess whether or not the chops are ready. If using an instant-read thermometer to check thick chops, aim for 125°F for rare, 135°F for medium-rare, and 140°F for medium.

247. PINEAPPLE BACON PORK CHOP

Servings:4

Cook Time:50 minutes

INGREDIENTS

PORK CHOPS

10. 1/2 Smithfield Boneless Loin, cut into 4 chops
11. 2-3 tbl Big Poppa's Sweet Money Championship Rub

PINEAPPLE BACON HASH

- 2 can 20Ounces Dole Pineapple chunks in juice, drained, with 1/3 cup of juice set aside
- 1 Pound Smithfield Bacon, cut into small pieces
- 1/2 Sweet white onion, diced
- 1 pat Salted butter
- 3-4 tbl Granny's BBQ Sauce

PREPARATION

1. Preheat the grill over indirect heat to 350 degrees Fahrenheit (you will be adjusting for direct heat later)
2. Both sides of the chops should be rubbed with Sweet Money Rub.
3. Cook the chops for 10 minutes on the indirect side of the grill, keeping an eye on the internal temperature.
4. After turning, cook for another 10 minutes at 100F internal temperature.
5. While the chops are cooking, make the pineapple bacon hash.
6. After cooking bacon pieces until crispy, set aside to drain on paper towels.
7. Remove most of the bacon oil from the pan, then add a dollop of butter and a pinch of Sweet Money spice to the pineapple pieces and sweet onion. Cook until the sugars have caramelized.
8. Return the bacon to the pan with 1/3 cup of the pineapple juice you preserved.
9. Before the liquids are reduced, pour Granny's BBQ Sauce over the hash.

10. Remove the hash from the skillet, season to taste with Tabasco, and set it aside.
11. Check the internal temperature of the pork chops and remove them when they reach 130 degrees Fahrenheit, then preheat your grill for direct-fire grilling.
12. Sear the chops on both sides until grill marks emerge and internal temperatures hit 145 degrees Fahrenheit when the direct heat for searing is ready.
13. Remove the chops from the grill and lay them aside to rest for a few minutes before topping with the hash and serving!

248. TANGY PORK CHOPS

Prep: 15 min. Cook: 5-1/2 hours

4 servings

Ingredients

- 4 bone-in pork loin chops
- 1/8 tsp pepper
- 2 medium onions, chopped
- 2 celery ribs, chopped
- 1 large green pepper, sliced
- 1 can (14-1/2 ounces) no-salt-added stewed tomatoes
- 1/2 cup of ketchup
- 2 tbsps cider vinegar
- 2 tbsps brown sugar
- 2 tbsps Worcestershire sauce
- 1 tbsp lemon juice
- 1 tsp beef bouillon granules
- 3 tbsps cornstarch
- 2 tbsps cold water
- Hot cooked rice or mashed potatoes

Directions

1) Add the chops to a 3-quart slow cooker after seasoning them with pepper. Combine the tomatoes, onions, celery, and green pepper in a large mixing dish. Over the veggies, add a mixture of ketchup, vinegar, brown sugar, Worcestershire sauce, lemon juice, and bouillon. Cook the beef on low for 5 to 6 hours, or until it is tender.

2) Blend the cornstarch and water until emulsified, then add it to the liquid in the slow cooker. Cook for 30 minutes on high, or until the sauce is thick. If preferred, serve with mashed potatoes or rice.

Nutrition

1 pork chop: 349 calories, 9g fat, 86mg cholesterol, 757mg sodium, 34g carbohydrate (24g sugars, 4g fiber), 32g protein.

249. HERB-CRUSTED PORK TENDERLOIN

Active:25 mins

Total:30 mins

Yield:4

Ingredients

- 6 tsp grapeseed oil, divided
- 1 pork tenderloin, trimmed
- 1 1/2 tsp chopped fresh thyme, plus leaves for Garnish
- 1 1/2 tsp chopped fresh sage

- 1 tsp chopped fresh rosemary
- 1 tsp fine sea salt, divided
- 1/2 tsp black pepper, divided
- 8 ounces mixed wild mushrooms, chopped
- 2 tbsps unsalted butter
- 1 garlic, minced (1 tsp.)
- 1/4 cup of dry white wine
- 1 cup of low-sodium chicken broth
- 1 tbsp all-purpose flour
- 1 red cabbage (about 9 Ounces.), shredded (about 4 cups of)
- 1 1/2 tbsp red wine vinegar
- 1 tbsp honey
- 1 tsp whole-grain mustard

Directions

1) Set the oven to 425°F (200°C) before using it. Spread 2 tbsp of olive oil over the pork; then, in a small dish, combine the thyme, sage, and rosemary with 1/2 tsp of salt and 1/4 tsp of pepper. Massage the herb mixture into the meat to coat it. A large skillet with 1 tbsp oil on high heat. The pork should be seared for 2 minutes total or until both sides are browned. On a baking sheet, roast for 10 to 12 minutes, or until a meat thermometer inserted into the thickest part reads 140°F. Before slicing, let the food lie on a chopping board for five minutes.

2) In the meantime, put the mushrooms in a pan with 1 tbsp of butter that has been heated to medium-high. Cook for 4 to 5 minutes, stirring periodically, or until one side is browned. Cook, often tossing, for 2 to 3 minutes, or until both sides are browned. Sauté until aromatic, approximately 1 minute, with the remaining 1 tbsp butter, 1/2 tsp salt, and 1/4 tsp pepper. Cook while often stirring until the liquid has completely evaporated. In a small basin, whisk together the broth and the flour. Pour the mixture over the mushrooms and simmer for 5 minutes, stirring occasionally, or until the sauce has thickened. Pour into a basin for mixing.

3) In a big pan, heat the last tbsp of oil to medium-high heat. Cook, often tossing, for 3 to 4 minutes, or until somewhat wilted. In a small bowl, combine mustard, vinegar, and honey. Stir the mixture into the cabbage. Add cabbage and a mushroom sauce to the pork before serving.

250. APRICOT LAMB CHOPS

Prep/Total Time: 30 min.

6 servings

Ingredients

- 12 lamb loin chops (1 inch thick)
- 1/4 tsp salt

- 1/4 tsp garlic powder
- 2 tbsps Dijon-mayonnaise blend
- 2 tbsp brown sugar
- 1/2 cup of apricot nectar
- 2 tbsps minced fresh mint
- 2/3 cup of dried apricot halves, cut into 1/4-inch strips

Directions

1. Before serving, season lamb chops with salt and garlic powder. The chops should be rubbed with a Dijon-mayonnaise mixture and dusted with brown sugar on both sides. In a large nonstick pan coated with cooking spray over medium-high heat, brown chops on both sides.
2. Combine the apricot nectar and mint in a mixing bowl. Cook for 12-15 minutes on low heat with the lid on. Toss in some apricots. Cook uncovered for another 5 minutes, or until the meat is done to your taste and the sauce has thickened somewhat. With the lamb, serve the sauce.

251. GARLIC BUTTER PORK CHOPS (THE BEST!)

PREP TIME5 minutes

COOK TIME10 minutes

TOTAL TIME15 minutes

INGREDIENTS

- 1 Pound. (0.4 kg) bone-in pork chops
- Coarse salt
- ground black pepper
- 1 tbsp cooking oil
- 2 tbsps unsalted butter, melted
- 3 sprigs thyme
- 4 cloves garlic, minced
- 1 pinch salt
- Lemon wedges

INSTRUCTIONS

1) Season the pork chops on both sides with salt and freshly ground black pepper.

2) Turn up the heat on a skillet to medium-high. Cooking oil, melted butter, and thyme should all be combined in a mixing basin. The pork chops should be cooked in a hot pan for 3 minutes on each side or until they are light golden brown.

To the same skillet, add the garliCup The garlic should lighten in color as you flip the pork chops and continue to sauté it. To taste, add a little salt. The pork chops should be taken out of the pan and served right away with lemon wedges.

252. BASIC PAPRIKA PORK CHOPS

Prep:5 mins

Cook:10 mins

Total:15 mins

Servings:4 servings

Ingredients

- 4 pork chops
- 1 tsp paprika
- 1 tsp fine sea salt
- 1/2 tsp freshly ground black pepper
- 2 tbsp vegetable or canola oil

Make

1. Dry the pork chops well with paper towels.
2. In a small bowl, combine the paprika, salt, and pepper.
3. Season all of the pork chops with the spice mixture on both sides. Set aside the chops while you ready the pan.
4. A big frying pan should be heated over medium-high heat. When the pan is hot, drizzle in the oil and cook until it shimmers. If the pork chops do not immediately create a magnificent sizzling sound when touched, remove them from the pan and let the pan and oil heat up a bit further. Reduce the heat to medium-low and cook the chops, occasionally stirring, for about 4 minutes, or until they're well-browned and released easily from the pan. Turn around and repeat the process on the other side.
5. Remove the chops from the pan and cover them loosely with foil for 10 minutes. Serve right away.

253. CLASSIC MOROCCAN LAMB OR BEEF KEBABS (BROCHETTES)

Prep:30 mins

Cook:15 mins

Marinating time:2 hrs 30 mins

Total:3 hrs 15 mins

Ingredients

- 2 1/2 pounds beef or lamb (cut into 3/4-inch cubes)
- 1 large onion (finely chopped)
- 3 tbsps fresh parsley (chopped)
- 3 tbsp fresh cilantro (chopped)
- 2 tsp paprika
- 1 tsp cumin
- 1 tsp pepper
- 2 tsp salt (or to taste)
- 1 tbsp vegetable oil
- 1 tbsp lemon juice

Make

1. Gather the required materials.
2. Put the meat in a large mixing bowl.
3. In a large mixing bowl, combine the onion, parsley, cilantro, spices, oil, and lemon juice.
4. With your hands, combine the meat and seasonings, kneading it gently to achieve even distribution.
5. Refrigerate the bowl covered in plastic or aluminum foil for two to three hours to marinate (or overnight)
6. Remove the meat off the wooden skewers and set it aside.
7. Preheat the grill or the broiler to medium-high temperature.
8. Cook the kebabs in batches for five minutes on each side, flipping once or twice, or until done to your preference.
9. To keep the grilled kebabs warm, place them in a bowl and cover them with aluminum foil.
10. Serve with salads, slices of bread, and condiments on the side.

254. LAMB CHOPS WITH GARLIC & HERBS

Prep Time30 mins

Cook Time30 mins

Total Time1 hr

Servings2 Servings

Ingredients

- 2 pounds lamb chops, cut ¾" thick, 4 pieces
- kosher salt for seasoning
- black pepper, for seasoning
- 1 tbsp minced garlic

- 2 tsp chopped rosemary
- 2 tsp chopped thyme
- ½ tsp chopped parsley
- ¼ cup of extra-virgin olive oil, divided

Instructions

1. Season both sides of the lamb chops with salt and pepper.
2. Combine the garlic, rosemary, thyme, parsley, and 2 tbsp of olive oil in a small bowl.
3. After spreading the mixture to both sides of the lamb chops, let them marinate for at least 30 minutes at room temperature.
4. Preheat a large 12-inch frying pan over medium-high heat. Once heated, add 2 tbsp olive oil and the lamb chops.
5. Sear for 2 to 3 minutes, or until browned on top.
6. Cook for 3 to 4 minutes, or until the internal temperature of the beef reaches 125°F (51°C) for medium-rare or 135°F (57°C) for medium.
7. Allow the lamb chops to rest for 10 minutes before serving.

255. CHARRED SQUASH & SPICED LAMB

Prep:15 mins

Cook:25 mins

Ingredients

- 1kg squash, deseeded and sliced into rounds about 1cm thick
- 3 tbsp rapeseed oil
- 1 tsp ground coriander
- 3 tsp ground cumin
- 4 lamb leg steaks, fat trimmed
- 2 tbsp pomegranate molasses
- 2 lemons, juiced
- small bunch of parsley, finely chopped
- 2 tbsp pistachios, toasted and roughly chopped
- 30g pomegranate seeds
- 40g feta, crumbled
- mixed salad leaves to serve

Method

1) Boil the squash for 5 minutes, drain, and then steam-dry it before placing it in a basin. 2 tbsp of oil, cumin, and coriander should all be combined in a mixing bowl.

2) Grill the squash for 8 to 10 minutes on each side, or until it becomes tender and blistered. Cook the lamb for two to three minutes on each side. Slice the chicken thinly after removing it from the

pan. Alternately, cook the lamb and squash over high heat on a griddle pan for the same length of time, flipping once.

3) Arrange the lamb, pomegranate molasses, and lemon juice on top of the squash on a serving plate. The top is garnished with feta cheese, parsley, pistachios, and pomegranate seeds. Separate salad plates should be served.

256. GRIDDLED LAMB WITH SPICED NEW POTATOES

Prep:10 mins

Cook:30 mins

Ingredients

- 1 ½kg new potatoes, halved (or quartered depending on size)
- 2tbsp olive oil
- 1 large garlic clove, crushed
- 2 preserved lemons (we used Belazu), flesh removed, and skin finely chopped
- 1 heaped tsp cumin seeds, crushed
- 8 lamb chops
- bunch mint leaves chopped
- peas or salad, to serve

Method

1. Bring a large pot halfway full of water to a boil with a pinch of salt. Cook until the veggies are soft, about 10-15 minutes. Half of the water should be drained and the other half saved for tomorrow. In the drained pan, add the remaining potatoes, 1 tbsp oil, garlic, preserved lemon, and cumin. Keep yourself warm while you wait for the lamb to cook.
2. With the remaining oil, season the lamb chops. In a heated griddle pan, cook for 3 minutes on each side or until done to your liking. Season the potatoes with salt and pepper, then add the mint just before serving with the grilled lamb and peas or a salad.

257. LAMB CHOPS SIZZLED WITH GARLIC

Active:10 mins

Total:20 mins

Yield:4

Ingredients

- 8 1/2-inch-thick lamb loin chops (about 2 pounds fatty tips trimmed)
- Salt and freshly ground pepper

- dried thyme
- 3 tbsps extra-virgin olive oil
- 10 small garlic cloves (halved)
- 3 tbsps water
- 2 tbsps fresh lemon juice
- 2 tbsp minced parsley
- crushed red pepper

Directions

3. Season the lamb with salt, pepper, and a little dusting of thyme. In a big pan, heat the olive oil until it shimmers. Cook the lamb chops and garlic for 3 minutes over moderately high heat, or until the bottoms of the chops are browned. Cook until the chops and garlic are browned, about 2 minutes longer for medium meat. While moving the chops to plates, leave the garlic in the pan.
4. Cook, scraping up any browned bits from the bottom of the pan, for approximately 1 minute, until the water, lemon juice, parsley, and crushed red pepper are sizzling. Serve the lamb chops with the garlic and pan sauce right away.

258. GARLIC BUTTER LAMB CHOPS

Prep Time: 5 MINS

Cook Time: 12 MINS

Inactive Time: 1 HR 15 MINS

Total Time: 1 HR 32 MINS

INGREDIENTS

- 4 tbsp extra virgin olive oil divided
- 2 tsp minced rosemary
- 2 tsp minced thyme plus more for Garnish
- 1 tsp cumin
- 1 tsp salt
- ½ tsp black pepper
- 8 New Zealand Grass Fed Lamb Chops (from 1 rack), cut into individual ribs
- 4 tbsp unsalted butter divided
- 4 garlic cloves minced and divided

INSTRUCTIONS

1) In a small bowl, combine 3 tbsp oil, rosemary, thyme, cumin, salt, and pepper.

2) Drizzle the herb mixture over the lamb chops in a baking dish.

3) Combine all the ingredients and toss until the chops are well coated.

4) Allow cooling for an hour after covering.

5) Take the chops out of the fridge and give them 15 minutes to come to room temperature.

6) Place the remaining oil in a large pan and heat it over medium-high heat. Sauté one minced clove of garlic for 30 seconds.

7) For about 3 minutes, fry the lamb chops in a pan (this can be done in 2 batches if needed).

8) Sear each chop for one minute on the opposite side. When the meat is medium-done (internal temperature of 130°F after resting), lower the heat to medium and cook for an additional 2 to 3 minutes.

9) Set the chops on a heated tray after taking them out of the skillet.

10) While the chops are resting, clean the skillet and put it back on the heat. Melt the butter in a medium saucepan over medium heat. Until all of the garlic is roasted, sauté for a further 2 to 3 minutes. Add butter to the pan before adding the chops. Turn off the heat under the pan.

11) Drizzle additional garlic butter over the chops on a serving plate.

12) Garnish the chops with fresh thyme before serving.

259. GARLIC AND ROSEMARY GRILLED LAMB CHOPS

Prep Time 15 minutes

Cook Time 10 minutes

Total Time 25 minutes

Ingredients

- 2 pounds lamb loin or rib chops thick cut
- 4 cloves garlic minced
- 1 tbsp fresh rosemary chopped
- 1 1/4 tsp kosher salt
- 1/2 tsp ground black pepper
- zest of 1 lemon
- 1/4 cup of olive oil

Instructions

1. Combine the garlic, rosemary, salt, pepper, lemon zest, and olive oil in a measuring cup.

2. Pour the marinade over the lamb chops and flip them to coat them evenly. Cover the chops and place them in the refrigerator for 1 hour or overnight.
3. 7-10 minutes over medium heat, or until the lamb chops achieve an internal temperature of 135 degrees F.
4. Allow the lamb chops to rest on a bowl covered with aluminum foil for 5 minutes before serving.

260. GRIDDLED LAMB WITH FRESH PESTO, CELERIAC MASH & RATATOUILLE

20 MINS 45 MINS

INGREDIENTS

- Celeriac 350g (12Ounces), peeled and diced
- Lemon juice 3 tsp
- Salt and freshly ground black pepper
- Olive oil 4 tbsp
- Red onion 1 small, peeled and sliced
- Fennel 1 small head, cored and thinly sliced
- Courgette 1 small, trimmed, and thinly sliced
- Baby plum or cherry tomatoes 4, halved
- Chopped basil 4 tbsp
- Chopped mint 4 tbsp
- Garlic 1 clove, peeled and crushed
- Pine nuts 1 tbsp, toasted
- Lamb steaks or chops 2, or 4 if small
- Butter 15g (½Ounces)
- Nutmeg grated

INSTRUCTIONS

1) To prepare the mash, put the celeriac in a pan with 1 tsp of lemon juice, add cold water, and season with salt. Bring to a boil, lower the heat, and simmer for an additional 20 to 25 minutes, or until the potatoes are tender.

2) Prepare the ratatouille in the meanwhile. A frying pan with one tbsp of oil on medium heat. The onion should be cooked for 5 minutes or until soft. Cook the fennel and courgette for approximately 15 minutes, stirring regularly, until they are just beginning to soften. After taking the pan off the heat, season it with salt and pepper as desired.

3) To prepare the pesto, mix the herbs, garlic, pine nuts, remaining lemon juice, and 2 tbsp of oil in a mixing bowl. Use salt and pepper to taste to season.

4) Heat a griddle or frying pan to high heat before cooking the lamb. Fry the remaining food in the oil for 2 minutes on each side, then turn the heat down to low and continue cooking for an additional 3 to 4 minutes on each side.

5) After the celeriac has softened, drain it and place it back in the pan over low heat to finish drying. Well, incorporate the butter. Add nutmeg, salt, and pepper to taste.

6) Distribute the mashed potatoes, ratatouille, and pesto on heated plates.

261. GREEK BUTTERFLIED LAMB LEG

Prep: 5 mins

Cook: 25 mins

Ingredients

MARINADE

- 1 tbsp dried oregano
- 3 large garlic cloves, minced using a garlic press
- 2 tsp salt
- 1 tsp black pepper
- 1/3 cup of fresh lemon juice
- 1 tbsp zest (= zest of 1 lemon)
- 1/2 cup of olive oil

FOR COOKING

- 1 tbsp oil (for brushing BBQ or for stove sear)

SERVING OPTIONS

- Lemon, for Garnish
- Oregano leaves, optional Garnish as pictured
- Flatbreads or store-bought pita bread
- Greek Salad
- Tzatziki (use recipe in Gryos) or just use plain yogurt
- More ideas are listed in the post

Instructions

1. Combine the marinade ingredients in a large ziplock bag.
2. Add the lamb to the bag and knead it well to ensure that the marinade gets into all of the meat's cracks and crevices.
3. In a sealed bag, marinate for 24 hours (3 hours minimum).
4. Remove the lamb from the fridge 1 hour before cooking (to take the fridge chill out for more even cooking).

264. LAMB KOFTA MEATBALLS IN CURRY SAUCE

SERVES4

PREP TIME 15MINS

COOK TIME 20MINS

INGREDIENTS

- Juice & finely grated zest of 1 lemon
- 1/4 cup of (60ml) olive oil
- 1 white onion, thinly sliced
- 500g lean lamb mince
- 1 brown onion, coarsely grated
- 2 garlic cloves, crushed
- 1/3 cup of (25g) fresh white breadcrumbs
- 1/4 cup of coriander leaves, chopped, plus extra leaves to garnish
- 1/4 cup of mint leaves, chopped
- 1/3 cup of (100g) korma curry paste
- 1 tbs finely chopped ginger
- 400g can of chopped tomatoes
- 400ml can of coconut milk
- 1 cinnamon quill
- 1 telegraph cucumber, roughly chopped
- Pappadams, to serve

METHOD

1) One tbsp each of oil and lemon juice The sliced onion should be taken out of the pan and kept aside.

2) In a mixing bowl, combine the mince, grated onion, garlic, zest, breadcrumbs, and herbs. Add the salt and pepper, then mix everything together. After washing your hands with cold water, form the mixture into 16 little balls with wet palms.

3) Set a deep nonstick frypan to medium heat to preheat. When the oil is heated, add the meatballs and cook, turning them over occasionally, for 4–5 minutes, or until both sides are attractively browned. Place a plate for cooling.

4) After adding the curry paste and ginger, go back to the stove, add the last 1 tbsp of oil, and stir continuously for 1 minute. Combine the tomato, coconut milk, and cinnamon in a mixing bowl. When it boils, season to taste, turn the heat down to low, and let it simmer for three minutes. Once

the sauce has decreased and the meatballs are well cooked, add the meatballs back to the pan and simmer for an additional 10 minutes.

5) After incorporating the cucumber into the white onion combination, season with salt and pepper.

6) To assemble the meal, divide the meatballs and sauce among four bowls and top with fresh coriander. Serve with cucumber and onion salad and pappadams.

265. CLASSIC RACK OF LAMB

PREP TIME10 mins

COOK TIME25 mins

MARINATING TIME90 mins

TOTAL TIME2 hrs 5 mins

Ingredients

- 1 or more Frenched lamb rib racks with 7 to 8 ribs each (1 1/4 to 2 pounds for each rack)
- For each rib rack:
- 2 tsp chopped fresh rosemary
- 1 tsp chopped fresh thyme
- 2 cloves garlic, minced
- Salt
- Freshly ground black pepper.
- 2 tbsps extra virgin olive oil

Method

Marinate the lamb

1. Rub the rib racks with the rosemary, thyme, and garlic mixture. To taste, season with salt and freshly ground black pepper. Fill a big plastic bag halfway with olive oil.
2. Slather the lamb rack(s) with oil all over with your hands. After squeezing out as much air as possible, seal the bag. To catch any leaks, fill a container halfway with water.
3. While the lamb gets to room temperature in the next step, marinate overnight in the refrigerator or for 1 1/2 to 2 hours at room temperature.

Bring lamb to room temp.

1. To let the lamb get to room temperature, remove it from the fridge 1 1/2 to 2 hours before cooking. If the meat is not at room temperature before cooking, it will not cook evenly, and the inside may stay raw while the outside is cooked.

2. Preheat the oven to 450°F. Arrange the oven rack so that the lamb is in the center of the oven.
3. Season the fat with salt and pepper, cover the bones in foil, and place them fat side up in the pan:
4. To score the fat, cut shallow, pointed cuts into it, spaced approximately an inch apart.
5. The rack should be rubbed with more salt and pepper. On a foil-lined roasting pan, place the bone side down (fat side up) lamb rack. To keep the exposed rib bones from burning, wrap them with foil.
6. To brown, roast for a few minutes over high heat, then reduce the heat to finish:
7. Preheat the oven to 450°F and roast the roast for 10 minutes (or more if cooking several racks), or until thoroughly browned.
8. Reduce the temperature to 300 degrees F. Cook for 10 to 20 minutes more (depending on the size of the lamb rack, if you are roasting more than one rack, and how rare or well done you want your lamb). When inserted into the thickest part of the meat, a meat thermometer should read 125°F for rare and 135°F for medium-rare.
9. Check the temperature of the meat with a meat thermometer. A multitude of factors influence cooking time, including the shape of the roast, fat marbling, and the characteristics of the oven. This roast is just too lovely and delicate to be overcooked.

10. Allow the roast to rest for 15 minutes before serving:
11. Cover and leave aside for 15 minutes after removing from the oven.
12. Separate the lamb chops off the rack by slicing between the bones. Serve 2-3 chops per person.

266. GREEK LAMB CHOPS WITH TZATZIKI

Prep Time: 10 minutes

Cook Time: 15 minutes

Total Time: 25 minutes

Ingredients

- 1 kg lamb chops
- ½ cup of olive oil
- 1/3 cup of fresh lemon juice
- 3 tsp dried oregano
- 2 t chopped rosemary
- 4 garlic cloves minced
- salt and pepper to taste
- Tzatziki to serve

Instructions

1) In a big mixing basin, combine all the marinade ingredients.

2) Give the lamb chops at least 10 minutes to marinate in the marinade (a few hours is preferable).

3) On a grill or griddle, cook the lamb chops until the exterior is caramelized and the inside is pink. To ensure that the fat renders and turns crisp and brown, position the lamb chops so that the fat side is up.

4) Allow the meat to settle for five minutes before serving with tzatziki.

Nutrition

Calories: 368kcal | Carbohydrates: 1g | Protein: 33g | Fat: 24g | Cholesterol: 110mg | Sodium: 120mg | Potassium: 468mg | Calcium: 32mg | Iron: 3.1mg

267. PEPPERCORN GARLIC PORK CHOPS

Cook Time:30 minutes

Total Time:30 minutes

Ingredients

- 4 pork chops (approximately 8 ounces each)
- 1 Tbsp garlic powder
- 2 tsp fresh cracked black peppercorns (or coarse ground black pepper)
- 1/4 tsp salt
- 2 Tbsps vegetable oil

Instructions

1. In a large, deep skillet, heat the oil over medium-high heat.
2. On both sides of the pork chops, season with garlic powder, salt, and black pepper.
3. Once the oil is hot, add the pork chops. Cook for 3 minutes, or until golden brown.
4. Cook for 3 minutes on the other side, or until the pork chops achieve an internal temperature of at least 145 degrees Fahrenheit. Make sure the bowl isn't overcooked.
5. The pork chops should be removed from the pan. Cover and place in the refrigerator until ready to serve.
6. In a mixing bowl, add the following ingredients to make the sauce. Reduce the heat to a medium setting. Warm up the remainder of the oil in the same skillet. (Remove anything that seems to be burned first, but leave everything else in the pan!)
7. Cook for 30 seconds, or until the garlic and black pepper have released their aromas.
8. Cook, stirring periodically, until the sauce thickens, about 7 minutes after adding the liquid and thyme. Scrape up any bits that have stuck to the bottom of the pan and toss them into the sauce.
9. Pour in the vinegar and whisk it around. If necessary, season with additional salt and black pepper. Add extra water or stock if the sauce is too thick.

Nutrition

Serving: 1chop | Calories: 368kcal | Carbohydrates: 6g | Protein: 31g | Fat: 24g | Cholesterol: 92mg | Sodium: 298mg | Potassium: 631mg | Fiber: 1g | Sugar: 1g |Calcium: 27mg | Iron: 1mg

268. CAPRESE STEAK

YIELDS:4

PREP TIME:0 HOURS 15 MINS

TOTAL TIME:0 HOURS 30 MINS

INGREDIENTS

- 3/4 Cup balsamic vinegar
- 3 cloves garlic, minced
- 2 tbsp. honey
- 2 tbsp. Extra-virgin olive oil
- 1 tbsp. dried thyme
- 1 tbsp. dried oregano
- 4 (6-Ounces.) filet mignon, or 4 large pieces of sirloin
- 2 beefsteak tomatoes, sliced
- kosher salt4
- slices mOunceszarella
- Fresh basil leaves

DIRECTIONS

1. In a small mixing bowl, combine balsamic vinegar, garlic, honey, olive oil, dried thyme, and dried oregano.
2. Allow 20 minutes for the steak to marinate.
3. Salted and peppered tomatoes are a must.
4. Set the grill to high. Grill the steaks for 4 to 5 minutes on each side, then sprinkle with mOunceszarella and tomatoes, cover, and cook for another 2 minutes, or until the cheese has melted.
5. Toss with basil just before serving.

269. COFFEE-CRUSTED BEEF TENDERLOIN STEAK

Prep:10 mins

Cook:10 mins

Additional:35 mins

Total:55 mins

Ingredients

- ¼ cup of finely ground espresso beans
- 3 tbsps brown sugar
- 2 tsp ground cinnamon
- 1 pinch of ground cayenne pepper
- salt and ground black pepper to taste
- 2 (6 ounces) beef tenderloin steaks
- 1 tbsp canola oil

Directions

1) In a mixing bowl, combine the ground espresso beans with brown sugar, cinnamon, cayenne, salt, and black pepper. Each steak should have the espresso mixture applied on both sides. Place the steaks on a tray and chill for 30 minutes to allow the flavors to meld.

2) Set the oven to 200 degrees Celsius (400 degrees Fahrenheit) (200 degrees C).

3. Heat the canola oil in a large oven-safe pan over medium-high heat. For 1 1/2 to 2 minutes, or until the bottoms of the steaks are browned, cook the steaks in the hot oil. Place the pan in the preheated oven after rotating the steaks.

4) Bake the steaks in the preheated oven for 4 to 5 minutes, or until medium-rare. 140 degrees Fahrenheit should be shown on an instant-read thermometer in the room's middle (60 degrees C). Allow the steaks to rest for at least 5 minutes after removing them from the skillet using a tent made of aluminum foil.

270.LEMON GARLIC ROASTED ARTICHOKES

PREP TIME5 minutes

COOK TIME1 hour

TOTAL TIME1 hour 5 minutes

Ingredients

- 4 globe artichokes
- 1 lemon
- 8 cloves garlic
- 2 tbsp olive oil

Instructions

1. Set the oven to 400°F.
2. Cut the stem and the top third of the artichoke off. Place two garlic cloves in the center of each artichoke after slightly separating the top leaves.
3. The artichokes should be placed on top of a sheet of aluminum foil in a baking pan before baking.
4. Lemon juice should be squeezed over artichokes.
5. 12 tbsp of olive oil per artichoke should be drizzled over the top.
6. Artichokes should be baked for approximately an hour or until an outside leaf may be removed with ease. As cooking times might vary, check to make sure it hasn't burned after around 45 minutes.
7. Use your teeth to scrape the "meat" off of the leaves after dipping them in melted butter or another dipping sauce. Using a spoon, remove the heart's hairy portion once all the leaves have been taken off. Rinse the heart well before eating.

Nutrition Information:

CALORIES: 138TOTAL FAT: 7gCHOLESTEROL: 0mgSODIUM: 74mgCARBOHYDRATES: 18gFIBER: 8gSUGAR: 2gPROTEIN: 4g

271. PARMESAN GREEN BEANS

total Time: 20 minutes

Yield: 4 servings

INGREDIENTS

- 1 Pounds fresh green beans, trimmed
- 1 Tbsp extra virgin olive oil
- 2 Tbsp grated Parmesan cheese
- 1/2 tsp salt
- 1/2 tsp freshly ground black pepper

INSTRUCTIONS

1. Set the oven to 400 °F.
2. Put parchment paper on a baking pan and set it aside.
3. Combine green beans and olive oil in a big bowl. Toss one more after adding cheese, salt, and pepper.
4. On the baking sheet, arrange the green beans in a single layer. Bake for 10 to 15 minutes, or until the edges are just beginning to brown. Serve hot.

272.MUSHROOM STIR-FRY

Prep:25 mins

Cook:15 mins

Total:40 mins

Servings:4

Ingredients

Sauce:

- 3 tbsp soy sauce
- 2 tbsp rice wine vinegar
- 1 tbsp sesame oil
- 2 tsps honey
- 2 tsps cornstarch
- 1 tsp Sriracha sauce

Stir Fry:

- 6 green onions
- 2 tbsp peanut oil
- 2 stalks of celery, thinly sliced diagonally
- 1 medium onion, cut into 1/2-inch wedges
- ¾ pound shiitake mushrooms, trimmed and cut into 1/4-inch slices
- ¼ pound beech mushrooms, trimmed
- ¼ pound enoki mushrooms, trimmed
- 2 cloves garlic, minced
- 1 tsp freshly grated ginger

Directions

1. In a small bowl, combine the Sriracha, soy sauce, rice wine vinegar, sesame oil, honey, and cornstarch; leave aside.
2. Green onions should be chopped into 2-inch chunks with the white and green sections kept apart.
3. A big wok with high heat is heating up with peanut oil. Stir-fry the celery and onion wedges for 3 to 4 minutes while continuously stirring. Stir continuously for 3 to 4 minutes after adding the white portions of the green onions, beech mushrooms, and shiitake mushrooms. Stir-fry for 2 more minutes while adding the enoki mushrooms, green portions of the green onions, garlic, and ginger.

4. Place the veggies in the pan on one side. After combining the sauce's components, pour the sauce into the wok. Stir into the veggies, then heat for about a minute to let the sauce thicken. Serve right after removing from heat.

Nutrition Facts

189 calories; protein 5.2g; carbohydrates 18.5g; fat 10.5g; sodium 775.5mg.

273.THE EASIEST VEGETABLE STIR FRY

PREP TIME10 MINUTES

COOK TIME5 MINUTES

TOTAL TIME15 MINUTES

Ingredients

- 1 tbsp olive oil
- 1 red bell pepper sliced
- 1 yellow bell pepper sliced
- 1 cup sugar snap peas
- 1 cup carrots sliced
- 1 cup mushrooms sliced
- 2 cups broccoli
- 1 cup of baby corn
- 1/2 cup water chestnuts
- ¼ cup soy sauce
- 3 garlic cloves minced
- 3 Tbsp brown sugar
- 1 tsp sesame oil
- 1/2 cup chicken broth
- 1 tbsp cornstarch
- chopped green onions and sesame seeds for garnish optional

Instructions

1. Over medium-high heat, add 1 Tbsp olive oil to a wok or big pan. Bell pepper, peas, carrots, mushrooms, broccoli, baby corn, and water chestnuts should all be included. Cook vegetables for 2 to 3 minutes, or until almost soft.
2. Combine soy sauce, garlic, brown sugar, sesame oil, chicken broth, and cornstarch in a small whisk.
3. Cook until the sauce has thickened, then pour over the vegetables. If desired, garnish with sesame seeds and finely chopped green onions.

274.EASY FRIED RICE

PREP TIME15 MINUTES

COOK TIME20 MINUTES

TOTAL TIME35 MINUTES

Ingredients

- 3 cups cooked rice
- 2 Tbs sesame oil
- 1 small white onion chopped
- 1 cup fr0uncesen peas and carrots thawed
- 2-3 Tbsp soy sauce, more or less to taste
- 2 eggs lightly beaten
- 2 Tbsp chopped green onions optional

Instructions

1. A big skillet or wok should be heated to medium. Fill the bottom with sesame oil. Fry the carrots, peas, and white onion until they are soft.
2. Pour the beaten eggs onto the opposite side, then slide the onion, peas, and carrots to the side. Eggs should be scrambled using a spatula. Combine the cooked eggs with the veggie mixture.
3. To the vegetable and egg mixture, including the rice. On top, add the soy sauce. The rice and vegetable combination should be stir-fried and cooked thoroughly. If desired, include finely sliced green onions.

275.EASY GARLIC PARMESAN ZUCCHINI NOODLES (ZOODLES)

PREP TIME: 5 mins

COOK TIME: 2 mins

TOTAL TIME: 7 mins

INGREDIENTS

- 1 tbsp olive oil
- 2 garlic cloves, minced
- 2 medium zucchini
- 2 tbsp parmesan, grated
- salt and pepper, to taste

INSTRUCTIONS

1. Slice the zucchini in half, then put it in your spiralizer. Spiralize zucchini and produce noodles.
2. On medium heat, warm the oil in a big pan. Sauté the garlic for 30 seconds after adding it.
3. After one minute of tossing and warming the zucchini noodles, remove them from the fire.
4. Give them one more toss in the pan, then season with salt & pepper and the grated parmesan.

NUTRITION

CALORIES: 119kcal, CARBOHYDRATES: 7g, PROTEIN: 4g, FAT: 8g, CHOLESTEROL: 3mg, SODIUM: 96mg, POTASSIUM: 511mg, FIBER: 1g, SUGAR: 4g, CALCIUM: 96mg, IRON: 0.7mg

276.SAUTEED GARDEN FRESH GREEN BEANS

Prep:5 mins

Cook:5 mins

Total:10 mins

Servings:4

Ingredients

- 1 ½ tbsp olive oil
- ¾ pound fresh green beans, trimmed
- ½ tsp onion salt
- ½ tsp garlic salt

- ½ tsp garlic powder
- freshly ground pepper to taste

Directions

1. Heat olive oil in a skillet over medium heat; cook and stir green beans, onion salt, garlic salt, garlic powder, and black pepper together until desired tenderness is reached 5 to 10 minutes.

277.4-INGREDIENT BABY BOK CHOY STIR FRY

Prep Time: 10 MINUTES

Cook Time: 5 MINUTES

Total Time: 15 MINUTES

Ingredients

- 18 Ounces (500 g) baby bok choy
- 1 tbsp peanut oil (or vegetable oil)
- 2 tbsp light soy sauce (or soy sauce)
- 1 tsp sugar
- 2 tbsp garlic, minced
- Toasted sesame seeds for garnish (Optional)

Instructions

1. Baby bok choy should be rinsed. Remove the rough ends by tearing apart the big leaves (see the blog post above for more detailed instructions and pictures). Drain in a strainer after washing well to get rid of any dirt stuck between the leaves.
2. In a large skillet (carbon steel or nonstick), heat 1 tbsp of oil until hot. Stir the garlic a few times till aromatic after adding it.
3. Baby bok choy should be added, stirred, and cooked for 1–2 minutes until well-coated with oil.
4. After stirring in the light soy sauce, add the sugar. To blend the sauce, give it a few stirs.
5. Cover and turn the heat down to medium. The baby bok choy should be cooked for 30 to 1 second until it becomes soft but not mushy. In the meanwhile, you can open the pan to check on the development.
6. Open the pan's lid. Taste the young bok choy thoroughly. Allow it to simmer for a further 30 to 60 seconds to absorb the sauce. When the young bok choy is finished, turn off the heat and quickly move it to a serving platter. If using, top with toasted sesame seeds.
7. Give as a hot side salad.

Nutrition

Serving: 1serving, Calories: 59kcal, Carbohydrates: 5.2g, Protein: 2.7g, Fat: 3.7g, Sodium: 314mg, Potassium: 338mg, Fiber: 1.4g, Sugar: 2.6g, Calcium: 142mg, Iron: 1mg

278.SAUTEED VEGETABLES

Prep10 minutes

Cook10 minutes

Ready in: 20 minutes

Ingredients

- 3 Tbsp olive oil
- 1 medium red bell pepper, chopped
- 2 medium carrots, peeled and sliced fairly thin (1 cup)
- 1/2 medium red onion, chopped (1 cup)
- 2 1/2 cups broccoli florets (cut into bite-size pieces)
- 1 medium yellow squash, thick portion halved, all sliced
- 1 1/2 tsp minced garlic
- 1 1/2 tsp fresh thyme leaves
- Salt and freshly ground black pepper
- 2 Tbsp chopped fresh parsley
- 1 1/2 tsp fresh lemon juice
- 1/4 cup grated parmesan cheese, optional, for serving

Instructions

1. In a 12-inch skillet set over medium-high heat, heat the olive oil.
2. Add broccoli, bell pepper, carrots, and onion. 4 minutes of sauteing (toss just occasionally so it can brown slightly).
3. Add squash and cook for 3 minutes.
4. Add the thyme, garlic, and salt & pepper to taste. 2 minutes of sautéing or until vegetables are barely soft.
5. Add parsley and lemon juice, then toss. If preferred, top the bowl with parmesan.

279.SUPER EASY STIR-FRIED CABBAGE

Prep:10 mins

Cook:5 mins

Total:15 mins

Servings:4

Ingredients

- 1 tbsp vegetable oil
- 2 cloves garlic, minced
- 1 pound shredded cabbage
- 1 tbsp soy sauce
- 1 tbsp Chinese cooking wine (Shaoxing wine)

Directions

1. In a wok or sizable skillet, heat the vegetable oil over medium heat. Garlic is added and cooked for a little while until it starts to brown. Once the cabbage is covered with oil, add it and stir, then cover the pan and simmer for one minute. Add the soy sauce, stir, and simmer for one additional minute. Stir in the Chinese cooking wine after turning the heat up to high. For an additional 2 minutes, cook and toss the cabbage until it is soft.

Nutrition Facts

65 calories; protein 1.8g; carbohydrates 7.4g; fat 3.5g; sodium 269.9mg.

280.PINEAPPLE FRIED RICE

Prep:10 mins

Cook:10 mins

Ingredients

- 1½ tbsp sunflower or vegetable oil
- 2 eggs, beaten
- 2 garlic cloves, crushed
- small bunch of spring onions, chopped
- 1/2 tsp Chinese five-spice powder
- 400g cooked long-grain rice
- 85g frOuncesen peas
- 2 tsp sesame oil
- 2 tbsp low-salt soy sauce
- 400g fresh pineapple, roughly chopped into chunks (about 1/2 medium pineapple)

Method

1. 1 In a wok, heat 1 tbsp of oil. To produce a thin omelet, pour in the eggs and swirl them up the edges. After the omelet has finished cooking, roll it up onto a cutting board and cut it into ribbons.
2. The leftover oil is heated. Add the five-spice, onions, and garliCup Add the rice, peas, sesame oil, and soy after stirring until sizzling (if using pouches, press the first to separate the grains). Stir in the pineapple and omelet ribbons after the rice is cooked from high heat cooking.

281.EASY BAKED ZUCCHINI

PREP TIME5 minutes

COOK TIME10 minutes

TOTAL TIME15 minutes

Ingredients

- 2 medium zucchini sliced into ½" rounds
- 1 tbsp olive oil
- ½ tsp Italian seasoning
- salt & pepper to taste
- ⅓ cup parmesan cheese

Instructions

1. Set the oven to 425 °F.
2. Slices of zucchini are mixed with a little over 2 tbsp of parmesan cheese, olive oil, seasoning, salt, and pepper.
3. Add the remaining parmesan cheese and place on a baking pan. 5 minutes of baking.
4. Then broil for 3–5 minutes, or until the cheese is melted and the zucchini is soft but still crunchy.

NUTRITION INFORMATION

Calories: 80, Carbohydrates: 3g, Protein: 4g, Fat: 5g, Cholesterol: 5mg, Sodium: 141mg, Potassium: 255mg, Fiber: 1g, Sugar: 2g,Calcium: 118mg, Iron: 0.5mg

282. GREEN BEANS AND BACON

Total: 35 min

Prep: 15 min

Cook: 20 min

Ingredients

- 2 1/2 pounds of green beans, trimmed
- Kosher salt
- 1/2 pound bacon, roughly chopped
- 1 small yellow onion, finely chopped
- 3 cloves garlic, minced
- 1 tsp red pepper flakes
- 1/2 cup chopped toasted pecans
- Juice of 1/2 lemon
- Freshly ground pepper

Directions

1. Green beans should be cooked for about 5 minutes until they are crisp-tender and bright green in color. Place them in a big saucepan of salted boiling water. To stop the cooking, drain the beans and shock them in a big bowl of icy water. Re-drain the beans, then pat them dry.

2. In a sizable, heavy saute pan, cook the bacon for approximately 5 minutes or until it is crisp. Transfer the bacon to a dish covered with paper towels to drain. Remove any extra bacon oil with a spoon, leaving 2 tbsp in the pan. Add the onion to the pan and cook for 4 to 5 minutes, or until very soft and tender. Add the red pepper flakes and garlic, and cook for a further minute or so until they are barely fragrant. Cook for another 5 to 6 minutes, or until the

pecans and saved green beans are fully cooked. Bring the bacon back to the pan, add the lemon juice, and stir. Add salt and pepper to taste.

283.MESA GRILL POTATO SALAD

Total: 50 min

Prep: 20 min

Inactive: 10 min

Cook: 20 min

Ingredients

- 3 pounds of new potatoes
- Kosher salt
- 1 cup prepared mayonnaise
- 2 tbsp Dijon mustard
- 2 tbsp fresh lime juice
- 2 tbsp ancho chili powder
- 1/2 tsp cayenne powder
- Freshly ground black pepper
- 3 scallions, white and green parts, chopped
- 1 large ripe beefsteak tomato, seeded and chopped
- 1 jalapeno, finely diced
- 1 medium red onion, halved and thinly sliced
- 4 cloves garlic, finely chopped
- 1/3 cup freshly chopped cilantro leaves

Directions

1. Place the potatoes in a big saucepan and add cold water to cover by an inch. Over high heat, add 1 tbsp of salt and bring to a boil. Drain carefully after cooking for 12 to 15 minutes or until fork tender. Slice into pieces that are 1/4-inch thick allow to cool somewhat, and then add to a large serving bowl.
2. In a medium bowl, combine the remaining ingredients. Warm the potatoes, then add the mixture, slowly stirring and slightly mashing the potatoes as you go. Before serving, season to taste with salt and pepper once more.

Made in the USA
Monee, IL
18 April 2023